To Vick Knight Jr.
who has played an
important role in the
UCA Friends of the
Library these 25 years!

April 29, 1990

$25,000 REWARD

JESSE JAMES

DEAD OR ALIVE

$15,000 REWARD FOR FRANK JAMES

$5000 Reward for any Known Member of the James Band

SIGNED:

ST. LOUIS MIDLAND RAILROAD

I, JESSE JAMES

by

James R. Ross

To a great M.C. and a very knowledgable
person – 4-29-90 – Vik Knight Jr.

James R. Ross

Acknowledgements

*The Publisher extends his thanks to the following
organisations and individuals for their invaluable help in
the production of this book.*

Ethel Rose James
James Farm and Museum Kearney Missouri
Library of Congress Washington DC
Professor Philip Davis
Saint Joseph Museum, St. Joseph Missouri
State Historical Society of Missouri, Columbia Missouri
Jack B. Wymore, Jesse James Bank Museum, Liberty Missouri
Christopher D. Allerbe

ISBN No. 0 946062 25 0
Library of Congress Catalogue Card No. 88-72112
First Published May 1989.

Publisher: David Chambers
Design & layout: Island Design
Typesetting: Concise Graphics Limited

Hand made black leather boots that were being worn by Jesse James at the time of his death.

 CONTENTS

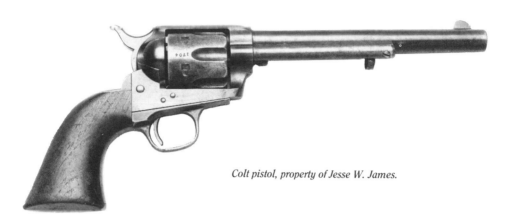

Colt pistol, property of Jesse W. James.

PREFACE

Every incident in this book is true, including all the surrounding circumstances with the actual people involved. I had three main sources of information upon which this claim is based.

The first and most important was my grandfather Jesse Edwards James (Jesse James Jnr.) with whom I lived the first twenty five years of my life, and called him "Daddy".

The second was my mother Jo James Ross, who in the thirties wrote an unpublished manuscript based upon careful research and discussions with relatives, friends and others who lived through the period in question.

The third source was rough handwritten notes scrawled by Billy Judson, who rode with my great-grandfather for eight years and was known as, and called by my grandfather and mother, "Uncle Billy". Both were absolutely convinced that Billy was telling the truth in his accounts, and my grandfather remembered him vividly from his childhood days.

The story of Jesse James will surely endure whether this book had been published or not, and it was certainly not my intention to further romanticize the tales of Jesse and Frank, nor for that matter to act as an apologist for them. I, and others of my family who are direct descendants of 'The Boys', wish only that they and their exploits be viewed once more, this time against the background of the times in which he lived, and with the additional benefit of the information contained in this volume. In this way, a new perspective may be obtained which will better qualify the reader to judge for himself whether the infamous 'James Boys' of Clay County Missouri, were saints or sinners.

Preface

No story is ever really finished, and so it is with the lives of Jesse and Frank James. Even as this volume was going into production, more information was found in the archives of the William Jewell College in Liberty Missouri that allowed me to expand and polish my text somewhat, and thereby make it more complete. This, in his own words, is the story of my kinsman Jesse Woodson James the Civil War guerrilla and outlaw. This is how it was handed down to me by my grandfather, his son, augmented by the research of my mother and confirmed by the testimony of Billy Judson, a member of the notorious James-Younger Gang.

James R. Ross
January 1989

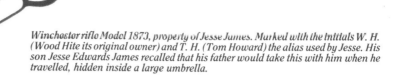

Winchester rifle Model 1873, property of Jesse James. Marked with the initials W. H. (Wood Hite its original owner) and T. H. (Tom Howard) the alias used by Jesse. His son Jesse Edwards James recalled that his father would take this with him when he travelled, hidden inside a large umbrella.

INTRODUCTION

Known the world over by name, the characters of Jesse and Frank James remain something of a mystery even though countless books, novels and pamphlets have been written about them, and a number of cinema and television productions dedicated to their legend.

More often than not, they are portrayed as wild and violent men who reveled in violence and destruction. But this was not the true nature of either of them. They were sons of a well educated Baptist minister, a founder member of William Jewell college. Jesse had a natural inclination to the church, and hoped to become a minister like his father. Frank, the older of the two, loved literature, especially the works of Shakespeare, and planned to become a teacher.

Losing their natural father at a young age they were raised by Dr. Samuel, a pleasant, mild mannered physician whom they loved as a father, and who returned their love. God fearing, property owning and reasonably prosperous members of the rural middle class, nothing indicated that they would grow up to be anything other than the successful products of a loving and stable domestic environment. But then the war came.

Along the border between Kansas and Missouri, the conflict was bitter and intense. Many Confederate sympathisers in Missouri were victimised, terrorised and robbed of all they possessed in the name of the Union. Countless smallholders saw their farms and crops burned, their children mistreated and their womenfolk abused by Northern Militiamen. The James family were no exception. Frank, as so many young Southerners did, took up with Quantrill the fiery guerrilla leader, and Jesse while still in his teens joined the band of William 'Bloody Bill' Anderson his lieutenant, to strike back at the North.

Jesse Woodson and Frank James spent their formative years astride fast horses a blazing revolver in both hands, as they and their companions at arms mauled the Union troops whenever the opportunity presented itself. Surrounded by men who would have made fitting companions for Attila the Hun and Genghis Khan, Jessed faced death daily, lived the life of a hunted man, and suffered many privations including wounds, grievous and otherwise. He became an accomplished horseman as well as a deadly shot with a revolver, the weapon of choice in the close quarters skirmishes at which Bloody Bill's men excelled. His fellow Americans became divided in the young man's mind, into on the one hand blood brothers for whom he would face any odds, and on the other sworn enemies whom he wished only to eliminate. Inevitably this would have a profound effect on one so young.

It is the nature of us all that we hate what we fear. And the Union soldiers feared the 'irregulars' greatly. When, in the many attacks they made on the Northern troops they would break cover and fearlessly charge down upon the Northerners, revolvers blazing and screaming like tormented souls, it was as if hell had opened its gates and disgourged those inmates that were too evil even for its fiery confines. The regular Union soldier, unable to act in the orthodox military fashion in which he had been trained, frequently died where he stood in the hail of withering fire from the mounted demons that rode under the black flag, or was cut down by accurate revolver fire during the rout that almost inevitably followed the initial guerrilla onslaught.

The losses and humiliation were not forgotten. The irregulars became for many Northerners the scapegoats for all their failures and set-backs. Consequently when the war ended, the guerrillas were not treated as former soldiers and permitted a dignified return to their wives and families. Rather, they were branded as common criminals, and deprived of the rights that had theretofore, and always subsequently been accorded a vanquished foe.

Stripped of their civil rights, second class citizens in their own communities, many moved away to escape victimisation. But the James brothers stayed on the land that they owned and that they loved. Being hunted, shot at and discriminated against persuaded them that the war would never end for former guerrillas, and so they returned to their previous mode of life and continued their war against the north by robbing its financial institutions.

The Japanese say that if a man has lived the life of a beggar for three days he will never again seek productive work. And this must hold true for bank robbers also. What started as a means of continuing the fight against the hated Union, became a way of life. A profession in fact, for which every minute and every experience of their young lives had ideally prepared them. The North had created the monster known as the James-Younger Gang, and now it would be savaged again and again by its own creation.

Yet these were not blood thirsty barbarians, but military men who planned and executed their raids with soldierly precision. Problems only ever seemed to occur when orders were not obeyed, or associates outside of their former guerrilla friends were chosen to ride with them. They were intelligent, well educated men who, unlike most members of the criminal caste in whose ranks they found themselves, married good women, raised families that loved and honoured them, and were held in such high esteem by their friends and neighbours, that the best efforts of the authorities over a sixteen year period failed to result in their capture. Only the assassin's bullet that killed Jesse, and the voluntary surrender of Frank James ended their careers as outlaws.

It can only be concluded that it was the war, and only the war that turned Frank and Jesse to a life of crime. After standing trial and being acquited twice, Frank lived out the rest of his life in peace, and never again troubled society. Jesse's son became a lawyer, and his great-grandson a judge. Prior to, and after the generation that was scarred by war, the James family produced at the very least upright citizens, and not infrequently pillars of society as well.

This is a story of Middle America in torment. The pages of this book are windows onto the lives of the families that lived along the Missouri-Kansas border during the wicked days of the Civil war when the only law that prevailed was the biblical one of an eye for an eye. The James Family is a microcosm of middle-class Missouri farming folk, who were caught up in whirlwind of hatred that the Civil War generated. By reading this account of their lives we can more fully understand not only the characters of Jesse and Frank James, but also the times in which they lived, and the way it shaped the history of the United States. We trust that you will profit from the experience as we have.

Major John Newman Edwards 1839-89.

Major John Newman Edwards 1839-1889

For many observers, it may seem passing strange that two men best known for acts of robbery and violence, should endure as public heros. If there is one person who is responsible for this it is John Newman Edwards, author, journalist and publisher; former confederate officer and adjutant to Gen. Shelby. Edwards championed the cause of the former guerrillas, and brought to the attention of his readers their plight. His powerful literary style shook friends and foes alike into at least recognising that a problem existed, and that the James boys were the perfect example of men whose lives had been ruined by it.

The staunchest friend and most loyal ally that any man could wish for, his only faults seem to have been an overly florid literary style, and wholesale surrender from time to time to the delights of grape and grain. He stuck with the James Boys through thick and thin, his belief in their basic honesty and decency unshakable to the end. When the attacks against them grew stronger and stronger, so the power of his prose grew tenfold in response, and he hurled literary javelins at his enemies in the manner that Zeus threw thunderbolts from Mount Olympus.

Major John Newman Edwards on the Assassination of Jesse James,

"We called him an outlaw, and he was, but fate made him so. When the war came he was just turned fifteen. The border was aflame with steel and fire and ambuscade and slaughter. He flung himself into a band which had a black flag for a banner and devils for riders. What he did he did, and it was fearful. But it was war. It was Missouri against Kansas. It was Jim Lane and Jennison against Quantrill, Anderson and Todd.

When the war closed Jesse had no home. Proscribed, hunted, shot, driven away from his people, a price put on his head, what else could he do, with such a nature, except what he did do; he had to live. It was his country. The graves of his kindred were there. He refused to be banished from his birthright, and when he was hunted he turned savagely around and hunted his hunters. Would to God he were alive today to make righteous butchery of a few more of them.

There never was a more cowardly and unnecessary murder committed in all America than this murder of Jesse James. It was done for money. He had been living in St. Joseph for months. The Fords were with him. He was in their toils, for they meant to betray him. He was in the heart of a large city. One word would have summoned 500 armed men for his capture or extermination. Not a single one of the attacking party need to have been hurt. If, when his house had been surrendered, he had refused to surrender, he could have been killed on the inside of it at long range. The chances for him to escape were as one to ten thousand and not even that; but it was never intended that he should be captured. It was his blood the bloody wretches were after, blood that would bring money in the official market of Missouri.

And this great commonwealth leagued with a lot of self-confessed robbers, highwaymen and prostitutes, to have one of its citizens assassinated, before it was positively known that he had ever committed a single crime worthy of death.

Of course, everything that can be said about the dead man to justify the manner of his killing will be said; but who is saying it? Those with the blood of Jesse James on their guilty souls. Those who conspired to murder him. Those who wanted the reward and would invent and lie and concoct any diabolical story to get it. They have succeeded, but such a cry of horror and indignation at the infernal deed is even now thundering over the land that if a single one of the miserable assassins had either manhood, conscience, or courage, he would go as another Judas and hang himself. But so sure as God reigns, there was never a dollar of blood money yet obtained which did not bring with it perdition. Sooner or later comes the day of vengeance. Some among the murderers were mere beasts of prey. These, of course, can only suffer through cold blood, hunger or thirst; but whatever they dread most, that will happen. Others, again, among the murderers are sanctimonious devils, who plead the honor of the State, the value of law and order, the splendid courage required to shoot an unarmed man in the back of the head; and these will be stripped to the skin of all their pretentions and made to shiver and freeze, splotched as they are with blood, in the pitiless storm of public contempt and condemnation. This to the leader will be worse than death.

Nor is the end yet. If Jesse James had been hunted down as any other criminal, and killed when trying to escape or in resisting arrest, not a word would have been said to the contrary. He had sinned and he had suffered. In his death the majesty of the law would have been vindicated; but here the law itself becomes a murderer; it leagues with murderers. It is itself a murderer – the most abject, the most infamous, the most cowardly ever known to history. Therefore, the so called executors of the law are outlaws. Therefore, let Jesse James' comrades and he has a few remaining worth all the Fords and Liddels that can be packed together between St. Louis and St. Joseph do unto them as they did unto him. Yes, the end is not yet nor should it be. The man put a price upon his head and hired a band of cut-throats and highwaymen to murder him for money? Anything can be told of men. The whole land is filled with liars, robbers and *assassins. Murder is easy for $100. Nothing is safe that is pure, or unsuspecting, or just; but it is not to be supposed that the law will become an ally and a co-worker in this sort of civilization. Jesse James has been murdered, first, because an immense price had been set on his head and there isn't a low lived scoundrel today in Missouri who wouldn't kill his own father for money; and second because he was made a scapegoat of every train robber, footpad and highwayman between Iowa and Texas. Worse men a thousand times than the dead man have been hired to do this thing. The very character of the instruments chosen show the infamous nature of the work required. The hand that slew him had to be a traitor's! Missouri with 117 sheriffs, as brave and as efficient on the average as any men on earth. Missouri, with watchful and vigilant marshals in every one of her principal towns and cities. Missouri, with every screw, and cog, and crank, and lever, and wheel of the administrative machinery in perfect working order. Boasting of law, order, progress and development, had yet to surrender all these in the face of a single man – a hunted, lied-upon, proscribed, and outlawed man, trapped and located in the midst of 35,000 people, and ally with some five or six cut-throats and prostitutes that the majesty of the law might be vindicated, and the good name of the State reeks today with a double orgy; that of lust and that of murder. What the men failed to do the women accomplished. Tear the two bears from the flag of Missouri. Put thereon in place of them, as more appropriate, a thief blowing out the brains of an unarmed victim; and a brazen harlot, naked to the waist and splashed to the brows in blood.*

Jesse Woodson James in 1864 (aged 17 yrs) while serving as a guerrilla fighter. Attributed to Schroder Photography Studio, St. Joseph Missouri. Property of Ethel Rose James, his grand-daughter.

Foreword

My name is Jesse Woodson James. I grew up in Clay County Missouri. I spent my formative years fighting the Civil War on the side of the South. As far as I was concerned, the Civil War never ended. I started out robbing banks to get back at the Northern carpetbaggers who were not content with having won the war, they wanted to run the Southerner's noses in the dirt. After the war, we Southern sympathizers were down but the Northerners put their dirty boots on our necks and pushed us even farther into the mud. I hated being branded a loser and I never accepted it. I robbed banks, railroads, mortgage companies and any other institution swollen with Union funds. You could say I got real good at it. I learned my craft during the Civil War, and afterwards when the Drake Convention forbade any Confederate from serving in a profession or in a church, I felt justified in thinking that the North had created me – now they would have to suffer the consequences.

My friends will tell you that I was the best shot in three counties, the fastest man on a horse, and that I always carried a well-thumbed Bible with me, read it, and quoted from it frequently. I also had a good head on my shoulders, inherited from my preacher father, who died when I was three. I was fearless, and this attribute, I think, I inherited from my mother. She was over six feet fall, and used to plow fields one-handed when the Pinkerton agents deprived her of her right arm. If "Ma" had been a man she would have been governor of the state.

I had one brother, Frank, four years older than men. I looked up to him. He had most of Shakespeare memorized and took pride in quoting from him when appropriate. He'd intended to become an English teacher, but fate had other plans.

I only had one sweetheart in my whole life and after we were married I never looked at another woman. I was tempted once when I was young, but I overcame it. My wife and my children were the center of my life.

My nickname was "Dingus". The reason will be explained in this book. Some people have described me as being left-handed. This is not true, otherwise I would not have earned my nickname.

I always tried to act as a gentleman should, no matter what the circumstances and my creed was never to kill a man – except in self-defense. (I was not always successful in following my creed.)

Much has been written about me and my outfit the James-Younger gang. This is my own story in my own words what I wrote. I hope it sets the record straight.

So let's get on with it, my first act of banditry, the first bank robbery ever.

Jesse W. James.

The James Family

Jesse Woodson James
B. 9/5/1847 – D. 4/3/1882

Jesse Edwards James
B. 8/31/1875 – D. 3/26/1951
M. Stella McGowan 1/24/1900

Josephine Frances James
B. 4/20/1902 – D. 4/19/1956
M. Ronald Ross 9/2/1925

James Randal Ross
B. 7/6/1926
M. Rosemary Henderson 9/2/1950

Jesse Woodson James. Born Sept 5th 1847, died April 3rd 1882. This photograph, probably the most famous of him in existence, is believed to have been taken around the time of his marriage to Zerelda Mimms in 1874.

The bank at Liberty Missouri (at the time of the robbery the Clay County Savings Association), believed to be the site of the first ever daylight bank robbery. Built in 1858, it was purchased in 1965 and restored to its original condition by Harold and Jack Wymore. The Bank museum was operated by the latter until 1987, when it was leased to the City of Liberty and the Clay County Parks Dept. Jack Wymore is considered to be a leading authority on the history of the area.

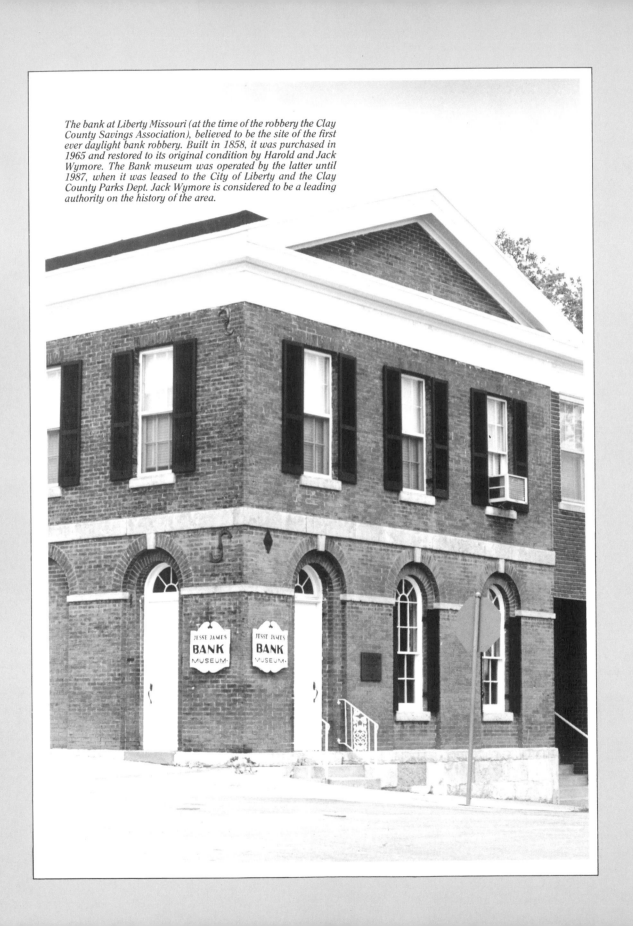

I

Liberty : Prophecy of the Two Bastards : The Reverend & Zerelda :
Little Pitchers Have Big Ears : A State Divided

As we were riding toward the town of Liberty, Missouri, my thoughts were mixed. Although I didn't know it at the time, we were about to create history by committing the first bank robbery.

As the leader, I was concerned and troubled by the thought that one of my outfit, which included my brother Frank, might be killed. Although all nine of my men were experienced raiders, none was over 25 years of age. Frank, who from my earliest memory had always carried a torn and ragged copy of Shakespeare's complete works with him and frequently quoted the bard, summed up my thoughts at that moment by stating characteristically, *"To be or not to be, that is the question."*

I shot Frank a stern look, but he just turned away with a slight smile. As we hit the outskirts of Liberty it was just Frank and me riding together. The others had split off into twos and threes as I had instructed them to do when I initially planned the robbery. All nine had been handpicked by Frank and me. They were all comrades-in-arms from our guerrilla days and I had absolute faith in each and everyone. Some of them were poorly educated, if educated at all, but their loyalty and resolution in action was unquestioned.

Although aware and alert for the possible danger that lay ahead, I must confess that like a typical 18-year-old part of my mind was on love, and my girlfriend, Zee, for it was February 13 – the day before St. Valentine's Day.

My horse seemed to have caught part of my ebullient spirits because he was dancing and prancing beneath me. I had not ridden my own horse "Stonewall" as he would be too easily recognized, but the horseflesh under me was the finest there was.

Although I was only 18 and still looked very young I felt that I had matured somewhat in the last year and a half since I had passed for a girl. Due to a round face, a nose frequently described as "button" and bright light blue eyes, I'd often been called "just a kid." I disliked my looks and as a result tried to develop a stern look in my eyes and practiced compressing my lips into a resolute grimace before the mirror. This year I had also begun to

shave – although I admit not too often. But I was now 5′ 10″ tall, and still growing. I hoped to catch up to Frank. He was different. He looked his age – four years older than me and was 6′ 2″ tall. Although lean and hard his bones were big and he looked older than his years. I was sure he would be much heavier in later life.

Liberty was similar to most midwest towns of 1866. There were about a dozen buildings facing the street including a hotel, restaurant, a general store, livery stable, blacksmith shop and an assortment of small shops and offices.

Back in 1849 – 1855 it had been the town for the outfitting of wagon trains. Many had started towards the gold fields of California from Liberty in those years. Although situated right in the middle of the bloody border war which developed into the Civil War, it was a prosperous town. Since it was the county seat, it was larger than most. The fact that it was the home of William Jewell College which was fast becoming recognized throughout the entire midwest, set Liberty aside from most of its neighbor cities.

As Frank and I approached the bank, which was lodged in a prosperous looking two-story brick building with green shutters and white wooden trim, we passed two boys about my age, walking along the wooden sidewalk with books in their hands. I envied them their leisurely attitude and their scholarly pursuits. I just knew they had nothing more weighty on their minds than Valentine's Day.

Later, I was to learn the name of one of those boys and quite a bit about him. He was Jolly Wymore and he was 17 years of age. He was one of the best liked young men in the town and at the college.

As our group began to arrive in the vicinity of the bank in seemingly separate groups of twos and threes – all pre-arranged – six of our outfit began to patrol the streets in front of the bank. Three took up strategic positions beside the main and side bank entrances and Frank and I dismounted and walked casually in.

Earlier research had indicated that at this hour the cashier, Greenup Bird, and his son William, would be within.

My older brother Frank flashed a bill in front of the elder Bird as we entered and inquired, "Sir, would it be possible to change this fifty dollar bill?"

The unsuspecting cashier replied good naturedly, "Oh, I think that is possible, assuming that it's not Confederate."

"Well, the bill may not be Confederate, but this is," said Frank menacingly as he whipped out a 45 Colt and pointed it right at the older man's head.

At this point what fleeting thoughts of the next day being Valentine's

The vault of the bank in Liberty as it appeared then, and now. Stacked in the safe at the rear of the strongroom was more than $60,000, possibly as much as $72,000 in currency, bonds and coin. Of the $42,000 worth of bonds stolen, all but $2,000 worth were redeemed.

Day may have been passing through young William Bird's head disappeared as I aimed a twin of Frank's Colt directly at him.

During the war both Frank and I had often been told that our blue eyes became like cold steel when we went into action. As I looked at the two bankers I saw something of that reflected in their frightened eyes. I was later to read that the Birds had described us in just that way – as having steel blue eyes to match the color of our Colts.

At any event, they moved rapidly to carry out our commands. Frank ordered, "Open the safe and put all of your money and other valuables in this here grain sack." Frank went over to the counter as I continued to control the bankers by pointing my Colt and my arctic eyes at them.

Realizing their danger, the cashier and his son quickly emptied the vault and cash drawer. The grain sack was soon full.

Never able to resist a pun, I grinned a little sadistically as I told them, "All birds should be caged. Get inside the vault, you Birds, and fly quickly." Slamming "the birds" into the vault, we joined our friends on the outside.

Unfortunately, in our haste we had not activated the spring lock of the vault correctly and before we knew it Greenup Bird had rushed to the window and began yelling at the top of his tonsils that the bank was being robbed.

As soon as he began shouting our men began galloping up and down the street shooting wildly to discourage anyone from interfering, so Frank and I could remount our horses.

As I was heading for my horse I espied the two young college boys I'd seen earlier. One was leaping for the nearest tree to hide behind, but the other was just standing there. He was just about to make a run for it when a bullet aimed by Arch Clement hit him squarely in the chest and spun him around into the dust of the street. It was Jolly Wymore, the young college student I had envied earlier.

To discourage any other citizen from trying to take action against us, all eleven of us began to yell as we mounted our horses. This was no ordinary yell. It was the well-known bloodcurdling rebel-guerrilla yell of the Missouri Confederate Irregulars who had ridden during the war under the black flag of Quantrill, Anderson and Todd. We kept up this unearthly screeeeeeeeeeeeeam until we were out of town and heading for Kearney, the next nearest town.

I didn't know it then but I learned later that before the screech of our rebel yell had died down the townspeople of Liberty were already speculating on the identity of the gang who had robbed their bank. Although none of us had been recognized, the gossip was that it was the work of guerrillas led by Jesse James. I was curious about this speculation.

George 'Jolly' Wymore.

The 'Variety Bazar', across the street from the bank that was robbed by the 'James Gang' and scene of the death of 'Jolly' Wymore. Arch Clements shot the youth through the heart as they made their escape, and he died three minutes later on the pavement in front of the store.

Was there something in my heredity or my previous conduct that would lead these good citizens – no matter how correctly – to suspect that the 18-year-old son of one of the founders of William Jewel College – the college of which they were so proud – was their bank robber?

But it must have been so, because of course they were right.

How they deduced this, though, amazed me because of course Frank and I practiced the greatest secrecy. And all of our men were 100% loyal – I was sure of that. But let me put down my complete story, without any gilding of the lily, without any moralizing, and you decide.

Robbery of the Bank in Liberty Missouri

THE STATEMENT OF CHIEF CASHIER GREENUP BIRD

Bank Robbery Committed in Liberty, Missouri on Feb 13th 1866

About two o'clock on the afternoon of the Tuesday 13th instant whilst I was writing at this desk and William Bird, my son was writing at the desk on my left, two men entered the Bank dressed in soldier's blue overcoats. They both came up to the stove. One of them turned and went to the place at which we receive and pay out money and said he wanted a bill changed.

William Bird left his desk and went to the counter to change it. On his arrival at the counter, the man on the opposite side drew a revolver and presented it at William Bird and demanded the money of the Bank. William Bird backed toward his desk. The man with the revolver in hand jumped on and over the counter, as also the other man drawing his revolver followed over the counter. One presenting his revolver at William Bird and the other man presenting his revolver at me, told us if we made any noise they would shoot us down, demanded all the money in the Bank, and that they wanted it quick.

William Bird not moving, one of the robbers struck him on the back with his pistol and said to him, "Dam you be quick" and shoved him toward the open vault door and followed him in, and drew out a cotton sack and made William Bird put the coin on the lower shelf of the safe into the cotton sack. (This coin was special deposit of Gold and Silver in rolls, bundles and bags). The other robber had me in tow outside of vault and demanded the Greenbacks. I pointed to a tin box on the table and told him they were in that box. He hoisted the lid of the box, took

out Greenbacks 7/30 and Bonds, and told the robber in the vault put them in the sack and to be in a hurry.

The robber in the vault told William Bird to remain in there. The robber at my side then told me to go in also. I hesitated and began to parley. He told me if I did not go in instantly he would shoot me down, I went in. They asked for the keys of the vault door. I told them they were in the door. They shut the door on us. This is the last we saw of them until we got out of the vault. After they left the vault door I found it was not locked. I opened the door a short distance to see if the robbers were out of the house and found they were out. We then opened the door, rushed to the front window, hoisted it and gave the alarm. As we were going from the vault door to the window, I saw several men on horseback pass the window, going east, shooting off pistols.

Prophecy of the Two Bastards

As Frank and I were growing up, especially after our minister father left home for the gold mines of California, there to die, Ma told us time and time again of the prophecy of the two bastards.

Our Stepfather, Dr. Samuel, did not seem to mind. In fact Dr. Samuel felt we should be told about our blood lines and our real ancestors. Yet, at the same time, Dr. Samuel always treated Frank and me as though we were his own.

Quite a man, my stepfather.

Ma would tell us the prophecy of the two bastards over and over again, usually after the supper dishes had been cleared and we were relaxing in front of a blazing fire in the room we called the parlor. We did not reserve this room for visitors only, or for Sunday use only as many did, but had made it comfortable and homey for the use of the family. Dr. Samuel had a rocking chair he was partial to – Ma would be seated on a straight-backed chair she had pulled close to the fire. Without arms, the chair allowed her freedom to roll the wool she was preparing into balls, later to be knit into a sweater for one of her boys.

The prophecy always began with Ma's description of those who had migrated to the Virginia colonies in the early years when the colonies were newly established in the land which was to become America.

Most came to live an exceedingly hard life, beset with Indian raids and always enduring under the threat of possible starvation. Often they were here in this new land because something or somebody who was more powerful than they were did not want them to stay in the mother country. Many in Virginia colony were running from something or somebody. Outcasts, robbers, bandits, bastards and the like were the backbone of the Virginia colony.

"Flowerdieu, Virginia, in September, 1622," ma would say, "was a place that harbored such people."

"The Indian raids of 1622 had devastated the settlers in that area. Those lucky enough to have escaped with their lives from the Indians had fled from their rough-hewn homes to the stockades where there was a chance to fight off the redskins and survive."

"In September of that long ago year two brothers, William and John, were arguing about William's future."

"William had insisted on returning to his land rather than staying in the stockades with his brother John and John's family."

As John tried to convince William to stay, William pointed out that he must return to his land "Because it is my job, John. It is my heritage – our heritage given to us by our father."

John replied, "Don't be bitter about duty, William. We both agreed before we left England that we were giving up any rights we had there in exchange for the land and our start here in the new world. But it's no use losing your life over your land."

William answered with considerable bitterness, "Yes, a lot of 'rights' either of us had as bastards, except for causing the good King James a lot of snickers at court!" William shook his head ruefully, as if to shake off an unwanted thought. "Oh I know in his way he thought he was doing the right thing," he continued, "And damn it all that's why I'm going to make it on my own land and sire my family under the name of James! If it's good enough for him, it's good enough for my family."

Ma's eyes would glitter with determination as she recounted the tale.

"No," (Ma's voice rose an octave with irritation), "That would be against our promise that neither of us would use the name 'James' here," said John.

William countered, "Sure, you can say that because you have Woodson, your mother's name. I don't even have a last name that I know of. You know there is quite a social distinction between your mother, who was a member of the King's court, and my mother, who was a chambermaid. If my mother was a Woodson I wouldn't be ashamed to use that name either. But someday when I'm lucky enough to have a son he will bear the last name of James. And if the good governor Yeardley won't register us, I'll let him go unregistered. But his name will be James."

Ma snapped a piece of wool between her teeth and tucked the stray end into the ball of wool she was winding. Frank and I were sitting on the floor wide-eyed, listening to the story, as we always did when she told us about our lineage.

"Poor John," said Ma. "He pleaded and pleaded with his brother William to stay at Flowerdieu in the stockade so he would not be massacred by the Indians. But William would have no part of it. "No, John," he would answer every time. "My horse is ready and my mind is made up. I'm going back to the land. There's just one more thing I wanted to tell you. Call it a premonition, call it a hunch, call it what you will. I've a feeling – a very strong feeling – that one of my descendants – descended from that son whose last name will be James – will become known in this new land. He's going to be famous and he's going to make the name of James famous, too."

John answered in a kindly fashion, "It's strange that you should mention that because I've had the same feeling many times. But I always felt that one of our descendants would be famous – but bearing the name WOODSON. I ask you to reconsider."

But William would not reconsider and rode stubbornly out of the stockade back to his land. He did survive the Indian attacks and he did sire a family and their last name was James.

Ma would finish the well-known story with a sigh and look meaningfully at me and Frank.

We knew William and John were our ancestors but she never spelled the royal significance of the story out for us. We were left to draw our own conclusions. But that we were the descendants of a bastard son of King James of England we never doubted.

Was this prophecy of the two bastards – either of whom would have been King of England if he had been legitimate – about to come to pass, about 250 years later?

Was the name of James about to become famous, or infamous?

When we were very young Frank and I would play games about this prophecy and exchange names.

Sometimes I was Woodson and Frank was James. Other times Frank was Woodson and I was James.

As we grew older, I sometimes detected a minute twinge of envy on Frank's part because I, in truth had both. For Pa had named me Jesse Woodson James.

Frank and I always called our stepfather "doctor" in front of strangers, but at home he was always "Pa."

Dr. Samuel was a kind and loving person and he treated us as though we were his own. Nevertheless, he wanted us to know our true heritage and he listened with a kindly twinkle in his eye as Ma would tell us about our real father, Reverend Robert James. After all, Frank and I had been seven and three years of age when he died, so our memories were almost non-existent.

After supper and chores, Ma would sit in the parlor, usually with some sewing in her hands, telling two avid listeners (three, actually, because Dr. Samuel never showed a twinge of jealousy and was just as interested) that those who made their living by converting others to Jesus Christ, did not have an easy time.

"Jesse, if you think you and Frank have a lot of hard work to do – well, it isn't anything like as hard as attending seminary. *That* is truly hard work for the studies are long and difficult. Your father had to learn ancient Greek so he could truly understand and read the scrolls of the original Bible. The studies take a long time and are not just done overnight."

Frank's and my eyes would widen at the idea of studying ancient Greek and a new respect would grow for the man we had scarcely known who had been our father.

"Your father," Ma would continue, "was a person who was committed to the Lord entirely. And because of this commitment he worked long and hard at the seminary for the Christian religion – and most particularly – for the Baptist faith.

"He believed with all his heart that a preacher was of no value unless he could convert others. And the Baptist teachings at that time were so strong that the Baptists believed theirs was the only true faith, especially for anyone who had his feet set on the path to heaven."

Frank chuckled when Ma said that, anticipating what she was going to tell us next. For we'd heard the story many times, but it was still our favorite form of entertainment, just like a child today will ask his parents to read the same old story from his favorite reading book over and over again.

"Go on, Ma," I'd prod, since Ma had paused to peer closely at a stitch she had taken that didn't please her exacting standard of workmanship.

"Well, even though it wasn't taught directly that anyone of another faith *would not* go to heaven, it was implied that a Catholic would certainly have a mighty hard time arriving there without first converting to the Baptist faith."

"But it *was* taught at the seminary that Catholics were very straight-laced and that marriage to a Catholic was forbidden. A Baptist minister could never marry a Catholic because he would be forced to convert to his wife's faith and all his children would have to be brought up in the Catholic religion. In other words, marriage to a Catholic was impossible for Robert James."

Frank leaned over and tickled me in my ribs to make sure I got the point.

"Hey," I said, "I may be young, but I'm no dummy. I understand what Ma's saying."

"Now boys," Dr. Samuel said, "Quiet down." He passed a wooden bowl of apples to us, and we each helped ourselves.

"Of course," Ma said, a twinkle in her eye, "the girls who attended the nearby Catholic convent were looked upon as unlikely candidates for courtship and marriage."

"Of course," Frank interjected, "And you were one of those girls, weren't you?"

"Hey, don't get ahead of the story" I told Frank, taking a crunching bite out of my big red apple. "Let Ma tell it her way."

"In May, 1840," Ma continued, "Robert Salee James had made so much progress in his studies at the seminary that one of his professors decreed he should attend a meeting where a group of young people of different faiths would be present. It was kind of a 'test' for Robert since this would be a good opportunity to see not only how he handled himself, but if he could begin to make some converts."

Here, in the telling of the story, Ma would pause and look at both Frank and me and beam with pride as she told us that as soon as Robert entered the room he was the center of attention of all the young people attending. Not only was he the most handsome man in the room, but his eloquent and polished college manner soon commanded respect.

Politely, but with great polish, he told the gathering of his calling to be an emissary of the Lord. He seemed to grow stronger and more confident as he realized everyone was listening with rapt attention. All but one. Ma's smile became a grin as she said, "Suddenly, his lecture was interrupted by someone who said, 'and just who are you to think that the Lord called you, or for that matter that a Baptist could or would be the chosen religion of our Lord or the Virgin Mary?'"

Robert's attention shifted from the group to a petite girl wearing the convent uniform.

He smiled condescendingly (after all, he'd been taught to be prepared for dissidents) and said, "Of course our Lord did not state in any scripture of the Bible that there was only one church, but I'm sure that the teaching you

Catholics have at the convent has already informed you of this fact."

Ma replied fast, "Your education is sorely lacking, Mr. James, if you believe that *only* Catholics attend the convent. I hope your knowledge of the scriptures is better than your knowledge of convents."

Much to Ma's surprise, Robert James looked at her and said softly, "I'm sure glad you're not a Catholic."

This brought forth titters and guffaws from everyone but the sharp-tongued girl in the convent uniform. She replied with a slight smile, "And I'm glad you're a Baptist."

The rest of the evening was not what either of them had been expecting. Robert learned that Zerelda Cole was a descendant of the Cole and Lindsey families of Virginia and Kentucky. This alone would have discouraged any average suitor for Zerelda's ancestors were famous for their courageous deeds during the Revolutionary War. However, this did not discourage Robert for he was quick to point out that he was descended from the James and Woodson families of the original Virginia colonies.

And so their courtship began.

But by the time school ended in the spring of 1841, Robert and Zerelda were not speaking. Their seemingly warm romance had hit an iceberg over one subject. Robert insisted that it was a wife's duty to follow and obey her husband as stated in the Scripture – 1 Timothy 2; 11 and 12, "A woman should learn in quietness and full submission. I do not permit a woman to teach or to have authority over a man; she must be silent."

Zerelda's reply was simply, direct and absolute. She told Robert that there were many other places in the Bible which she could cite which made a woman equal – and able to express her thoughts. Zerelda said she would say her piece where and when she wanted to regardless of whether or not it might cause a young reverend problems.

The summer passed without the two of them having anything to do with each other.

But just three days before the Fall, 1841 convent term was to begin, Robert arrived and proposed marriage to Zerelda. He told her he would never expect her to be subservient to him. Their legal union took place on December 21, 1842 when marriage vows were exchanged and a dowry of fifty pounds, in currency, not tobacco, was accepted by Robert.

Shortly after their wedding they purchased a farm near (soon to change its name to Kearney), Centerville, Missouri. There was no house on the land but they planned to remedy that fact in the spring.

On January 10, 1844, Ma gave birth to a baby boy, my brother Frank, while dad was finishing his last year of schooling before becoming ordained in Georgetown, Kentucky.

When the Reverend Robert James returned to Missouri, he built a small cabin on the farm he had previously purchased and he bought two slaves. He then began to farm and to preach. His preaching was good and so was his farming.

It was spring when Ma told Pa she was expecting another son. She never used the word "child" – it was always "son." As usual, she turned out to be right, because on September 5, 1847, I was born.

When it came time for "this baby to be named" said Ma, the Reverend said he had a hankering to give the baby boy a name that had been used many times in both ancestral lines.

"You're right, Robert," Ma said agreeably, "And a name we can both feel good about is "Jesse" (her younger brother's name) and I'm a hankerin' to give him that name."

She told us Pa let a goodly portion of time go by before replying as if "Jesse" had been his choice all along, "I agree. It's a good Christian name. But I think the middle name should be "Woodson" in honor of my ancestors. It's a good family name and I'm a hankerin' that *it* be used." Therefore, that was my name – Jesse Woodson James.

Between 1844 and 1850, life was good to the Reverend Robert James and feisty Zerelda. They had two healthy sons and a productive 275 acre farm. Weekdays, Robert and his slaves worked hard on the farm. Sunday was reserved for the Lord. When the Reverend James preached, people listened. He established two new Baptist congregations – one at New Hope and another in Providence – and often baptised as many as 60 new converts at one baptismal ritual. He was also one of the founders of the Baptist college, William Jewel, in nearby Liberty, Missouri.

In 1850, thousands of men were being lured by the promise of gold in California. Liberty, Missouri was an outfitting town for the overland trek. Because of Pa's connection with William College in Liberty, he began to be very interested in the wagon trains which were being equipped there. He noitced that there didn't seem to be any preachers in the groups which were heading westward, and by talking to others he established that there probably weren't any preachers already there. This bothered him because he felt that these men needed to hear and know of the Lord, particularly with the hard times which they were sure to face in their westward trek.

The Reverend decided that God had laid out a new path for him to follow – to the gold fields of California – so that these men would not lose sight of the Lord and his teachings.

Ma tried to overcome this decision, but this was one time that she did not prevail. Pa had made his commitment to a higher being. He promised Zerelda that he would go for two years only. After that, he would return to Missouri or have his family join him in California – however God saw it at the time. But he was firmly convinced that the families on the wagon trains needed him.

He began his trip on April 12, 1850. Ma told us how I cried bitterly when our father left and begged him not to go. I think I remember the incident, although maybe it's just because Ma had told us the story so many times. Ma also told us that on the morning she had a premonition she would never see him again. On August 12, 1850, just 18 days after arriving in the gold fields, the Reverend Robert James was dead.

Robert left a good estate. In addition to the 275 acre farm itself, there were 30 sheep, 6 head of cattle, 2 yoke of oxen, seven slaves and what was considered an enormous library – containing 60 volumes.

Little Pitchers Have Big Ears

All boys play games. Frank and I were no different.

One of our favorites was "Old John Brown." It went like this.

"Release your slaves. I'm John Brown. If you don't release them, Jim Lane will come and take your horses and furniture off to Lawrence for the auction."

That's the statement I shouted with as sinister a sneer as an eight-year-old boy could muster.

Then an older boy, usually Frank, would yell, "Grab him and whip him."

The other boys would grab me and throw me to the ground. They would begin to whip me with imaginary whips all the time shouting, "Old John Brown, you're going to hang for this someday. You're in Missouri, not Kansas. Now get back to Kansas you jayhawker[1] before we do hang you."

In keeping with the game's informal rules, I then got up off the ground and stumbled away, shaking my fist and yelling, "I'll be back and you'll be sorry, you bushwackers." The game ended with more threats and yells being called back and forth.

As Frank and I walked home he said, "Jesse, what would you do if you were really whipped and beaten?"

I shot back my answer as fast as Ma would have.

"Well, Buck (our family nickname for Frank), I know I would kill the man who did it."

Frank looked at me with disapproval. "But Jesse, wouldn't that be

[1] *A Member of a band of anti-slavery guerrillas in Kansas and Missouri before and during the Civil War.*

against the scriptures, and you planning on being a preacher like Pa?"

My temper boiled up and I snapped back, "No. The Scriptures say *'an eye for an eye'* and if somebody begins it first, then whoever beats me up or hurts or kills my kinfolk, then I can do the same to them or their kinfolk."

Frank didn't answer. Maybe he could sense my fierce intent and the sincerity of my remarks. For I believed it then when I was eight years old and I believe it now.

That same evening Frank and I sat in the background in our farmhouse at a meeting of many of our neighbors and heard the stories of the latest in the bloody border war between the anti-slavery forces or the abolitionists in Kansas and the slave owners in Missouri.

The topic was Governor Atchinson of Missouri and his embargo on traffic across Missouri to Kansas. What had happened is that the governor's embargo had turned up a consignment of 4,000 Sharps Rifles. These rifles were being sent by Doctor Samuel Cabot of Boston to A. A. Lawrence, the founder of Lawrence, Kansas and the leader of the anti-slavery movement for Kansas.

One of the neighbors at the meeting explained that it looked like the high and mighty Cabots of Boston were in league with the abolitionists of Kansas. One of our other neighbors broke in with the comment, "It's New England versus the South, all taking place in these raids upon our property."

Little did any of us realize it, but this statement was to foreshadow the Civil War.

One of the other men almost hesitantly remarked that with arms being sent to the anti-slavers by the East, more violence could only lay ahead.

It was a very solemn group assembled that evening in the farmhouse on which we small boys avidly eavesdropped.

Then one of the other farmers piped up. "By the way, if you want to see a beautiful coach made in Virginia which used to be owned right here in Clay County, Missouri, just go down to Lawrence, Kansas and watch Jim Lane's family brag about the coach and how they got it in the last raid from one of us slave-lovin' Missourians."

I had the feeling that the remark had been made to stir up the men present, but it was Ma who chimed in with "Well, if I were a man I'd go to Lawrence and bring it back."

It was another neighbor, old Bob Welles, who took a noisy suck on his corn-cob pipe and said, "You wouldn't say that if your first husband was here."

Ma replied quickly, "Oh yes I would. Because the good book says *'an eye for an eye'* and I'd do it even if it meant that Jim Lane would have to keep his appointment with the devil right then and there."

When Ma said the above, I elbowed Frank and as his cool blue eyes met mine I whispered, "See, Ma knows the right thing, too."

It was a patronizing Frank who whispered back, "O.K., you're right. But Ma's not a man."

I replied in a stage whisper, "Maybe we can do it for her when we get a little older."

Although I made the statement, little did I realize that Frank would actually be keeping that appointment in Lawrence, Kansas.

The heated discussion continued with another neighbor stating, "Yeah, all the governor does is stop people, just like when Colonel Cookel stopped the 'immigrants' near the Nebraska line headed for Kansas."

"What's wrong with immigrants?" questioned kindly Dr. Samuel.

Old Bob Welles replied, "Immigrants like hell. There were 223 persons in the company and only five women. No spinning wheels, no furniture or farm tools, few household goods. But there was a remarkable assortment of Halls Muskets, Sharps carbines, revolvers, bayonets, ammunition, kegs of powder and dragoon saddles."

"Well, I'm glad they were stopped before they got to Kansas, in that case!" replied Dr. Samuel.

"Stopped!" came the retort from Ma, "Yeah, stopped for one day. Scolded for one day and released to go on. After all, the guns, saddles and the rest were donated by the Iowa State arsenal for those 'settlers' to start life in the wilderness of Kansas!"

It was big Jim Ferguson, one of our neighboring farmers, who sighed and voiced what most everyone in the room had been thinking: "It's coming soon. War must occur."

Again it was Ma's voice, even more strident than before, who said, "So what? It's already a border war, so what's the difference, we might as well have the rest of the South with us."

The thoughtful silence that followed was broken by the low, calm voice of Dr. Samuel who told her, "you know, dear, that remark could get us all in trouble. Just talking about Missouri and the rest of the South seceding and fighting the northern abolitionists is not a popular thing to say."

"If that's treason, or somethin', then let it be" Ma stated loudly.

It was getting late for farmers, and although everyone at the meeting thought that something should be done, no one agreed what it would be or even had an idea of what could be done.

For the next two years, the border warfare between Kansas and Missouri continued and escalated in viciousness and violent deeds. However, it did not touch the area near our farm until one Sunday in late 1857.

It was dinnertime when we heard the noise of a horse arriving, followed by a banging on the door and someone screaming, "Please let me in, Dr. Samuel! Let me in!"

When the door was opened, the light from within shone on a pale lad of 17 with heavily bloodshot eyes. We immediately recognized him as the son of one of our neighbors.

In a voice shaking with anger and terror he exclaimed, "The Jayhawkers raided our farm. Pa's dead, the house and barn are burned and they've taken half of our slaves and stock! Just after they killed Pa and as they left the leader yelled out, "Slaveholders are not wanted around here!"

Before Dr. Samuel could speak, Ma gave the order: "Frank, Jesse, round up the neighbors right away. You know the ones. Tell them to report here at once. There's real trouble – bad trouble!"

Within two hours we had done our job and 18 grim-faced men had assembled in our home.

The story was a familiar one – another Kansas raid involving stealing, murdering, and burning of a farm which harbored slaves – but this time it has struck close to home.

The talk at first was of the authorities. But that died quickly as these angry men knew that past atrocities had gone unpunished.

After a great deal of discussion, one word was muttered over and over again and soon becomes a commitment. That word was "reprisal."

All 18 of the men present promised to return in eight days to begin the reprisal raid from our farm. Each not only promised to be there, but to bring other like-minded men.

As soon as the men left, Frank and I began pleading and begging with Ma to allow us to participate in the raid. However, as usual, Ma let us know in no uncertain terms that even though we might be growing taller with every passing year, she was still the boss, and she told us neither of us was ready to do "man's work." What we could do, she added, in an effort to take some of the "sting" out of her remarks, was to "remain alert to help protect the farm."

For the next week, Frank and I perfected our marksmanship with rifles in the nearby woods. Frank was unyielding in his efforts to get Ma to relent. As he pointed out, he was now 14 years old and tall for his age. He was ready, he said, to "be a man" which in Clay County, Missouri at that time meant being able to shoot, and shoot to kill. Frank could certainly shoot straight but Ma, as usual, won. Frank did not go on the raid.

His unhappiness at "not being a man" was to endure for almost four more years. Although the border raids upon Missouri slaveholders and retaliation raids back into Kansas were to continue, Ma was able to hold us both at home. That is until . . . .

A State Divided

I was 13 years of age when the Civil War began.

As predicted, the bloody border wars had escalated and now an entire nation was involved.

As war began, the James family and our neighbors were sure that Missouri would join its sister slave states in seceding from the Union and join the Confederacy. We soon learned, however, that there was more to the State of Missouri than Clay and Jackson Counties. The reports we received on the farm were often confused and divided. Governor Jackson, we know, was a Southern sympathizer. He was for secession and for joining the confederacy. He immediately appointed Sterling Price, former governor and hero of the Mexican war to organize and command the state militia. He gave Price the title of Major General. In addition, so-called state guards were formed of local militia. One of the state guard militia was organised in our town of Centerville (soon to be renamed Kearney). Frank enrolled immediately.

On the other side of this divided state, we found such luminaries as Frank P. Blair, General John C. Fremont, Captain Nathaniel P. Lyon and others. At the outbreak of war, Captain Lyon carried the title of Chief of Military Affairs in the state. These powerful men wanted just the opposite from the governor. They wanted Missouri to remain in the Union and to go to war against the South.

Unfortunately, as in all wars, battles were not fought by the politicians or in the political arena, but by real, live men who bled and died.

The first major battle of the Civil War was fought in Missouri, by Missourians.

It was the battle of Wilson's Creek which inconceivably saw Missourians killing Missourians. Often men from the same county or the same neighborhood had taken arms against each other. What side you fought on did not depend on where you lived, but on what you believed and upon what militia you had joined.

On August 10, 1861, forces under Major General Sterling Price, now commanding officer of the state guard of Missouri defeated the Federal Missouri force under now Brigadier General Lyon of Missouri. Casualties were high and the list of injured long. This battle pointed out as no other had that this war was to be a long and bloody one. Although General Lyon was killed and the Southerner General Price had been victorious during the battle of Wilson's Creek, the encounter was far from conclusive. One untested 18-year-old who fought bravely and happily and who was *not* injured was my older brother Frank.

After this battle furloughs were given and when his turn came, Frank came home. Of course he was given a hero's welcome. There was no doubt in our neighborhood on which side Mrs. Zerelda Samuel was on, or that of her entire family.

In Clay County when Frank arrived, everybody knew it. Ma was never one to keep quiet, especially about such an eventful occasion. Frank, himself, was very proud to have served under General Price and let it be known that as far as he was concerned, the "yankees" were the enemy and he would consider them as such, until they admitted the error of their ways. The South, said Frank, was more than equal to the North in every way.

It was just two days before his furlough was to end when a group of over 30 federal militia arrived at the farm while we were inside having supper.

They announced that Frank was under arrest for the crime of rebellion to the United States of America.

As soon as this announcement was made, I grabbed Frank to one side of the door and said, "Let's fight it out with them right here!"

Frank, however, showed his maturity and wisdom as he explained to his hot-headed brother that we were outnumbered 15 to 1, and more importantly, our family's safety was at stake, while the families of the men in the militia were at no risk.

I always admired Frank, but I found new reason to do so when he responded to the men in a cool, collected and resonant voice:

"Gentlemen, I am ready to allow you to arrest me because you have the manpower, but next time you'd better bring more men, as my brother here will be a year older and you just can't tell how many other 'rebs' might be around."

Frank was usually immersed in a copy of Shakespeare's plays, but I never gave any credence to his sometimes half-hearted confession that someday he might like to be Shakespearian actor. But on that day, I did.

Frank returned to the farm in only three days having been forced against his will to take the oath of allegiance at Liberty, where he had been imprisoned.

As he told us, Ma burst forth with a fiery condemnation of her son. Over the years I had learned that the only way to handle Ma when she did this was to let her blow off steam (like a volcano erupting), and then come back with a smile and make a light remark. When she finished lambasting Frank, I just smiled and said, "Aw, come on Ma, you don't think Frank is going to allow any forced oath to affect his real thinking?"

Frank grinned widely. "Jesse, sometimes I think you know me better than I know myself. I've just stopped by home to let you all know that I'm okay before I return to General Price under the flag of the Confederacy."

This information surprised and delighted Ma. She didn't like to eat crow, but this is one of the few times in her life when she did, and she did it graciously.

She actually begged Frank's forgiveness for ever doubting him.

Frank demonstrated the qualities I'd always admired in him when he answered, "Nothing to forgive. I know that you'll always be for us and with us no matter what we do. Blood *is* thicker than water."

Within the hour Frank was off to rejoin General Price under the Confederate flag. Frank always considered himself a Confederate soldier, whether a regular or irregular, fighting for the South's cause against the North.

I went with Frank when he rejoined General Price and did everything to enlist. I guess that I made a real ass out of myself, because it was General Price himself – and a very impressive man he was, too – who told me that although he had no doubt of my resolve and patriotism, that he would not accept my enlistment and that I would have to return home. What really hurt, though, was when he said, "we're not yet enlisting babies."

When he said this, everyone laughed except Frank. He stood up for me and said, "General, you can't tell a book by its cover. Jesse, there might look angelic, but he's really full of just plain old guts." However, the General prevailed and I was sent home, trying to fight back tears of disappointment.

It was true that my looks were against me. I had small, even features in a round "baby" face with pink and white skin, large blue eyes, and blonde hair. My lips were small and well-curved and would have better ehanced the looks of Sally Merriweather, the prettiest girl in the school, rather than a tough, young man, which is the way I considered myself. On the other side of the ledger, there were compensations. I could ride like an Indian, could tame and break-to-the-saddle the wildest cow ponies and broncs and on most days I could shoot as straight and true as Frank. I meant to close that gap between Frank's marksmanship and mine rapidly, and to that end I practiced every day. I also spent hours compressing my lips into a thin and determined sneer to erase some of the angelism. But nevertheless, most soldiers don't take "pretty boys" seriously, especially when they're only 13 years old.

With Frank gone, I was given the responsibility of running the farm. Dr. Samuel, of course, was nominally in charge, but he was away much of

William Clarke Quantrill 1837-1865.

the day attending to his medical practice. With the slaves, I worked long hours and it was backbreaking work. At the same time I continued my studies as best I could. I always tried to put my studies first because I intended someday to follow the career of my beloved father, whose memory I worshipped. I wanted to be a Reverend – just like him.

Letters from Frank and reports of General Price and his Southern Missouri brigade did not bring good news.

Price was greatly outnumbered, out-provisioned and supplied and he rapidly retreated to Arkansas, and then to Mississippi. Frank reported that many of the men from Clay and Jackson Counties were becoming very disillusioned. Their experience and expertise had been with the border warfare and they believed their duty was at home in Clay and Jackson Counties.

Finally, we were surprised to receive a letter from Frank in which he reported that those men who wanted to return would be allowed to do so, to continue fighting under the command of a man named William Clarke Quantrill. He was a former Dover, Ohio farmer, gambler, schoolteacher and desperado and he was commissioned by the Confederacy to form a band of guerrilla soldiers to fight as "irregulars" on behalf of the South.

Quantrill's raids on Federal troops were characterized by his brutal massacre of captives. His guerrillas fought under a "black flag." Many claimed that Quantrill's guerrillas were "outlaws" riding and raiding for their own purposes. The fact that they were always fighting against the Union forces seemed to escape the notice of these so-called "informed citizens" who branded Quantrill and his men rogue fugitives.

Frank, we soon learned, was serving under the leadership of Commander Quantrill. Their adventures during this period were recounted to me at great length by Frank and by many others in later years, especially by Cole Younger.

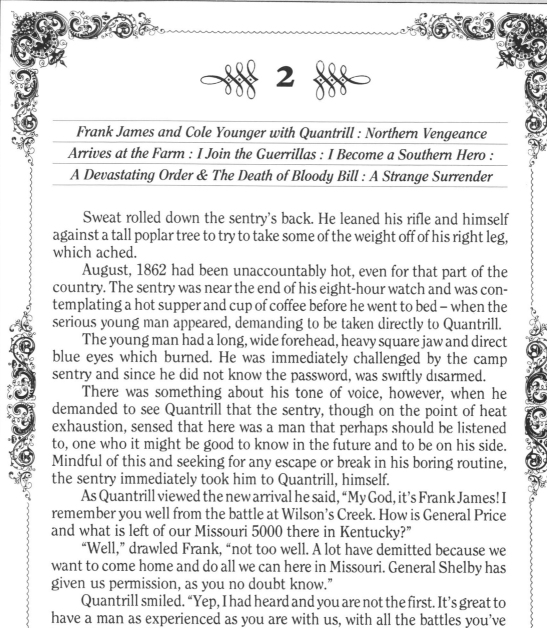

2

Frank James and Cole Younger with Quantrill : Northern Vengeance
Arrives at the Farm : I Join the Guerrillas : I Become a Southern Hero :
A Devastating Order & The Death of Bloody Bill : A Strange Surrender

Sweat rolled down the sentry's back. He leaned his rifle and himself against a tall poplar tree to try to take some of the weight off of his right leg, which ached.

August, 1862 had been unaccountably hot, even for that part of the country. The sentry was near the end of his eight-hour watch and was contemplating a hot supper and cup of coffee before he went to bed – when the serious young man appeared, demanding to be taken directly to Quantrill.

The young man had a long, wide forehead, heavy square jaw and direct blue eyes which burned. He was immediately challenged by the camp sentry and since he did not know the password, was swiftly disarmed.

There was something about his tone of voice, however, when he demanded to see Quantrill that the sentry, though on the point of heat exhaustion, sensed that here was a man that perhaps should be listened to, one who it might be good to know in the future and to be on his side. Mindful of this and seeking for any escape or break in his boring routine, the sentry immediately took him to Quantrill, himself.

As Quantrill viewed the new arrival he said, "My God, it's Frank James! I remember you well from the battle at Wilson's Creek. How is General Price and what is left of our Missouri 5000 there in Kentucky?"

"Well," drawled Frank, "not too well. A lot have demitted because we want to come home and do all we can here in Missouri. General Shelby has given us permission, as you no doubt know."

Quantrill smiled. "Yep, I had heard and you are not the first. It's great to have a man as experienced as you are with us, with all the battles you've been through. The next time you hear 'Boots and Saddles' you will be Sgt. Frank James of the Quantrill Rangers of the U.S. Confederacy; we've just been sworn in as partisan rangers. Bill Haller is our first lieutenant, George Todd is No. 2 and Bill Gregg serves as third lieutenant. We're organizing for a big raid and you'll be ready, or I've misjudged Frank James."

Frank James responded with determination and passion. "Yep, I sure as hell will. I just hope it's something we can all get a little revenge for what happened to our kinfolk here in Missouri." His cool blue eyes, which had so mesmerized the Quantrill camp sentry, held an icy steeliness which reflected the beginning of the hatred which was already simmering in him. Although only 19 years old, he was already a seasoned soldier.

The next two weeks passed as swiftly as an Indian arrow. Frank was quickly assimilated into the guerrillas, but as the day approached for the raid, he found himself thinking that there were too few irregulars for a successful attack. However, as each day passed, a few irregulars began drifting into camp. They seemed to appear out of nowhere – one or two hard-bitten men riding together, then a group of five or six, and finally larger batches of 10 to 15 at a time.

By early morning of the scheduled day for the raid, the original band had swelled to a goodly company.

As Frank and the other men mounted their horses, each had his own special memory which ignited his hatred and thirst for revenge.

George was from Butler. He vividly remembered his small town being completely sacked, every house burned. Of course the houses were not burned until Jim (now anointed as General) Lane, the famous abolitionist, had taken all the belongings out to be transferred to the "true" Americans from the great territory of Kansas.

Shep, from Parkvile, remembered returning home on furlough – to find that his home along with most of the others in Parkville had been destroyed, his horses gone to Kansas because he was a Confederate and all Confederate property was to be confiscated for use by the Federal Militia, or by the families of the Federal Militia.

Probably one of the most bitter guerrillas to swing up into his saddle that day was John, whose memory of the raid on his hometown of Osceola on September 22, 1861, had scorched a vivid picture on his very soul. The entire town of Osceola along with the surrounding farms were burned and sacked of any and all valuables. Twenty civilians were killed by the Federal Militia, including John's father, the town's beloved Baptist minister. During the looting, the chaplain of Lane's Federal Militia entered heartily into the spirit of the raid by stripping the altars of the Confederate church to be used to complete his own church in Kansas.

As the men made final adjustments to their stirrups and saddles and gave a last inspection to their guns, Quantrill gave them their orders.

In a stentorian voice which the men at the rear had no trouble hearing, he bellowed.

"It was the Good Book which stated *'an eye for an eye'* and it is the purpose of this raid to fulfill that Scripture."

With malice aforethought, Quantrill had deliberately selected a town in Kansas beginning with an "O" as the objective of the raiders' retribution.

At the end of his talk to his men, he announced that the town of Olathe, Kansas would bear the brunt of their revenge for the deeds of the Kansas Federal Militia. Frank James could never be absolutely certain if he heard it or sensed it, but later he was to report that he was fairly certain that Quantrill had chortled when he stated, "The Good Book says *'an eye for an eye'*, and we're going to give them an 'O' for an 'O' – remember Osceola!"

The signal to begin the raid on Olathe that early morning was a blood-curdling yell. It was terrible and frightening and awesome. It was the famous guerrilla yell that Frank was hearing for the first time. It was like a crazed banshee screaming from the depths of hell. It terrorized those who heard it – no matter how many times – and put added resolution into Quantrill's men.

The terrifying raid began.

The townspeople of Olathe, Kansas – men and women alike – were slaughtered like so many sacrifices on the altar of the Confederacy. No regard was given to either sex. This, after all, was total retaliation for the Federal Militia who had killed Missourians without regard to the victim's sex.

As the town was being looted and sacked and the screams of the dying mingled with the snorting of crazed and overworked horses and the guerrillas' terrifying yells, Frank James came upon the church which he recognized as a Baptist sanctuary. Frank could not desecrate the church. He could only think of his real father who would not have allowed a house of God to be destroyed. However, John, who was also a preacher's son, grabbed the lighted fireball from Frank's hesitating hand and threw it into the church, yelling "Remember Osceola!" Frank James believed that he had seen hatred in a man's eyes before – he had even seen a glint of it in his own when shaving some mornings – but the look in John's eyes was a new and frightening vision of malevolence. Their horrendous task completed, the raiding party began to leave Olathe. As the guerrillas departed, it was John who screamed so that all within earshot could hear, "The Lord has been avenged. An eye for an eye – or better yet, an 'O' for an 'O'."

A column of pure dread crept up Frank's spine. He shuddered. He had been in many battles, but he had never experienced anything as ghastly as the raid on Olathe.

After a major raid, it was the custom of the Quantrill forces to split up. Instead, this time they stayed together fighting skirmish after skirmish with

Federal troops in Kansas. Then they moved through the Osage nation and finally into Arkansas, joining up with Brigadier General John Marmaduke, the cavalry commander for the District of Arkansas. Quantrill's entire band of men were assigned to an old friend's brigade – Missourian Joe Shelby, who was headquartered at Cross Hollows, Arkansas.

During the months of November and December, 1862, Shelby's command fought in many battles. During one of the skirmishes, Joe Shelby was slightly wounded and captured when his horse was shot and killed under him. He was taken to the nearest detention house, which happened to be a schoolhouse. It was well guarded and thought to be escape-proof.

However, the Federal Militia, in buttressing their escape-proof prison, had not reckoned on a crazy, wild bunch of guerrillas who were part of Joe Shelby's command, and who would try anything to rescue him.

Five guerrillas rode to the schoolhouse, each approaching from a different direction so as not to arouse suspicion. When three of the riders were in good view of the schoolhouse, the other two slipped in the back way, surprising and overcoming the guards and rescuing Joe Shelby. When the two in the back left by the same route, the three men in the front of the schoolhouse began to give the guerrilla yell. This allowed just enough time for Frank James, riding double, to carry Joe Shelby to safety. None of the five men were captured. The most daring rescue to date had thus been accomplished.

While riding under Quantrill in the last days of 1862, Frank James, as it is so often with soldiers in time of war, found a comrade-in-arms and the two men cottoned to each other. His new-found friend was a big, overgrown man, named Thomas Coleman Younger, known as "Cole". Frank later learned he was the son of a wealthy and staunch pro-Union man – Judge Younger.

Because Cole Younger had joined Quantrill earlier than Frank, he had many tales to tell Frank of battles fought under Quantrill – how Quantrill had operated in each one, both in and out of the Confederate army system, how the raiders fluctuated in size, and most importantly – how Charley Quantrill had become a guerrilla in the first place.

Frank was fascinated by these stories and listened avidly to them.

"In 1859, Charley Quantrill had come to Kansas from Maryland to join his older brother on a trip to California," Cole told Frank. "However, the brothers were waylaid by the Jayhawker, Montgomery. Charley's brother was killed and Charley was left for dead. After two days, Quantrill was found at the brink of death by Cherokees who nursed him back to health. He became a blood brother to the Cherokees, and then, after fully recovering, had sworn to avenge his brother's death by killing Jayhawkers one at a time."

The Younger family, children of the wealthy landowner Henry W. Younger of Jackson County. Henrietta centre. Front Row, Robert, James and Thomas Coleman 'Cole' Younger. 'Cole' was driven to join Quantrill's band by the persecution of his family. After becoming a guerrilla, his father was robbed and murdered by Union troops, and the family home put to the torch.

As Cole finished the chilling story, Frank said, "Yeah, I remember Quantrill with his Cherokee friends at Wilson's Creek. He was more savage than any Indian."

Cole nodded. "That's Charley Quantrill, all right. Wild, but completely without fear. And filled with lots and lots of hatred. He won't be satisfied until all three leaders of the Jayhawkers – Lane, Montgomery and Jennison, are dead by his doing."

" *'In time we hate that which we often fear,'* " Frank responded, quoting from his beloved Shakespeare's "Anthony & Cleopatra."

"Shakespeare?" asked a tentative Cole.

"Shakespeare" affirmed Frank.

"You're a learned man," Cole said in a tone of wonder.

"No," Frank replied. "I'm a dabbler. But I *do* know Shakespeare pretty well. I've read him often enough."

Cole continued to regard him with a degree of awe. "My Pa is for the Union," he told Frank. "But the Redlegs, Lane and Jennison, were so violent and preyed upon him for tribute so hard, he vacated his post as Judge in Jackson County and moved to Harrisonville. Still, he hoped for a reconciliation between the Union and Confederacy. You know, Frank, he even had parties where the Federal officers came to our home. He also sponsored dances and allowed my sisters to attend."

There was a long pause. Cole seemed deep in thought. After a while, Frank nudged him and said, "Well, what happened?"

Cole's tone was apologetic. "My sisters were always polite and well behaved, mind you, but they were just unmoved by those pretty blue uniforms." Then a smile crept over Cole's face. He seemed to be absorbed in a distant vision.

"And . . .?" Frank prodded.

"Well," Cole continued, "There was this dance over at Harrisonville and this Federal Captain, Walley, asked my sister to dance. When she refused, the Captain blamed her turndown on me. We were lucky to get out alive. The captain just wouldn't let go of the incident. The next day he came to our home saying he was going to hang me cause I was a friend of Quantrill. The funny thing is, Frank, I didn't even know Charley then."

"But he put in bee in my bonnet, so to speak. When he said that I thought well, Cole, you might as well be hung for a ram as a lamb, so I looked up Charley and here I am."

Frank raised his eyebrows in surprise. He snapped his fingers. "And he took you in, just like that?" (Snap).

"Yeh, but he almost didn't. Hell, if it hadn't been for George Todd and the Shepard boys, Oliver and George, vouching for me, I would have been in the soup, in the middle of both sides. And what still worries me is that I sure hope these asshole Feds don't take it out on my Pa and the rest of the family back home."

"Yep, me too. But I have my doubts that they will."

If these too hopeful comrades-in-arms could have peered into a crystal ball they would have seen events which would have dashed their beliefs.

In store for the Younger family was the death of Judge Younger. He was robbed and killed in cold blood by Federal troops led by Captain Walley. Cole would also have seen himself kneeling beside his father's body and swearing a terrible oath of vengeance.

Next, Cole would see Captain Walley, who had heard of his oath of vengeance against him, arresting Cole's cousin and three sisters. He imprisoned them and other Southern sympathizers in a two-storey house. The house was deliberately undermined until it cracked and collapsed, pinning many of the women beneath heavy wooden timbers and brick walls. Cole's cousin was killed, together with the sister of another guerrilla leader. Many of the women who lived were maimed for life, paralyzed from the neck down.

This bloody retribution on the Younger family came about because a young girl refused to dance with the gallant (?) Captain Walley in his Union blue.

The future that Cole and Frank might have seen if they'd been gifted with a gypsy's foresight was soon to be played out at the James/Samuel family farm.

Northern Vengeance Arrives at the Farm

It was a fine Spring day in 1863. My stepfather, Dr. Reuben Samuel and I were working in the fields plowing corn.

I looked up from the row I was working on to see a band of Northern militia as they rode into the field. As they rode in, I couldn't help but notice that their guns were unholstered. Immediately, several guns were aimed at the doctor and myself. Neither of us were armed, nor were any guns nearby.

The officer in charge cocked his revolver at Dr. Samuel's head and in an imperious tone demanded, "I'm Captain Culver and I want to know the location and whereabouts of Quantrill."

"I don't know," stammered Dr. Samuel. He was immediately struck in the face by the Captain's whip. As Dr. Samuel vainly tried to stem the flow of blood from his face wound, Captain Culver urged his horse a few steps forward. He loomed over us.

"Your step-son, Frank, is riding with Quantrill and all you slave lovers know where they are camped." He raised his whip preparatory to striking the doctor again. But Pa said (truthfully), "I don't know where either Frank or Quantrill are."

With that reply, the orders came fast and viciously. The doctor was taken from the plow and driven by bayonets to the mulberry tree near the barn. Two bayonets were applied to me and I swiftly followed. After arriving at the tree he was asked the same question and replied the same way. The next thing I knew, a rope was taken out of one of the saddlebags and one end was put around his neck, the other thrown over the tree limb. Pa was hoisted into the air and left to hang until almost dead.

However, just when I was sure he'd breathed his last, he was lowered and asked the same question. When he answered the same as before, he was once again hoisted up into the air. The Northern militia did this four times until blood began flowing, not only from his face, but from his neck as well.

It was my turn next. The Captain turned his attention to me and snarled, "I'm Captain Culver. Where is your brother, boy?"

I really didn't know exactly where Quantrill and Frank were, but I had a general idea of the area where they might be. However, I was determined to be the man Ma and Frank would have wanted me to be, so I answered the truth, "I don't know." The Captain's face broke into an ugly mask of frustrated fury. "Well," he growled, "maybe you'll remember with a little help from my boys here."

I began to run through the corn rows. As I did, each soldier unleashed his black whip and snaked it over my back. Time and again the biting whip dug into me, and my body was soon covered by my own blood. Finally I could take it no longer and I collapsed between the rows. However, there was apparently nothing in the game which stated that just because I'd collapsed, the game would stop. The deadly whips hit me again and again as the lashing continued. Finally I heard the great "humanitarian," Captain Culver, give the command to stop, saying, "Stop! He's no good to us dead." He leaned off his horse and nudged me in the ribs with one of his black boots. "Where is your brother Frank?" he demanded. "Tell us or you die here."

All I could mumble was, "I don't know."

I firmly expected a gun to go off to end my life. As I turned over onto my stomach, all I could think of was that the dreams I had been having lately of being shot in the back, were about to occur. After about five minutes passed, I began to think that maybe my dream would be fulfilled at a later date.

Golly, I just might live to be 16. I looked up and saw that the militiamen had left the field. I struggled up to see if there was anything I could do for Pa.

As I did, I saw the Federals dragging a semi-conscious Dr. Samuel to the farmhouse. At least he was still alive! Ma come out of the house. Even though she wasn't armed, the chivalrous bluecoats pointed their guns at her and again the good Captain Culver intoned, "You had better tell me all you know."

What the Captain did not know, but I did, was that he was demanding something of a woman who was not scared, nor intimidated and the only thing that frightened her was God. She was as tough as any frontier woman ever born. She stood over six feet tall and she had a glance that could wither a gabby stranger faster than he could make a fool out of himself.

She responded tartly. "I'm like Marion's wife. What I know I will die knowing."

The Captain's face was now a bright crimson. He was being thwarted by obviously inferior farm people. Not only didn't they realize they were flaunting the Federal Militia, but also an obviously superior individual such as himself.

But the Captain's viciousness had not been fully expended as yet. He gave a command, "Bring that man around here and let him say goodbye to his wife."

Dr. Samuel was dragged around to the front of the house and when Ma asked what they were going to do with her husband, the Captain replied, "Why, kill him of course. Unless you change your tune in a hurry."

As Ma glared at this remark, the Captain snapped "Take him out behind the hill in back. I'll be along in a minute as I want the pleasure of the kill." He had gone mad with power and authority. As he turned his horse in the direction of the hill, he turned and blazed at Ma and me on the porch, "If either you or the boy want to follow, we'll do the same to you."

I was tempted to follow so as not to leave Dr. Samuel alone with these monsters. But Ma grabbed me. She said simply, "Jesse, I won't sacrifice either you or me to this madman and his authority; don't worry Jesse. Some-day our time for what has been done here today will arise and the eye for an eye will be returned."

Deuteronomy 19:21 flashed in my mind.

"Thus you shall not pity; life for life, eye for eye, tooth for tooth, hand for hand, foot for foot."

We grasped each other's hands as we stood there on the porch. We heard three shots fired. After that, Ma finally got a good look at me and realised I was badly hurt.

She ripped off my shirt and examined my back which was covered with red stripes oozing blood. When Ma saw this, it was the straw that broke the camel's back. Even women of steel must sometimes falter. Ma began to weep. My thoughts were very simple. They were of hate. There and then I took the vow that from that day forward, any man – wearing the blue – whether militia or not – would be my sworn enemy and would have to be killed.

"Ma, don't cry. I'll not stand this again. I will join Quantrill and kill some blue bellies to even the score."

Between sobs my mother protested, "But you are so young. You're only fifteen years old. Besides, they've stolen all our horses and all our money!"

I straightened by painful back and stood as tall as my 5′ 8″ would allow.

"Time will bring us both," I resolved.

After the Federals had gone, we both crept fearfully behind the hill. I was dreading seeing the body of the only father I had really known well lying there in the dirt with his life's blood draining away.

But there was no body!

For three unbelievably long and trying days there was no news whatsoever. Then we learned that Pa was not dead. He had been taken to Liberty jail and imprisoned for resisting arrest by a Federal officer. We also learned that no medical aid had been given to his neck from the hanging. What we did not know at that time was that this neck injury was so severe, that Dr. Samuel would suffer from it greatly and be in constant pain as a result for the rest of his life.

Not everybody in Clay County was a Southern sympathizer. There were a few who were for the Union. One of these Union men had an excellent gray mare that was not only fast, but had a great deal of endurance. I "borrowed" this horse from the Union sympathizer. I say "borrowed" because I did not have any money to pay for her. I just plain forgot to tell the man that I was borrowing his horse. I felt in some way it was a "payback" to the Federal people who had stolen our horses from us.

I arrived at Quantrill's camp on the gray mare.

Frank not only vouched for me, but told Quantrill what an excellent shot I was. But matters were little different from when I'd applied to General Price. The only difference was that Charley Quantrill was more genial than Price and he laughed when he said, "Boy, I haven't come down to accepting babies, at least not yet." Charley thought it was a good joke.

But Frank realized how deeply I was affronted and rejected. He summoned all the psychology he knew on me by trying to tell me how important it was for me to go home to protect Ma and our three little siblings, our sister Suzie, age 13; our half-sister Sallie, aged 4; and our half-brother, John, aged 2. Now that Pa Samuel was in jail, Frank said, it was a more important job than riding with Quantrill.

I gave in to Frank's urging. But I felt deep inside that this was the last time I would give in to anyone's will – including Frank's.

When I arrived back at the farm, it was to an empty house. I discovered to my utmost horror that Ma and the children had been taken to St. Joseph and imprisoned for the terrible crime of having a son and brother fighting with Quantrill.

All I had was a gun and a horse, yet I thought there had to be some way of obtaining the release of my family.

I devised a plan.

I went to St. Joseph. When I asked boldly to see the person in charge, for some reason it was granted.

I pleaded for my family's release. Of course my request was immediately denied.

With that denial and my dismissal, I put my plan into action. I brashly stated, "Well, I've at least warned you. Quantrill will kill one Union sympathizer for every day that his lieutenant, my brother Frank's family, is in jail."

Of course Quantrill had said no such thing to me or anyone else, but the earnest way I said it, and perhaps coming from such a baby-faced innocent-looking youth, seemed to take the Commanding Officer aback.

I knew when I left the jail that I was being followed. I headed straight back to Quantrill's camp. My follower trailed me right up to the campsite and then I heard his retreating horse's hoofbeats.

For some reason my family was released from jail the very day my follower returned to St. Joseph! My ruse had worked!!

Of course, I immediately told Quantrill of my boast. He didn't seem displeased. He merely stated that it was time to move camp anyway and he did so that night.

Before they left, Frank patted me on the back and praised "the guts I'd had to gain the release of Ma and the children."

Now I know what Shakespeare meant in Henry VI," said Frank solemnly, "when he used the term 'worthy brother and valiant brother'."

He carefully explained to me that there were two other bands of guerrillas who operated in a loose arrangement with Quantrill. He told me that sometimes all three bands got together and rode as one group, but mostly how each group rode alone. Frank said, "Me, I usually stick with Charley, but why don't you try to hook up with either Anderson or Todd? Maybe one of them will take you on. Tell them you're my brother."

Frank also detailed to me how the guerrillas were able to operate so successfully in federal controlled territory when they were so vastly outnumbered. The bands of guerrillas would operate in comparatively small groups of 30 to 80 men, he said, with the ages of the men ranging from 19 years of age to 25. After a raid, he expounded, the entire raiding party would disperse into single riders, or at most, two or three riders, and then assemble again at a predetermined place for another raid.

I wanted to be a part of it. I knew in my heart that someday – and a day not too far distant – I would.

I Join the Guerrillas

Bill Anderson lived for just one thing – to kill yankees. His blood lust was manifested by a high, wild satisfied laugh as he killed, killed, killed. He carried a silk scarf which had a knot in it for every federal militiaman he had dispatched. I didn't know it at the time, but I was later to learn that his scarf had 54 knots in it. Anderson's ruthlessness quickly earned him the sobriquet, "Bloody Bill".

When I left Frank and Quantrill, rejected by them – or by Quantrill, at least, as "too young" – I became determined to find another rebel group and join up. Ma always said I was as tenacious as a low-grade infection and this time I summoned all my determination and tenacity to the forefront and confronted "Bloody Bill" Anderson.

I looked him right in the eyes and told him what was happening at home, with the homes and barns being burned out, people being killed, and slaves kidnapped. It wasn't easy to look "Bloody Bill" in the eye because his stare sliced out at you like a scalping knife. He was a handsome man with long black hair, a beard and moustache, and light grey eyes. But the look in those eyes told you he had been to hell and back and seen things that no man should ever have had to experience.

Something about my mulish and dogged intent must have been conveyed to him because I was totally surprised when he snapped at me, "Okay, cub, you're assigned to Fletch Taylor. He'll teach you. But you give him one problem and it's out you go."

It was a relief when he turned those pale, scalping-knife eyes away from me.

I found Fletch Taylor. He just smiled at the likes of me and said, "Well, I guess it's my turn to babysit. But as the lieutenant said – one problem and OUT you go."

That first night around the campfire I asked Fletch Taylor what had brought out the devil in "Bloody Bill."

"Well, Cherub, it's a short story. Bill had two sisters who were arrested for the crime of cheering the Confederate soldiers as they marched down their hometown street. The sisters were taken to a ramshackle house outside Kansas City. The arresting redlegs under Jennison undermined it. The house collapsed. One sister was killed and the other had her spine crushed. She died, too, but lived long enough to tell her brother what had happened."

"When Bloody Bill heard what had occurred, he swore to kill every yankee he came upon for the rest of his life. He also vowed to see to it that each of them bled – scalped if necessary."

Fletch's explanation made a powerful impact on me. But deep in my guts I vowed that though "Bloody Bill" and I might have the same motivation, I would never become a savage, as he had.

As I rolled into my bedroll beside Fletch, he asked, "What's the matter Jesse? Is it too much for your sensitive stomach?"

Not wanting to reveal my innermost thoughts, I just gave him a derisive snort – and changed the subject.

"Were you at Lawrence?" I asked him.

"I'm God damn proud to say that I sure as hell was and your brother Frank was great that day. In fact, he saved many lives. He was just the opposite of *our* leader. Every time "Bloody Bill" killed he screamed, "I'm here for revenge and *I've got it!*"

My thoughts were sober as I settled into my bedroll. Fletch made the final statement of what had been a long, long, day. "You remember, Jesse, that if you ride with 'Bloody Bill' there are three rules: One, you kill every bluecoat, no wounded and no prisoners. Two, keep your horse well groomed and ready to ride at all times, *night* and *day*. Three, keep your guns clean and ready to fire at all times. If you follow those three rules, you may be able to stay alive out in the brush."

These were hardly comforting thoughts on which to fall asleep, but nevertheless, I did.

I had sought combat and I got it.

Between August 4 and September 21, 1864, we took part in 10 actual battles between our guerrilla group and the federal forces. I, myself, participated in eight of them. It soon became evident that in these barbarous encounters, there was no clemency of not killing a defeated enemy. No wounded were taken alive and we took no prisoners.

During one of the battles I was shot through the right lung. I was sure I was a goner, but somehow Fletch Taylor led me and my horse from the battlefield. Fortunately, Fletch knew of a doctor in the immediate area who was a Southern sympathizer. Dr. John A. Rudd of Carroll County was an excellent physician. He not only saved my life, but brought about a quick and miraculous recovery.

I made two important discoveries during the period that I rode with Fletch and "Bloody Bill" and his men. I believed that no one should drink alcohol, as it was the devil's water. My comrades-in-arms did not so believe. I also strongly believed that no one should take the name of the Lord in vain. I strictly adhered to no swearing whatsoever. All of the guerrillas swore without letup and drank as often as the occasion allowed. Despite this, and our close association, I pledged not to let their behaviour sway me from what I believed devoutly were the teachings of the Lord.

At the time that I was recovering from my lung wound, an incident occurred which was to eradicate my childhood nicknames of "Cub", "Cherub" and "Babyface" forever and give me a permanent adult nickname.

Adhering to Lt. Bill Anderson's admonition to keep my gun clean and ready at all times, I was working diligently on my pistol when the thing went off unexpectedly and accidently, despite my experience with cleaning guns. The bullet shot off the tip of the third finger of my left hand.

Several of my fellow guerrillas were watching me, so without flinching I shook my hand and said, "That's the doddingus pistol I ever saw."

From that day forward I was known to each and every guerrilla that ever rode with Quantrill, Anderson or Todd as "Dingus" and only "Dingus".

Oh well. It was a lot better name than "Cherub". It was a painful price to pay for a new nickname, but Fletch had begun to call me "Cherub" in front of the other guerrillas and I was very pleased to know that I had heard the last of that ridiculous and childish name.

I Become a Southern Hero

The mode of operation for Anderson's guerrillas was to separate after each raid or skirmish.

We would ride off in small groups in different directions so as to confuse and addle the enemy. I began to ride off with a guy named Jim Younger who seemed compatible. We just sorta drifted together because we both had older brothers who had been with Quantrill.

We already knew how to shoot fast, but now we learned how to talk fast.

Since we were irregulars we did not wear the usual grey southern uniform. A common occurence was for Jim and me to ride up to a farmhouse, usually dressed in blue. If we sensed the occupants were glad to see us and were probably Northern sympathizers, we would state we were Union soldiers who had been fighting the guerrillas and were ambushed.

On the other hand, if we discovered that the farmer was a Southern sympathizer we quickly shifted our story and told him we were guerrillas who had taken the uniforms of the yankees because we had none of our own.

At times it got ticklish, but we always managed to pull it off. Needless to say, if we were mistaken in our estimation of the farmers whose homes we invaded, we would be dead.

This is the way we survived – not with our guns – but with our mouths. The fact was, we never stayed more than one night at any one place. We usually slept in the barn. That way, if the farmer or any member of his family decided to ride to alert the authorities, he'd have to do so by walking, because we were bedded down with his horses.

Little did I realize at the time that Jim and I were learning and perfecting skills which were to serve us well in the future. All I knew at the time was that our "Northern sympathizer" – "Southern sympathizer" – stories were enabling us to survive.

My lung injury was completely healed by September 27, 1864 when one of the biggest groups Lt. Bill Anderson could assemble, rode with him into the town of Centralia, Missouri. This town was famous for the help it gave to the Union soldiers. The inhabitants were almost all Northern sympathizers. Two of the men who rode with us, however, were from Centralia and they had told Anderson how their families – because of their Southern sympathies – had been driven from the town.

"Bloody Bill" didn't like to hear their stories. So grim-faced and with his light eyes flashing, we rode to Centralia.

Centralia became a blood bath. We robbed and killed all the Union sympathizers; we left alone those we had been told were neutral. As usual, we left no wounded alive and took no prisoners.

Just as we were about to ride out of town, a train pulled into the Centralia station with 22 Union soldiers aboard. Anderson took these soldiers off the train and in accordance with his rule shot and killed every one.

We were riding complacently and leisurely out of town when I noticed a large cloud of dust behind us. We reined our horses to a trot to see what it was. It was a large group of about 300 Union soldiers. The troop quickly shortened the distance between them and us and they were soon within firing range. The leader, whom I later learned was a Major A. V. E. Johnson, ordered his men to dismount and load their rifles. Only he stayed astride his fine gray horse, a little in advance of his men.

Then he yelled, "We are ready. Come on, you damned cowards!"

When I heard this I became infuriated. *I* was not a coward, let alone a "damned coward."

I turned around and started my horse toward the captain. He had come forward and was less the 50 yards straight ahead of me. His men were standing ready and alert waiting for we "cowards" to attack.

Some inner voice told me that no one could catch me as I was mounted on the fastest race mare in the group. I wanted to get to the man that had called us "cowards" before anyone else did, so I rode directly towards him. Some instinct told me he would not shoot. And of course, I believed in my recurring dreams that I would die by being shot in the back. I galloped to within five feet of the captain and shot him through the brain. He threw out his hands as if trying to say something – then pitched forward – a corpse.

This singular act seemed to demoralize the Union forces and to give renewed courage and determination to our band. We "cowards" charged into that mob of Union soldiers and killed over 230 of them. Those who were not killed in the charge quickly mounted their horses and attempted to flee. Six of us, Arch Clements, Harrison Trow, Ben Morrow, Peyton Lang, Jim Younger and I pursued 60 Union soldiers. Of the 60, only eight escaped and we killed the other 52. At the end of the battle the score was Federal dead: 282 – Guerrilla dead: 4.

The news of this battle spread quickly through Western and Southern Missouri and far beyond. I became the hero of the battle. It was quite an ego trip for a boy who just three weeks before had achieved the ripe old age of 17.

The battle, however, created instant retaliation and an all-out pursuit by the Federal forces against our relatively small band of guerrillas. We had less and less time to split up and seek sanctuary. It seemed that every two or three days we were involved in another skirmish, if not a full scale battle.

Because of my actions after the battle of Centralia, and because I was mounted on the fastest horse, that wonderful gray racing mare, I always ended up at the head of our charge. As a result, my gray horse became almost as famous as any of the guerrilla leaders. And of course I garnered quite a bit of that fame for myself.

Soon our notoriety spread and other guerrillas began to join us from Quantrill and Todd's groups. Despite casualties, our total numbers seemed to remain almost constant.

Also, after my success with the Union soldiers outside of Centralia, "Bloody Bill" never once attempted to stop me from leading a charge. He usually rode second in the charge and he always gave the orders, but when someone would try to rile him by observing that perhaps the bloodiest person in the outfit was not "Bloody Bill", but the guy they called "Dingus", he merely smiled indulgently.

Needless to say, with my edict against drinking or swearing, I had little in common with any of the guerrillas, except for Jim Younger. While the rest drank themselves into oblivion after an encounter, I read the Bible. I didn't give a hoot what anyone thought. If they thought this made me "soft" or "strange" – so be it. They all knew better anyway, when we were in a battle.

Gradually, however, I began to talk seriously to Lt. Bill Anderson. His questions were always the same – whether or not I thought he would go to heaven. I would read from the Scriptures and explained to him that the Good Book said, "an eye for an eye". Bill would shake his thick mane of black hair and stare at me with those baleful, chilling grey eyes and opine as how he thought he was too far gone with the devil to be saved.

I felt differently. As I contemplated Bill and all the things he had done and the reasons for them, I sincerely felt that if he would turn to God he could be saved. I, myself, fervently believed that I was doing what I was doing only because of the war and that I would end up in heaven because I had not killed, except as a soldier.

A Devastating Order & The Death of Bloody Bill

We all had become adept at living off the land.

This meant either conning the farmers out of their eggs, chickens or vegetables, or "borrowing" them. This is the way we survived without being supplied like a normal army. Obviously, the Union Army was aware of how we existed, but "Bloody Bill" and I and the rest of our guerrillas did not see any way the Union Army could put a stop to it.

We were wrong.

What happened was the enactment of what we considered one of the most inhumane orders ever passed. It was Order No. 11. This order, issued by the Union Army, decreed that all residents of Clay, Jackson, Cass, Bates and Vernon Counties – amazingly enough, whether Union or Confederate – were to abandon farm and stock, sell nothing, and betake themselves to fortifications within the jurisdiction of the Union Army. All who disobeyed the order were outlawed or imprisoned.

Order No. 11 quickly turned a once prosperous-looking countryside into a scorched and dried piece of hellish earth. It was stripped bare. What a sight we all beheld – babes in their mothers' arms whimpered, children cried, wagon wheels creaked dismally, and in the distance one could hear a deserted dog howling mournfully as the fugitives left their homesteads, looking back fearfully to see their homes in flames, their stock driven off by looters, and complete desolation where a green and thriving community had once been.

When the feat was accomplished, it was obvious that the effect the Union forces wished to take place had indeed occurred. Now our living off the land was impossible – there was just no more meat or vegetables to be had.

On October 26, 1864, Jim Younger and I were ordered to a place in the brush just outside Orick, Missouri. There we found our leader and 12 guerrillas. But what made my heart leap with elation was discovering that my brother Frank was among them. Frank and I had never ridden together and I really wanted to ride with him. There was just a good feeling which came over me when I saw him. I loved my brother and of course I was anxious to prove to him that his little brother could do everything he could.

Frank and I had a lot of personal things to discuss, so we walked out a short distance away from the rest of the group. Frank make me feel like I was 10 feet tall when he said, "Well, little brother, you've become quite a hero."

I felt I could be completely open and honest with Frank so I told him, "Gosh, Buck, I've just tried doing the best I can to make sure it's 'an eye for an eye.' Like I once said, every bluecoat is my enemy and always will be. Heck, I'm not afraid of any of them, as long as they are not at my back."

"Do you still have that dream of being shot in the back?"

"Frank, it's not a dream, it's as plain as God's word. My life will end by being shot in the back. It is written. You do believe that it is all written down beforehand, don't you?"

Frank patted me affectionately on the back and gave me a half-smile. "Yeah," he said, "But I am sure that I do not know what is written about me."

In spite of his effort to lighten up the conversation I felt a chill around my heart. I could not laugh at this premonition of mine. I knew it was true. I forced a lopsided smile as I told him, "Sometimes I wish that I did not know. But I do."

I was going to go on and elucidate about my dream to him but he interrupted. "Look, Jesse, a big group coming up the trail. Better tell Bill."

I followed Frank's gaze and then yelled, "They are not ours, Frank, it's Feds and there are a slew of them!"

We both began to run towards the camp to give the alarm.

This is one time that I was thankful that Bill Anderson had made us strictly abide by his three rules. Our horses were ready and well-rested. We all quickly mounted. However, in an instant, the Federal forces which I estimated to be about 300-strong, were upon our small group.

"You have been surrounded. Give yourself up or you will be killed"

Alexander Franklin James as a guerrilla.

shouted the commander of the Federal forces.

It was true. The Federals had broken their charge and were surrounding us.

Suddenly, a high screaming voice with devilish overtones which I had learned to easily recognize as "Bloody Bill" shrieked, "I will never give up!" Bill started to charge right through the line of the Federals. I was next behind him. The remainder of our band of guerrillas was right behind me. Each of us was charging and firing in the guerrilla way, with sixguns blazing in both hands riding low on our horses with the bridles held between our teeth.

Our charge was successful except for one of our guerrillas – who I never found out – who fell from his horse. And Bill did something that was uncharacteristic and not in keeping with our code. When he saw our fellow guerrilla fall, he reared his horse and started back. I followed him. I knew you could charge a line of Feds once, but not twice. But as Bill leaned over to pick up the fallen guerrilla, the Union captain yelled, out "He is mine," and he shot Bill right through the head. I got only a fast short look at the captain, but it was enough.

How I ever got out of there, I shall never know. But once Bill and our fallen guerrilla were down, I rode back through the Union lines again. When I got through I spurred my horse to his fastest pace and that mare really flew. Before I knew it, I was up in front with the others and we escaped without further injury to anyone. As we rode I thought, "How in God's name did I ever make it? Surely there was ample opportunity for my dream to come true as there had been plenty of shots at my back. But I guess this was just not my time."

Later, we learned that Bill's body was dragged across the countryside and into Orick, where his head was removed and mounted on a stick and set in the square for all to see. Below it, a sign read:

> *BLOODY BILL ANDERSON*
> *LET IT BE A WARNING TO ALL GUERRILLAS*
> *AS TO HOW THEY WILL END UP,*
> *UNLESS THEY SURRENDER.*
>
> *– CAPTAIN COX*

The grisly exhibition of Anderson's head caused quite a stir throughout the area and scores of people came to see it, including many soldiers. Jim Younger and I dressed in the uniform of the Northern soldiers and went to see what everyone was talking about. As we rode away from the gruesome scene Jim asked, "Did you see who shot Bill?"

"Sure did. It was their captain, the same man who beheaded him and put his head on display. I think his name is really Sheets, not Cox. But in any event, I will kill him someday. This I swear on my father's grave."

Jim later told me that when I said that, an icy spasm went up and down his spine and he thought, "Well, Cox or Sheets, whatever your name is, your death warrant has just been signed."

Not long afterwards Lt. Todd, a grave and fearless guerrilla leader, joined Anderson in death. Each bloody battle saw more and more of our men being killed or badly wounded. Each time as a meeting place for a raid was designated, fewer and fewer men kept the appointment. We began to hear almost daily stories of the death or maiming of our comrades. This, together with Order No. 11, began to take a serious toll of the Southern irregulars.

A big meeting of all the remaining guerrilla forces was arranged. Everybody who could possibly walk or ride his horse was there. As we conferred, the decision was made to retreat for the winter, reform perhaps in the Spring, and come back to fight on another day when it was hoped many of us would have regained our strength. The only remaining decision to make was where to retreat. There was a great deal of indecision and conflict as this point was debated. Of the three guerrilla leaders, only Quantrill remained, and he had been out of serious action for a period of time. No one knew for sure exactly why, but there was a lot of innuendoes and rumors and grumblings about "Charley" and a certain woman.

At last it was decided that we should split into two groups. One group, led by Quantrill, opted for Kentucky. The other, more or less led by George Shepard and Arch Clements, chose Texas. Frank threw his lot in with his longtime chief, Quantrill, and he wanted me to join up with him. But I guess because of Quantrill's earlier rejection of my offer to join, I decided to throw in my lot with Shepard and Clements and head for Texas.

As we rode towards and then actually into Texas we rode together as one unit at all times. No longer did we split up into two and threes. One thing we were all in agreement on was that the area was huge and sparsely populated. In fact, there was a lot of banter that if things went poorly for us when we returned to Missouri, we could always retreat to Texas and nobody would ever find us.

Everyone liked the area's quietness. In fact, George Shepard expressed all of our thoughts when he said, "This is a peaceful area. Maybe someday I will come here and farm or ranch as they say down here." I, myself, had the same thoughts. I started day-dreaming of establishing a ranch and calling it simply, "Peace". Good Lord, all of us, I think, were dreaming, hoping and even praying for peace.

In Texas, something occurred that made me learn a great deal about myself. For some reason I had always had a mind that remembered everything that happened, remembered every little detail, and remembered it accurately. As we rode I hadn't missed one little bit of the territory through which we travelled and could remember each and every little turn that our group took. There was no question in my mind that I could easily start back, and with no markings left by us to guide us, I could retrace our ride every horse step of the way. Today, this type of mind is called a "photographic memory" but then all I could figure is that it was a mind that was just meant to store up the facts and remember 'em.

I learned that this was not so with many of my brother guerrillas. There would be discussion at night around the campfire about past raids, who was there, what happened, who did what, who said what – and the stories were often totally conflicting. I began to correct what was said because my brain had every detail catalogued. Unfortunately, this did not set too well with some of the others.

One night I got into a heated arguement with a couple of the men which would have escalated into gunplay if Arch Clements hadn't stepped in. After we had cooled down, Arch took me aside and explained that although I had been entirely correct in every detail, that I always was, and went on to comment, "What the hell are you Dingus, a person or a machine who merely repeats what it has learned beforehand?"

I was a little piqued at the time but not too upset so I answered tartly, "Well, doggone it, I figure that my eyes were meant to see and my ears to hear and my head not to forget what my ears heard and my eyes saw."

Arch told me like an older brother that he was sure this was true, and I was right, but that the other men did not have the education or background I had, and it might be better to conceal and temper my observations when around them. "After all," he said, "What does it really matter who's right or wrong? They're just shooting off steam."

I allowed as how Arch was right and when one of the guerrillas began reminiscing and coming up with facts which were totally wrong, I kept my mouth shut. It was hard for a 17-year-old hothead to do, but I managed. Part of the discipline of growing up, I guess.

After a few weeks riding through the desolate plains of Texas, we finally met up with the Texas Confederate Regulars and were accepted as part of the regular Confederate Army. We served and fought for the Confederacy for the rest of the winter and on toward Spring.

*Fletcher Taylor, a lieutenant of 'Bloody Bill' Anderson
with Frank and Jesse James. Circa 1864.*

All the news was terrible. The South was losing badly and things looked depressing.

We all heard of Sherman's march through Georgia and when we contemplated the complete devastation of five of our counties, we felt that the havoc and ravagement must have been similar.

Finally, a small group of us decided since it was almost Spring we would return to Missouri and do some good in protecting our families. We were given permission to leave and promptly did so. However, many of our initial group stayed on and went to Mexico, riding under General Joe Shelby. They had offered to fight for Maximilian. The Emperor was having his own troubles against the popular republican leader, Juarez.

I was one who went back to Missouri. It was my home and I was determined that if I were to live or to die, it would be in Clay County, Missouri.

A Strange Surrender

"Well, what the hell, we're back in Missouri at least!" Little Archie Clements was speaking to a confused bunch of tired and disgruntled men. Archie was now in charge of we irregulars since George Shepard had gone to Mexico with General Joe Shelby. Archie was "little" only in stature – being only 5′ 5″ tall. He was uneducated, often vulgar, but he was a real rebel in every sense of the word.

Now in this Spring of 1865 we were deciding what to do – with Archie's help and guidance. We knew the war was over. We knew that General Lee had surrendered the Confederacy and that under the terms of the surrender, Confederate soldiers were to be pardoned. What we did not know was how this affected us as irregulars. And what gnawed at most of us was what we should do as a group – and what we should do as individuals.

Finally we decided to have a meeting to air our feelings. Arch had summed up our general frustration by trying to be positive about being back in Missouri. But this wasn't enough. Never at a loss for words I blurted out, "It's true we're home. But what next? Do we fight or surrender?"

That kicked up a ruckus. Everyone had an opinion. The talk swung wildly from some who wanted to continue to fight – to take on the whole Union Army – and others more sanguine who pointed out the futility of this tactic and urged that we all surrender.

Finally one of us, and I don't remember who, came up with the sage thought that in order to make a final decision, we should determine the conditions of surrender. Then, and only then, would we be equipped to make a final decision.

Arch displayed his leadership qualities by ordering us to be on our own for one week and then meet in order to travel to Lexington, Missouri, to seek out the officer in charge and to find out exactly what the surrender conditions would be.

So ended our first meeting. Those who had been dissenting and grumbling seemed to fall in line with this sensible suggestion, and one by one they mounted their horses and rode off.

Those who didn't want to surrender were mollified when Arch suggested that after we found out the conditions, we all ride away as a body. Those, then, who wished to surrender could go back and surrender – but not until we irregulars had shown our joint solidarity by leaving together.

No one could pick any holes in this argument so the heated discussions had died down as fast as a campfire doused with water.

When I arrived at the farm I found that the house and barn were completely gutted, although their foundations were still visible. I toured the neighborhood and found all the farmhouses as deserted as mine. Surprisingly, I found that the town of Kearney was still standing. Why it hadn't been put to the torch I do not know. Several people were still living in Kearney and from them I learned that my family had gone to Rulo, Nebraska.

I returned to the burned-out farm and camped there for three days trying to decide what to do. War makes men make difficult moral choices and I was facing mine now. I wanted to surrender and start life anew. I still wanted to be a preacher. However, I had made a vow on my father's name to kill Captain Cox or Sheets or whatever his real name was, for what he'd done to Bloody Bill. I had an earlier vow to kill every bluecoat I met because of what Captain Culver had done to Dr. Samuel and me. Were these vows only to be made in the heat of anger and then to be ignored? I didn't think so.

As I lay on the floor of our former home in my improvised sleeping bag I had a strange dream.

I clearly saw my father that night. He told me that I should surrender and that my vow to kill all bluecoats had been forgiven. But that my vow to avenge Bloody Bill by killing Captain Sheets must be fulfilled. After the dream I slept better than I had in years, as though a great weight had been taken off my mind and an important decision made. As indeed it was. I rode back to our prearranged meeting site and arrived one day ahead of time.

We met just outside of Lexington, Missouri. It was a cool, clear morning. Arch informed the 28 of us who had assembled (a surprisingly small turnout), that the Union officer in charge was Captain C. E. Rodgers, and that there was no reason to keep on waiting for others of our group to show up since we were merely going to meet with Captain Rodgers to determine the terms of surrender.

For a little guy, Arch had a fiery glance. He turned it on me and said, "Dingus, you lead the way and carry our white flag of truce."

As we rode single file with the white flag fluttering on high towards headquarters, we caused quite a bit of commotion. I was riding the same horse that I had ridden when I led the charge at Centralia and I was recognized. Since we were all heavily armed, the good citizens of Lexington were wide-eyed as we cantered into town. But no incident occurred.

Captain Rodgers came out of headquarters and looked us over.

I noticed immediately that he was calm, dignified and of a mien which just plain commanded respect. I liked him on sight which immediately set up another conflict within as I thought, "My God in heaven, there are men who wear the blue that are *fair!*" I watched him with fascination. His stern visage immediately took in the fact that we were all heavily armed, but this fact did not seem to faze him.

"Does your decision to surrender or not apply as a group?" he asked.

Arch spoke immediately. "Nope. It's an individual decision after we hear the terms and conditions."

The Captain looked us over even more carefully and I almost thought I could sense his thoughts at having to deal with the rag-tag bunch. We all had on different outfits. None had a full Confederate uniform. Oh, here and there you could spot a Confederate jacket, or a Confederate cap, but truth to tell, we were not an imposing group if you judged us from our clothing.

"Are any of you actually Confederate soldiers?"

This struck Arch's sore spot and in an irritated tone told the Captain, "Hell, no, we've just fought with Confederates and killed Federals as best we can. It has been war you know. I believe you Union boys calls us "irregulars" when you're making a statement to the newspaper people. But we are Southern all the way and we ain't apologizing for nothin' we did."

Arch had expressed the tension that we all were feeling. But the Captain didn't flinch a bit. In his same calm voice he stated firmly, "You get the same Federal surrender rights that any Southern soldier gets, no more, no less."

This mollified Arch, but down the line I heard some grumblings, "Yeah, but how about that damned Drake Constitution here in Missouri where the Union soldier is pardoned for any crimes he committed, but we ain't?"

Again, there was a ripple of tension down the line as others heard the complainer. So had the Captain. But to my relief, without the slightest inflection of annoyance in his voice, he dispassionately stated, "Look, that's a state problem. There is nothing I can do about that. All I can do is give you a military pardon for the Federal government. It's your decision."

For a split second the whole world stopped on its axis. I realized that the time for decision that would affect my whole life had come. And I was torn.

Arch broke the spell into which I had drifted.

"Well, I'll never surrender," he bawled. "Do we get safe passage out of here?"

I heard my voice say, "I have not committed any crimes, so I'll part from you Arch, for the first time, and surrender."

Arch comes right back at me and says, "Dingus, that's not our argreement. This meeting was just to find out the conditions and terms of surrender. So we'll all go out together, and those who want to surrender can come back later."

Before I can reply, the Captain speaks up.

"All right. In one week each of you that wish to surrender, and any others of your kind that also wish to surrender, will return here and be pardoned. That will give the Captain here – he gestured towards Arch – and others a chance to change their minds. The war is over."

He walked up to Arch and extended his right hand which Arch automatically, but somewhat hesitatingly, took. Then Arch murmured with the stubbornness for which he was known, "I ain't surrendering, but I won't try and convince anybody else not to."

I knew right then that Arch would never surrender and I admired him for it. A part of me agreed with him. Each man must do what his conscience tells him and except for my dream, I might well have been making the same statement.

As we filed out of town I was again in the lead, but my thoughts were not on what I was doing. They were on my dream and how I was going to fulfill its bidding. The white flag dipped and it's possible was not visible to all.

Just at that time 60 Federals came riding into town, saw us and immediately opened fire. We reacted quickly and returned the fire while attempting to break through the Federal lines. Strange as it may seem, everyone made it with one exception. Me.

A Wisconsion cavalryman charged at me from ten feet away and we both began firing. I saw him grasp his heart and go down, but another rider charged and I shot his horse. But his bullet found my right lung, the same lung that had been so sorely wounded just eight months before. Also, my horse was killed.

Somehow, I struggled out from under my horse and stumbled for the timber. Five Federals pursued me. I thought, "If only I had stayed and surrendered, this would not be happening. But I am not going to die now." So I turned and shot the Federal who was leading the pack and he dropped in his tracks. This caused a momentary halt by the pursuers so I stopped and emptied my boots, which were nearly full of blood.

As I went further into the woods, I again spotted the pursuers coming up fast behind me. I turned and fired shattering the right arm of one of them. The other three were not deterred, however, and their leader shouted, "Damn your soul. We have got you at last." And he added, somewhat ironically I thought, "Stop and be killed like a gentleman."

I knew I was no gentleman, and besides this wasn't the way I was going to die, I knew it. So I calmly lifted my dragoon pistol with two hands, took careful aim, and shot the trooper who had cursed me, through the heart.

One of the remaining two pursuers yelled, "This is one devil that cannot be killed and the war is over. I'm not going to be killed by him!" and he and his partner turned around and took off.

I staggered on for about another 500 yards before I fainted on the bank of a creek.

For two days and two nights, I lay by that creek bathing my wound when strength would allow and drinking the water. All the time I kept thinking that the soldiers would find me and finish the job. But something, I know not what, kept me from dying. The pain became so intense that there was many a moment when I wished they would find me and finish the job. I began to have feverish dreams in which I dreamed I was shot from the back and this was the doom I had long thought about.

There were other dreams. In some, I was back laying between the rows of corn waiting for Captain Culver and his men to thwack me again with their black whips. But suddenly a voice broke through my hallucinations.

"Well, Mr. Guerrilla, I do not know your name. But I am a Southern-cause man and you sure don't look like you are going to make it without some help. I saw you while I was out ploughing before planting my corn."

I summoned all my fast-waning strength and mumbled, "Do you know a Mr. Bowman in this area?"

"Yep, I know him. And he is a Southern man, too. Why do you ask?"

I again replied feebly, "If you can just get me there, I have a friend who will come and take care of me."

With that last mustering of strength, I passed out.

I remember, but vaguely, the trip as I lay there in the haywagon. The next thing I remember is looking up into Arch Clement's bearded and grizzled face. I later learned that the good farmer had taken me to the Bowman's and that Arch was there. Arch took over immediately and nursed me the best he could.

I laid there at the Bowman's for some period of time. And although Arch did the best he could, I do remember telling him over and over that I wanted to be with my family when I died. I told Arch they were in Rulo, Nebraska, banished there by Order No. 11. I pleaded with Arch to somehow get me there.

One day I awoke and was starled to find that I was looking up at Captain Rodgers.

I was still weak and my first thought was that he had come to take me away and hang me for shooting the Federal soldiers. I saw Arch standing right beside him, and that was confusing.

Captain Rodgers explained that 137 irregulars under Dave Poole had surrendered to him. He also added with a smile that Arch Clements was not one of them.

I asked him if I was to be taken back and put in prison, or what was to happen to me.

He explained carefully that as far as he was concerned I had made my surrender when I was first in Lexington, and he was here to help in getting me to my family in Nebraska. He went on to say that while he could not officially help, he felt that what had happened to me was partly his fault. He was the one who had told us we were safe in Lexington as we were under the white flag of truce.

The converstion whirled around me. I did, however, clearly hear the Captain explain that he could not allow Arch to go with me to Nebraska by boat, for then we would be out of his jurisdiction, and Arch, as an un-surrendered irregular, would be fair game for all.

It was finally decided that guerrilla named Richard West, who had been pardoned, would accompany me to Nebraska by boat.

What really surprised me was that Captain Rodgers, himself, paid for the passage for both Richard West and myself out of his own pocket.

My initial estimation of Captain Rodgers had been right. I was learning a lesson, and a painful one it was too. Not all bluecoats were like Captain Culver and Captain Cox. Here was a man I could like and respect. And he was a Union man!

Arch took me to the steamboat and got me safely ensconced together with Richard West. Arch was still aboard when a Union trooper came on the ship and recognized me. He told me that he was the man who had shot me that day outside Lexington. He explained that he had not seen the white flag. He asked me if I had been pardoned. I replied that I had been, by Captain Rodgers himself, and that I was merely going home to die.

I noticed that Arch was warily watching the trooper who had given us his name. He was John E. Jones of Company E, 3rd Wisconsin Cavalry. He told me and Arch he was now discharged and starting home himself.

I knew that if Trooper Jones made one untoward move towards me, there would be one more Federal added to Arch Clement's list. Arch was still at war. He had not surrendered.

Somehow, for the good of all of us, nothing occurred and no more blood was spilled.

The trip up the river, thank God, was uneventful. And although Arch was not with us, Richard West took over my care with careful and constant attention, which allowed me to make it as far as my mother's home in Rulo, Nebraska.

The news at Rulo was good. Dr. Samuel was doing well and in fact all the family was healthy and prospering.

For eight weeks I lay close to death. And despite my stepfather's loving care and medical knowledge, he could do little to cure that terrible wound in my chest and lung and I made little progress.

3

Back to Missouri & A New Love : The Planning of Liberty :
After Liberty the Meeting : Remorse

Better than the good doctor's treatment in saving my life were the continual prayers and steadfast resolve of my mother.

Resolute, stubborn as a Missouri mule, and at times downright ornery, Ma nevertheless had the strength of will and purpose to pull me through.

I lost 30 pounds. I coughed blood into my fist. I sank into fevers that made my teeth chatter. I frequently fainted, even while lying back on a stack of pillows in my bed. Ma did not cry. But frequently as she put her ear to my chest to see if I was still breathing, she would have tears in her eyes.

Finally, as she did this one morning, I mustered my faltering strength and whispered, "Ma, take me home. I don't want to die here in the North. Please Ma."

She didn't answer. But I knew by looking at her that she would find a way to do so.

When the family gathered for the midday meal, Ma matter-of-factly stated, "We're going home. Jesse don't want to die here in the North. He suffered 21 wounds fighting for the South and for all of us. And if he wants to go home, it's home we go – back to Missouri."

It did not surprise me then, nor did it ever, that what Ma said went.

Dr. Samuel let Ma make all of the family decisions. Why, I never knew. Here was a man who married a widow with two boys, who suffered a severe injury because of one of them, who never complained, and never once stood up and made a decision contrary to one made by his wife, my mother. If, as stated in the Bible, "The meek shall inherit the earth," then Dr. Reuben Samuel would certainly be one of those who did. I called him "Pa" and proudly so.

So it was back to Missouri. We travelled downriver by boat, leaving it in North Kansas City, Missouri. The plan was to proceed to the farm by wagon. The farm would take a lot of work to once again make it habitable. But on the boat I had a severe relapse, coughing up blood, fainting, and wracked with high fevers. It was Dr. Samuel who convinced Ma that I was

not physically able to make the trip.

Ma decided that I should be taken for a spell to her cousin's house, John Mimms.

When we arrived at the Mimms house I required around-the-clock nursing. This was undertaken by my mother, my sister, and my first cousin, Zerelda Amanda Mimms. Her mother was my father's sister and my Ma, Zerelda, was the source of her Christian name. She was always called "Zee."

Zee nursed me through pneumonia and spooned up gravied vegetables and noodles and homemade soups while I constantly hacked into a tin spittoon.

Zee was a pretty woman of considerable refinement and patience. She was conventional in her attitudes and pious in her religion, a diligent, quiet, self-sacrificing good daughter. I was embarrassed by my condition in front of this beautiful cousin and I frequently apologized to her for my lack of appearance and strength.

While my Ma and sister Sallie nursed me with loving care, it was Zee's cool hands I looked forward to having on my forehead and Zee's shy smile I wished to see. Gradually I began to fall in love and my will to live grew as I realized some day I wanted to hold this girl in my arms when I had recovered my full strength as a man.

I guess I must have worn my heart on my sleeve because my feelings soon became evident to all, especially Zee. To my surprise, my feelings were returned!

While neither of us said anything while anyone else was present, when we were alone we plighted our love and troth. I had read somewhere that young love can cure anything. While I was not yet cured I did regain sufficient strength to return to the farm.

And I immediately sank into a deep depression.

Dr. Samuel opined that it was because the trip was so strenuous. But I knew it was because Zee and I had been parted.

Ma sensed that my depression was not solely because of a physical relapse and when we were alone she came right out and asked me about it. I had the impression that she had already guessed the answer.

I told her I was in love with Zee and that we two were going to be married.

Ma's response was immediate and fiery.

"I'm opposed to you marrying Zee." Then for the first time of my life, I told her – instead of asked – in no uncertain terms, "Ma, I said I'm going to marry Zee, and that is what I'm going to do."

Ma undoubtedly could see the resolve in my eyes. For as strong-willed a person as she was, she must have realized that no amount of persuasion, cajoling, coercion, or threats would change my mind. She said nothing. And the subject was never again mentioned by either of us.

During this period, from September to December, 1865, I was almost continually bedridden. I had some good days, but most of them were not so good. I was still hacking up blood, still beset by fevers, still weak and trembling. I had plenty of time to think about my future, if indeed I had a future.

The future that I perceived between bouts of fever was one of working in the fields of the farm. I thought of the Drake Convention, which on April 8, 1865, had become the State Constitution of Missouri. It had clearly stated that all Confederate soldiers or Confederate sympathizers, whether civilian or not, were fully responsible for all their acts from January 1, 1861, but that Union soldiers were granted full amnesty for any of their acts. It went on further to strictly forbid any Confederate soldier or sympathizer to practice any profession, or to act as deacons of any church.

And what of my unresolved vow to kill Captain Cox in order to avenge Bloody Bill?

At times it felt as though there were two equally strong forces pulling me apart and often I felt as though I were two different people.

A part of me was the law-abiding, God-loving son of a Baptist minister who wished to obey all of God's Laws.

The other part of me wanted to continue fighting for my own rights, to avenge what had been done to me and mine.

One day it all fell into place. I knew that when I recovered I would be hunted. So why not be the hunter, I figured, and take those things from others who had taken them from me?

How could I accomplish my goals? How could I even things up? How could I avenge the hanging of Dr. Samuel, the whiplashing I'd received in the cornfields, the burning of our farm and barn, the killing of Bloody Bill? I had a long, long list and those guerrilla-fighting years had sowed a heavy seed of hate within.

I took a cold look at my assets. The only things that I could do really well, better than just about anybody, was to ride and shoot. There were two other things I knew I had – I knew I had more daring than most – inherited from Ma, no doubt. I also knew I had leadership. Why had Bloody Bill never questioned my leading the charge? Why had Arch Clements not complained when I spoke up? Because of one thing, I was convinced, they knew that in spite of my age, I was a leader. Right then I decided that I would never again follow anybody. I would lead.

While I lay there doing my best to recover my strength and figure things out, the neighbors began to drift back to our area. Like ourselves, they were all penniless after the war.

All of them had mortgaged themselves and their property to the carpet-baggers from the North, who had set up their own banks to finance the mortgages. The rates of interest and repayment schedules were so high and outrageous that all of us would be working for the Northern banks for the rest of our lives. We were being victimized by the bankers, who were enjoying an undeserved prosperity and extraordinary profits at the expense of the unfortunate Southern farmers.

As the family reported to my sickbed with these tidbits of news from the neighborhood and environs, it suddenly came to me that perhaps I was ordained in a different way from my father. Perhaps I'd been ordained to right the scales of justice. Maybe I was the one to fight the bankers and restore the balance of inequity. When this thought occurred, I felt an immediate sense of rightness, of virtuousness. I now knew what I must do.

While my mental conflicts were being resolved I began to make a slow but sure improvement from a physical standpoint. My fevers abated. Day by day I gained a little strength. My worst problem was that every few hours I would have to drain the pus from my lung into a vessel. At first, I would have to be propped up by one of the family, but later I could do it for myself. There were even a few days when I could actually get up out of bed and walk a few steps.

Encouraged by my improvement, but still concerned about the pus in my chest, Ma arranged for a specialist from Kansas City by the name of Dr. Lankford, to inspect my lung wound.

He came every few days. Slowly, a plan evolved in my head which would make the good Dr. Lankford an unknowing and unwitting vital accomplice.

As Christmas grew near, my condition took a turn for the better. But I insisted that Dr. Lankford be kept unaware of my improvement.

The very next day after his visit I arose from my bed, drained my wound, and announced, "Ma, I'm going for a short ride."

Ma protested vigorously, complaining that although she agreed that I was better, this did not mean I could ride. However, I assured her the ride would be a very short one. I was not going to be deterred – even by Ma. For I had a mission.

The Planning of Liberty

I got up, dressed, prepared my horse, mounted and headed off towards Kearney for my "short ride." However, as soon as I got out of sight of the house I veered across country towards Liberty.

I rode casually and slowly down the main street. I didn't see anyone I recognized, nor did anyone recognize me. I observed everything in minute detail, making mental notes as I slowly rode down the street. Just as I had remembered it, there in the middle of Liberty was the bank. I dismounted in front of the bank, peered in, but did not actually enter. I then slowly remounted and left town. During my sick-in-bed days I had grown a beard which was a help in case someone in town thought they'd recognized me.

As I got back to within a mile of the house I ran into a farmer who recognized me and blurted out, "Why, Jesse, I thought you were bedridden. I sure didn't know you were up and about."

I replied in a pained voice, which wasn't difficult, because by then I was in considerable pain. "I'm up, but not sure about being 'about.' I could not even ride into Kearney. I just hope I can make it home."

Our neighbor was most considerate and he went with me that last mile back to the farm. As I dismounted, I collapsed into his arms. I was taken into the house, bedded down, and my wound drained, with the help of the neighbor. I knew that in this way, news would get around that Jesse James was still bedridden, and in a bad way, unable to ride.

As I lay in bed I made my final plans. I knew that I would rob the bank at Liberty, which I perceived as a blow in the right direction for the Southern farmer. I felt in so doing, justice would be served. It would not be a crime. It would be merely the righting of one small wrong inflicted upon us Southerners by the carpetbaggers and by those who had passed the rules of the Drake Convention.

Seeing that I was convalescent, Ma decided that it was time to have the entire family together for Christmas. She especially wanted Frank home for Christmas. Frank had been staying with relatives in Kentucky. He had gone there with a band of guerrillas under Quantrill. When Quantrill had been ambushed and killed near Smiley, Kentucky, Frank had surrendered and been given parole. He had not come home to Missouri because of the Drake Convention, but Ma wrote to him and asked him to come home for the holidays. He wrote back and said he would.

He arrived the day before Christmas. As we talked, he seemed to sense that I had something important on my mind.

"What's up Jesse?" he queried.

I wasn't quite ready to blurt out my entire plan, so I stalled by exploring his feelings.

"Buck, what do you think of our future here on the farm under the conditions established by the radicals in this state?" I asked him seriously.

Frank grinned as he replied, "Well, by George, I think that if I'm not murdered within the first six months after returning, I will be within one year. That's why I stayed in Kentucky."

"Yes, that's already happened to four of our guerrilla comrades who rode with us under the black flag. I guess the only reason I'm still alive is that they all think I'm dying – so why waste good bullets on a dying man."

Frank's face became stern. "Yeah, I sure don't want anybody to know I am here and I ain't staying here long after Christmas day."

"Frank, if they're going to treat us like criminals maybe we could give them good cause."

Frank peered at me intently, knowing I wasn't one to make idle conversation.

"What have you got in mind Dingus?"

"I just got a hankerin' to rob a bank," I answered.

Frank's blue eyes twinkled. "You mean like Bill Anderson did during the war?"

"Yep, that is what I'm talking about. Just like Bloody Bill did."

Frank's eyes steeled. "Hell, Jesse, that's never been done except during the war. You know that?"

I replied with utter confidence – in myself and in my plan.

"Yep, I know that, but what's the difference? Same people. Same guns. Same horses. Same operation. Except *we* keep the money."

Frank seemed to be thinking hard on this statement. He said he'd like a little time to think it over. Knowing that Frank never made a decision under pressure, I agreed to wait until after Christmas to bring up the subject again.

The holiday came and went. The next time Frank and I had a chance to compare notes, he remarked,

"Little brother, you gave me a lot to think about. I've got some questions, but I'll go along with you. There's two things that bother me though, and bother me a lot. For one, we're sure to be recognized, and secondly, in your condition, you would not last a day in the saddle before you were dead."

I was real happy that Frank was dealing himself in.

"Buck, I've thought it all out and not only won't we be recognized, but we would have perfect alibis. Everyone knows I'm too sick to ride and everyone knows you're in Kentucky. I've been doing nothing for months but thinking about this – not knowing whether I was going to live or die. And realizing if I did live we'd be working here on the farm in constant fear of someone sneaking up on us and killing us before we could get to our guns. You know this time it won't be a rope or bayonet that they take to us.

*James Younger. One of the four brothers who with Jesse and
Frank made up the 'James-Younger' gang.*

This time it'll be the death of Frank and Jesse. And the killing will be in the name of the law – Missouri radical law. Damn it Frank, we just don't have no other choice."

Frank's blue eyes became resigned. "Ok, ok. I agree. And knowin' you, you've already got a plan. What is it?"

"Yep. I plan to rob the bank in Liberty. It's got a lot of money in it. Northern money. We ride in, rob the bank, and ride out. I went over there the other day and nobody recognized me and I didn't recognize anyone. But we'll need good and trusted men to help us. We'll need protection on the outside while we go inside."

"Who do you have in mind, 'ceptin' me?"

"To do it right it would take 10 to 12 men. And I feel they should be brother guerrillas who have the same attitude as we do, that this is really the only way to go."

"You got any thoughts as to just who?"

"The two I really want are Jim and Cole Younger."

Frank can find no objection here and he merely stated, "There're not two better in this world than those two. I agree. Who else?"

For some period of time we discussed names, discarding some, keeping others. This decision was so important, for when you're going into battle, and this is just what we two considered it to be, we wanted the best. Each man we discussed had his good points as well as his bad. We carefully considered every aspect of each man's character before finally deciding on seven more names, in addition to the Youngers. They were Bud Pence, George and Oliver Shepard, John Jarette (the Younger's brother-in-law), Arch Clements, Red Monkers and Bill Chiles.

Our talk then turned to when we would rob the bank and Frank pointed out, "Okay, Jesse. Just remember when we do this I'll need some time to contact all of the boys."

I was happy at the way my plan was progressing and I smiled as I told him, "I figure the day before Valentine's Day. After all, don't you figure we deserve our own Valentine's gift – money?"

Frank wasn't in a light mood. "Damn it, Jesse," he said, "it's no joke. Don't forget it's winter and I'll have a lot of travelling and convincing to do before I get everyone to agree."

I reassured him. "The way you ride, even with your hip still bothering you, you'll be able to contact the boys and get them here on time. I know my brother. Your eloquent tongue will be able to convince each and every one of them."

"Oh hell, Jesse you know these boys'll be all for it. Arch will never

Robert 'Bob' Younger.

surrender and he'll feel he'd just as soon die with money in his pants than broke as a skunk. I'll wager we won't have one turndown. No siree."

Next, Frank wanted to know about our alibis.

"It's like this," I told him. "This here doctor from Kansas City keeps coming out to see me every few days. I'll get him out here a couple of days before the raid and he'll think I'm so bad off that I couldn't even mount a horse, let alone ride one. He's a talker. And he's got a good reputation. So everyone will believe what he says. By the way, after you've contacted all the boys, head back for Kentucky and be seen by as many people as you can. Then scoot back here just for the raid, then back to Kentucky, like you never left."

I think even Frank was impressed by my forethought.

"You know Dingus," he said, "you just might become a great bandit leader with the way you think. That is, if you don't get us all killed or captured."

I flared up when he said that. "Captured? Not me, Frank. Not ever. I may be killed, but never captured!"

"You still having that dream Jesse, about being shot in the back?" he asked with concern.

"It's no dream, Frank. I know just how I'll die. I see it when I'm wide awake, as well as when I'm asleep. But the only way to guard against it is to be on constant alert and surrounding myself with only those whom I can trust."

Frank nodded. "Yep, that makes sense. And with the boys we've chosen, you sure don't have to worry none about being ambushed from the back."

The only thing left for us to decide is the meeting date. I told Frank to have each one of the boys ride in singly two days before Valentine's Day. I told him to have them meet in the brush here on the farm, where we've hid out so well over the years. Our meet day would be conducted just like a normal round-up for "boots and saddles" – the usual guerrilla password – and the same requirement would be in effect – guns and horses ready to shoot and ride."

Then I cautioned him, "But be sure no one comes to the house, except you, cause that could arouse suspicion if a lot of new people are seen hanging around the house."

"That's a good thought," Frank approved. "You know you sound like you got a promise of being what I said before – a good leader – for an 18-year-old!"

For the next six weeks until four days before February 13, I drained my pus into the vessel and cleaned my wound religiously. However, the next day I did nothing so that the area around the wound began to swell up and become repugnant. It looked awful. Finally, I hollered for help to Ma. "You'd better get that Dr. Lankford out here to look at me, Ma. I just feel real poorly."

As always when one of her children needed help Ma responded quickly. She got the doctor to ride out from Kansas City in the morning. Two days before Valentine's Day, the doctor found his patient in mighty bad shape. He drained the pus, put compresses on the swelling, and after being assured that I had not made any changes in my daily regime opined that I had had a serious setback, which made it obvious that I couldn't get up and about at all. The doctor said I would have to remain in bed, almost motionless, or suffer serious consequences. He also observed the extreme pain that I was experiencing and the debilitating weakness I was suffering. There was no doubt in Dr. Lankford's mind that I was very bad off. After opening the wound for natural drainage, he gave orders that I should not even get up to go to the outhouse.

Later that same afternoon, a dusty but elated Frank rode in to inform me jubilantly that not one of the boys had said "no" to our plans. In fact all of them were assembled in the brush on the farm and were ready to ride tomorrow.

I replied with a grimace of pain and the news that the doctor had given orders I could not even get up to go to the outhouse.

But when I did so, I had a twinkle in my eye which readily told Frank the truth. I told him that I would outline the final details of the plan just before dawn the next day.

Frank told me later that when he left the house to rejoin the men in the brush he thought to himself. "That kid brother of mine sure has a crafty mind. An alibi for both of us, the right men, and a plan to make all of our saddlebags heavier with what we all want and need – money. I wonder what else he has up his sleeves?"

As the first rays of the morning sunlight began to show from the East, ten men were ready to ride once again. This is not too different from a guerrilla raid, they're thinking. But they've had no final instructions. They don't know anything except they're going to rob a bank.

They're beginning to be a bit restless and a bit uncertain without their leader. "Where the hell is Dingus," I heard as I rode up. "It's time."

Frank answered, "Stay calm Cole. He'll be here."

Just then I came out of the brush and after a quick but warm greeting to each man, I laid out the plan, drawing a map of the city, the street and the bank in the dirt with a nearby stick. Only Frank and I would enter the bank. The rest would remain outside with specific instructions as to how each man was going to conduct himself. I drew each man's route in the dirt with my stick and explained each man's position which he would take during the robbery.

The men listened carefully, even those who were older and more experienced. It was a good plan and I knew they would follow it to the letter. Finally Jim Younger voiced his disquiet. "Damn it, Dingus, its a good plan all right, but ain't you supposed to be flat on your back?"

"Yep," Frank answered him in an exaggerated Southern drawl. "He's so damn sick I may have to come back from Kentucky to look after him." This brought out loud guffaws from the assemblage.

Then Arch Clements asked, "When do we begin to shoot?"

I had been dreading this question, but it was unavoidable. I answered quickly and firmly, "Doggone it, Arch, let's hope there is *no shooting* until we're leaving town. If any of the town folk realize what's going on and attempt to interfere, then we ain't got no choice but to shoot. But remember this isn't war – it's business." Then I added, "By the way, I got a good old Missouri grainsack right here that will look awful good when it's filled with those carpetbaggers' money from that there Northern bank."

With all the preliminaries out of the way, it was "boots and saddles" time again, with Liberty our destination. This time, though, it was not a raid against the Federal militia and a fight for a cause, it was for a more selfish – and it was to be hoped more rewarding – reason. Each man riding in this raid is not mounted because of some atrocity that has befallen him or his family, but each rides with the same thought – that since each is considered an outlaw by the terms of the Drake Convention, which is now the law of Missouri, that each just as well might be that – an outlaw.

My thoughts were a little different. I had already made my peace with God. This bank robbery was only a small slice of vengeance for the atrocities we had suffered. There was no thought in my mind that in leading this outfit, that I was doing anything that was not correct. There was no wrong in this act, in my mind. It was only a small attempt to begin to even the scales, to make things right in the world after the Civil War. I was convinced that I would still go to heaven, as nothing I was doing was wrong. I love God. I do not swear. I do not drink. And I know God will accept me for I love Him. I know eventually I will join my earthly and celestial fathers in Heaven. Knowing the conditions which have brought about my actions, God will forgive.

After Liberty – the Meeting

No sooner had the last ghastly brays of the guerrilla-rebel yell died down than we began to scatter – each taking a different trail. The distance from Liberty to the farm was short and even though we each rode through highly-covered brush trails it was not long before we reached the farm.

Each dust-covered and tired man was curious (and excited), about the amount of cash that was in the grain sack that Frank James was holding. However, no one ventured a word about it because true to our guerrilla rules, everyone must wait until the leader arrived.

But where the devil was Jesse? They each seemed to be thinking, as they dismounted from their horses and sat on their heels in a small gulch near the farm. Even Frank told me later he was concerned with my late arrival, knowing the weakened condition I was in. Had Jesse passed out? Fainted? He wondered.

Most of the men had a look of uneasiness on their faces when I popped out from behind a tree with a gun levelled at them. In my stoniest voice I yelled, "What the dickens, if I was a posse you'd all be dead ducks by know. I thought better of this lot than I find."

You never saw such sheepish looks on probably one of the toughest, roughest bunch of free riders ever assembled.

"Aw hell, Dingus. We're safe here on your farm," allowed Bud Pence.

I was damned angry at their laxness. And I'd meant what I'd said.

"Nobody is safe at any time, Bud. Nobody should ever put themselves in the position to let anyone get the draw on him. Especially from the back, like I just got on you. The next time I get the drop like I just did on any of you, there'll be no more ridin' with me, understand?"

Arch Clements' jaw line clenched and he drew his gun, "Look, Dingus, I nurtured you when you was just getting started with Captain Bill. I'll be damned if I'll let you talk to me like that."

I knew then that I was going to have to fight for the right to be the leader of this group. Former leaders do not allow a new chief without a battle.

Well, I was more than willing to stand up for my rights. I knew in my heart that I was born to command and I was ready to meet the challenge.

"Arch," I said sincerely, "I love you like a brother, but I ain't going to take one word back. What I said goes. I'll never ride again with a man who gets careless, drinks before a raid, or in any way betrays one of us, even if the betrayal is an accident."

All the time I'm speaking, Arch is looking at me intently. "Now, Arch, put that gun away and let's find out just how much is in that grain sack Frank's aholdin' over there. Hope its more than a bushel – like it says on the outside." I gave Arch a friendly, boyish grin, but my eyes never left his gun.

But before he could holster his weapon, I deliberately put mine away first, making sure everyone observed this gesture.

My remark about the money and deferring to Arch by putting my weapon away first seemed to break the tension.

Arch, completely chastised, broke out into a big grin. Years later when he discussed this incident he told me he'd been thinking, "Damn it, Dingus, young as you were, there was somethin' about you that said *LEADER* all over you. At the time I didn't know where or what we'd be headin' into, but I thought, By Gosh, Dingus is right. And being right, he's got the privilege to be our chief."

As we began to count the loot, it soon became clear that there was a great deal of money in the sack – more than any of us had ever seen in our entire lives.

Cole, who had assumed the responsibility for the counting, was putting money into one stack and a stack of bonds into another pile. It looked as though he didn't give the bonds any importance because he was stacking them off negligently to the side.

Finally Cole said, "As I count it boys, there is $24,316 Union dollars. Now all we got to do is split it up. What's the split, Dingus?"

"That's cash, Cole," I told him. "But what about them bonds?"

Red Monkers looked disgusted. "Hell," he chimed up, "those things aren't worth nothin' cause them bankers have them numbers posted in all of the banks by tomorrow morning, you can bet on that!"

I caught Frank's eye and sent him a silent message which he seemed to understand.

"The split's an even one," I said, "Except I'll take a half share if me and Frank get the bonds."

Frank added, "Yep, if we get the bonds, me and Jesse will both take a half share along with anyone else who wants to split the bonds with us."

The two Shepard boys spoke up almost as one. "It's a deal. We don't want none of them damned bonds. Don't know how you can get rid of them – but good luck!"

Cole and Jim Younger opted for the bonds.

And so the decision was made. The cash was divided into nine equal portions and then two of the portions were divided in half. Each rider with a full share had over $2,700 in cash. In 1866 that would buy a farm, horses and much more.

But what was more important to me and Cole Younger and Frank was that the face value of the bonds was in excess of $40,000.

After the rest of the guys had gone, Cole Younger put a voice to what he'd been thinking, "Just what in hell is going on here," he said in his deep and resonant voice. "Frank, these bonds ain't worth anything if we can't cash 'em in."

"Well," I said in my sweetest voice with a hint of a smile in it, "You could have taken the cash."

Cole almost whined as he defended himself. "Lookit here, Jesse, I don't know what you and Frank are up to but I saw that look pass between you two. I'll go by your rules, all right, but damn it, I just want to know what's goin' on."

I thought of Captain Rogers' cool and calm demeanor and I tried to emulate him as I said, "Cole, these bonds are bearer bonds which means anybody can sign 'em with any name they want and they're just as good as cash in any big bank you go into. I figure with a little bit of bluffing, people with nice manners like we got could cash 'em after waiting a little bit of time, in any big city. Like New York."

"Hell, Jesse, none of us ever been in a big city like New York," argued Jim Younger.

"That's right," Frank said with pride, "And nobody ever robbed a bank before today either."

Cole was mollified. "Okay, you're right. As I figure it we got 'bout four times as much as the others by taking the bonds. Iffen we live to cash 'em!"

"Don't worry about that, Cole," I reassured him. "We'll live to cash 'em, all right. But there's one more thing we need to think about. If we are going to build us a pot to operate out of as an outfit, we got to put a little aside for expenses when we need it right?"

"Right on, Dingus," says Jim. "I'll go for that and Cole can hold onto our half and we'll be able to ride a good distance and go to New York or somewhere, easy enough. We got enough cash out of this whole deal to go for quite a spell."

So that's how it all began.

Later, we were to realize that the start of what would become a legend – The James-Younger outfit – had its beginnings with the bank robbery in Liberty, Missouri. But at the time we were not a legend. We were just simple farm boys from Missouri. And although I was by far the youngest, I was still their undisputed leader on that hot and sultry day before Valentine's Day in 1866 so long, long ago.

Remorse

As I'd already planned to do, for the next three days I did not drain the pus from my wound. I allowed it to become inflamed and swollen.

On the third day Dr. Lankford arrived and saw with his own eyes what bad shape I was in. He determined that I was unable to walk, even to the outhouse.

The concern in his eyes told me that my plan had succeeded because I looked worse than I had just four days before. My alibi was working perfectly.

After the doctor's careful examination, he talked things over with Ma. He gave her strict orders. I was not allowed to walk, even to the outhouse. Ma would have to be my chambermaid. She would also have to do the actual draining of the pus from my wound. The doctor explained carefully how this was to be done. Without Ma adhering strictly to his orders, he said I might not survive.

Outwardly I was a physical mess, but inwardly I felt very good that I had completely fooled the doctor. The raid had gone according to plan – my plan. With one exception – the killing of the young college student, Jolly Wymore.

The next time Dr. Lankford came he seemed to approve of the care Ma had been giving me. I looked a great deal better. Ma had drained the pus from my wound every day and kept me completely flat on my back.

As I lay there day after day I reviewed each detail of the raid in my mind, seeing each man at his appointed post, watching the action in the bank, and unfortunately seeing once again the untimely death of young Jolly.

I had never wanted that to happen. In fact in my planning I had never contemplated such an event. I had, of course, told my outfit that if anyone interfered we would have no choice but to shoot them. However Jolly Wymore had not done anything. But as the leader, I was responsible.

On the occasion of his third visit after the Liberty robbery, the doctor seemed quite pleased with my progress, but I also noticed him giving Ma concerned glances.

"Mrs. Samuel, I could not help but notice that you don't look too well, yourself. Is something bothering you?"

Ma would never confide in a stranger, even a doctor, so she answered simply, "Oh maybe not up to snuff. You know, what with worrying about Jesse and not having seen my other son since last Spring, I'm a little weary. But warm weather is just around the corner and I'll be perkin' up real soon."

Wouldn't you know it! Ma, without really knowing the truth, was providing an additional alibi for Frank, protecting him as well as me.

After the doctor left, Ma came over to my bed.

"Jesse, are you awake?" she asked.

I was. "What is it, Ma?" I asked.

"Jesse, I know that it was you and Frank in that bank robbery. I understood all this fighting before and during the war, but Jesse, you just ain't been smiling since the robbery. What is wrong? Neither you or Frank were hurt."

I patted her hand. "Ma, that's true, none of us were hurt. But what happened is that a boy – an innocent bystander was killed – and there was no need for that to happen. I was the leader and I'm responsible. It's put a black smudge on my soul and I'm worrying something fierce about it."

Ma smoothed my hair back off my forehead and offered comforting words, "But Jesse, you didn't do it. I know that. And there must have been a reason for any of you boys to shoot and kill that boy."

Ma's kindness had opened the floodgates I'd been holding back for so long, and I started to weep.

"Oh Ma, he was just standing there and Arch shot him and then told us that he thought he was going for a gun. So instead of just shouting to scare him, as I had ordered, he shot and killed him. But what is important is that I was the leader of the outfit and the leader is always responsible. So I feel that I killed that boy just the same as if I'd pulled the trigger myself."

As my loving mother tried to comfort me, I wept even harder. The tension, the pain of my wound, the guilt of taking an innocent life – had all caught up with me.

Ma started to cry along with me, but finally she said,

"Jesse, we got to pray son, and hope that in your father's memory, God will listen and forgive. Remember 1 John 1:9 – *'If we confess our sins, he is faithful and just to forgive our sins, and to cleanse us from all unrighteousness.'*"

I joined Ma at the side of the bed in kneeling position and she and I prayed out loud to our God and Saviour asking forgiveness for my part in the death of Jolly Wymore. In my prayers I promised over and over again that I would rejoin the church and follow Christ for ever and ever.

After we both had prayed long and hard. I crawled back into bed and propped myself up and stared ahead while Ma took a seat in the chair next to my bed. Neither of us spoke for quite a spell.

"Jesse, we must let the parents of that boy know that it was an accident and that you grieve."

It was probably what I wanted and expected to hear because I heard myself saying in a very humble tone, "You're right. I've been thinking the same thing. I'll write the letter for both Frank and me if you'll deliver it to his family."

"I promise you that I will, first chance I get." She then got up, went to the desk and got the pen, ink and paper and brought it to me. I wrote the following:

> *We regret the death of your son and hope that*
> *you will believe it was an accident as we had no*

cause to kill him and never meant to do so.
You have our deepest sympathy.

Frank and Jesse James

When I finished, a great weight of remorse and sorrow seemed to have been lifted from me. I handed the letter to Ma and went peacefully to sleep. When I awoke, I had dismissed the entire matter from my mind.

The heart has its own reasons for what it does that the head knows nothing about. What I had done came straight from my heart and it eased my internal turmoil considerably. But my head told me it had been a right foolish thing to do – and as usual, although I didn't fully realize it at the time, the head was right.

Zerelda Samuel, as she was by this time, the mother of Jesse and Frank James. The 'boys' greatest ally, she defended them with the ferocity of a tiger protecting its cubs.

4

It was a cool Autumn morning when we five met in the brush just west of Lexington, Missouri on October 30, 1866.

As always before a raid – or as now a robbery, we were dead serious. Our preparations had been the same as before a guerrilla raid, which we all knew so well. Our very lives depended upon the careful attention to detail. Needless to say, and most important, our guns were checked and re-checked to make sure they worked without a hitch.

Even more important, if possible, the plan of attack and retreat had been reviewed minutely. Each man's responsibility during the robbery was outlined clearly and carefully.

The most crucial aspect of each raid or robbery, in my opinion, was the retreat. We always entered the town from at least two different directions, and often more. We had thoroughly scouted and familiarized ourselves with the route to take out of town. We also had at least one alternate route in the event something went wrong with the original plan.

The only difference between our robbery preparation and our black flag guerrilla preparations was our wearing apparel. At a few minutes before noon, five men wearing dusters which were popular male apparel during that time, sauntered into town. We came from different directions. We looked just like normal riders of the era. Nobody could tell that under the dusters each of us was heavily armed.

The first three men in our outfit to arrive in town took up positions that gave them complete rifle coverage not only of the bank, but of all possible places from which trouble could emerge. As Frank and I approached from different directions and dismounted, I felt extremely confident. No one seemed to be paying us the slightest heed.

As we entered the bank of Alexander Mitchell & Company, there was only one other person present and he appeared to be a cashier. Frank asked him if he could change a $50 bill. He nodded and opened the cash drawer.

Frank James as a young man of approximately 21 years of age.

When he looked up he was staring straight into two Colt 45 revolver barrels. Just at that moment of truth, two others of our outfit sauntered into the bank and immediately drew their revolvers from under their dusters.

"Who are you?" stuttered the terrified cashier.

I was feeling mighty cocky and I just couldn't let the opportunity slip. "We're bank examiners," I grinned.

"And put it right here in this nice grain sack to be examined," said Frank. The money from the cash drawer was quickly deposited in the grain sack.

"Now we'll have that $100,000 in the vault" threatened Frank, waving his Colt under the cashier's nose.

The cashier's voice shook. "I don't have a key. Only the manager has the key and he's not here."

I glared at him with as much ice as I could put in my eyes as I cocked my pistol and put it to his head. "If that key don't appear in ten seconds, you won't have no head to connect to your body."

A very frightened voice answered that he didn't have no key. He added that he could be searched and no key would be found. Cole, who had entered with Jim Younger, did just that and then said, "Dingus, there's no key on this man."

I uncocked my Colt and managed a genuine smile. "My good man," I said graciously, like the lord of the manor, "I believe you. This will be your lucky day. You still have your head," then I sniffed at him repugnantly, "but I might suggest that you change your longjohns."

We all four holstered our guns with a shrug of resignation about not finding the key, and calmly walked from the bank. Jim Younger shot a parting remark on the terrified cashier, "If you show your face outside of this bank within the next ten minutes, your family will have a funeral bill to pay!"

We later learned that the cooperative cashier's name was Mr. Thomas. Not wanting his family to have a big debt at the mortuary, he waited the full ten minutes before emerging from the bank.

As prearranged, John Jarrette had quietly gathered up the horses and brought them into the area in front of the bank. We mounted and slowly rode out of town.

As we were riding out of town, I told John about the disappointing turn of events regarding the absence of the key to the safe. John began to cross-examine me in a way I didn't like, which gave me the impression he was not entirely convinced of my explanation.

I felt that this was the time to put my foot down and to assert my rights as a leader, so I stopped my horse and looked at him straight in the eye and said, "John, your friendship means more to me than money. And if you question me that I'm telling the truth, you can have my share – but we'll never ride together again." Jim Younger told me later that the sincerity of my statement not only quelled Jarrette's doubts, but solidified my leadership.

I had one more point to make with Jarrette and I did so as we jogged along. "In the future, I'll stay outside as I believe that is where any danger will arise. Hereafter, we need only two men actually inside the bank, just as we did at Liberty. And anybody, including you John, will have my trust to the fullest."

We five were still riding out of town in a group, not having split off in different directions as yet, because we thought we had gotten away scot free. But lo and behold if we didn't hear the clattering hoofbeats of a posse riding hard up behind us. As soon as we spotted the posse and they spotted us, we split up rapidly, going off in five different directions.

Later, we found out that the posse was being led by Dave Poole and his brother, John, both of whom were former guerrillas. Dave Poole later told us that when we split up as we did, both he and John knew immediately it was a group of guerrillas, and all of a lickety-split sudden, the posse just ran out of steam and somehow lost its fervor to catch us. Because no way, were ex-guerrillas going to exchange shots with their former comrades.

This taught me a very important lesson. While all of us black flag boys might have gone in different directions after the war, there would always be a tight bond between all guerrillas. It was a kinship that would always be there. As outlaws – which the Drake Convention had made us – we needed kinfolk. I would design all of our future operations based upon that knowledge.

As I thought of kin, I thought also of 1 Kings 12:24, "Thus says the Lord, *'you must not go up and fight against your brothers the sons of Israel; return every man to his house, for this thing has come from me. So they listened to the word of the Lord and returned and went their way according to the word of the Lord'*."

That's what the Lord meant – that kinfolk should not fight. And that passage from my beloved Bible was clearly demonstrated by Dave and John Poole.

An Attempt on My Life

After Lexington I returned to the farm while Frank went back to Kentucky.

The ride home after we split up had drained my strength. By the time I reached the farm I knew I wouldn't have to pretend to have physical problems to Dr. Lankford. It puzzled me how I could change so rapidly from apparent robust health to that of an almost-invalid. Peculiarly, while the outfit was in action I felt strong as a horse and in complete command of myself. As soon as it was over, I reverted to a pale, weak, constantly-coughing individual.

By the time I reached the farm I had a fever. I actually had to be helped to undress and get to bed. I was so bad off that Ma immediately summoned Dr. Lankford and when he arrived he found his patient had deteriorated. I couldn't stop coughing and with every spasm my entire body was wracked with intense pain. And, of course, my lung wound was swollen, red and angry-looking and the wound was draining pus.

Of course Dr. Lankford was spared the truth about my activities. All he was told was that I'd been getting worse for the last week to ten days. After he examined me he stated firmly that he should have been called sooner. He also added that he hoped I hadn't done any exercise for the past week before (which was true), and he chastised me strongly for that.

The interesting thing about this entire story is that I didn't really have to fabricate my physical condition. Although it made a tremendous alibi for me, I was truly suffering in the worst way from my lung wound. It was strange how I could rise to the occasion when I needed to (the occasion being a Northern bank filled with Northern loot), and then fall back into a swift relapse almost in minutes. Was it because I was part Devil?

For three months, throughout the winter, I was unable to do anything for myself. It even came to the point (which I never thought it would), that I was unable to go to that little outside room decorated with the crescent moon. Ma and my sisters cared for me as best they could. I was put in the little room upstairs and I'm sure everyone thought it was just a matter of time for me.

And on many a discouraging day followed by a pain-filled and discouraging night, it would have been easy to succumb. But the one thing that kept me going was thoughts of Zee. If only she were here, I thought, then I *would* get better. But of course, there was no Zee. Oh, how I longed for her.

I was at a very low point the night of February 18, 1867 when I heard a commotion downstairs, outside on the porch. Dr. Samuel came upstairs to tell me that there were Federal militia at the door and that they wanted me, dead or alive. It didn't seem to matter to them.

I somehow mustered enough strength to drag myself to the small bedroom window. There were five militia on the porch and five horses out by the fence. They were yelling for me to come out or they would come in and get me. I sure didn't want any of my family to get hurt because of me. So I had no choice.

The door leading onto the porch at the James' Farm. Locals believe that the holes repaired with wooden plugs are those made by the bullets from Jesse's gun that killed the first militia man on the night of February 18th 1867.

I realized that surrender would mean I'd be dragged to the nearest tree and hung. And of course following the hanging there might be a trial, but it wouldn't matter one way or t'other to me. I felt like a trapped animal. And my reactions were the same. Like any trapped animal, I must fight my way out. Kill or be killed. I'll be darned if I was going to join so many of my guerrilla comrades in being hung to the nearest tree.

The porch of the James' farm as it appears today. The door in the centre is the one through which the fatal shots were fired.

I grabbed my two revolvers which were fully loaded and went down the stairs. I made a couple of general comments from just inside the door as I wanted to judge exactly where the men were outside on the porch. As soon as I determined this from their replies, I fired through the door. There was an instant yowl from the porch. Almost at the same instant I threw the door open and continued firing.

In addition to the first man I'd shot, one of the others dropped, never to rise again. The other three ran hell-bent for leather for their horses. I shot two of them, but I did not aim to kill, only to wound. The third militiaman was able to mount and ride away. Whether I'd wounded him or not, I just did not know.

I had so thoroughly taken all five of them by surprise that they had been unable to fire even one shot in retaliation.

The family and I dragged the two wounded militaimen out of the bitter winter cold and into the house. Dr. Samuel got busy tending to their wounds and I was happy to learn later that they both lived.

However, I knew that when the militia came back the next day, that this wouldn't help me one bit and I would be hung for murdering the other two. It might be self-defense, but would I get a fair trial? I seriously doubted so. I would be hung and questions asked later.

Those were my innermost thoughts as I went upstairs and packed. As usual, when push came to shove, I was able to summon up the strength from somewhere – I knew not where.

For the next nine days I relied on kinfolk on whom I felt confident I could depend. One type was relatives. My father, Robert James, had nine brothers and sisters living throughout Missouri and Kentucky, and I had many, many cousins. The other type of kinfolk was that closely knit and fierce band of Southerners, mostly ex-guerrillas, who would never refuse help to a former Confederate, whether a regular or an irregular, as I was. This was especially true in the State of Kentucky which, although a slave state, had remained in the Union but was home to many ex-Confederate soldiers.

After nine days of travelling from one kinfolk to the other, receiving all the help that each could give, I finally arrived at the home of one of my Kentucky cousins. Here, I was given the same loving care that I would have received in my own home.

When you are "kinfolk" in the South, you are "kinfolk," and no questions are asked.

If an outsider might get nosy and inquire as to who the stranger is, the answer would be that it's just Cousin John who is "visiting for a spell." You're treated as though you were a close member of the family and had always lived there.

The North may have won the war, but to the vanquished, there was always the consolation of "kinfolk."

Of course, even greater consolation would have been the presence of one beloved cousin – Zee – but that was not to be for a time.

Ma wrote to me. She told me that the day I had left, the militia had come out with their captain and retrieved the two wounded men, that the five who had come to the house and demanded my surrender were not acting under official orders, that they were acting entirely on their own. But the best news of all was that my actions had been adjudged as self-defense and there were absolutely no charges outstanding against me at all.

My immediate thought was that these findings were all to the well and good. But would it have gratified me if I'd been hung that night?

Not at all.

The Savannah Bank Robbery

I had been at my cousin's in Kentucky for just about a month and was beginning to improve when I heard about a bank robbery in Savannah, Missouri.

From the newspaper accounts the robbery sounded very much like the Lexington robbery, which I had planned. However, there were two significant differences. The first was that no money had been taken. And the second, and most important, was that I had not been there.

No names as to who the perpetrators of the robbery might be were mentioned in the paper. But the description of the mode of operation alerted my suspicions.

About two weeks later Arch Clements arrived. After getting off alone and out of earshot of anyone else Arch admitted that he had been present at Savannah.

"Dingus," he confessed, "We rode in just like we always do, like you and the boys did at Lexington, but before we knew what was happening that cashier was firing at us. We returned the fire and four bullets hit him and down he went. But God damn it, Dingus, that didn't help us at all, because he had shut down the vault. Not only that, but his damn son-of-a-bitch ran out of the bank yelling to the townsfolk. And that really started things up in a hurry. We were lucky to get out alive."

Arch's mouth was moving a mile a minute so to calm him down I said, "Whoa there, Arch. Just slow down a mite and tell me who was in the outfit, and what exactly did you do that was just like we did it at Lexington?"

"Well, there was just myself, Ol and George Shepard, John Jarrette and Bill Chiles. And the reason we know . . ." I cut him off with the question, "But who was the leader?"

Arch, for the first time since I'd known him hung his head and meekly answered, "Dingus, it was me. And I led us right in the bank, and I got a bullet along my side – but it ain't serious."

Before answering I took note of the fact that Arch was pretty dismayed to be in his position and although I didn't want to embarrass him I felt a point had to be made.

"Doesn't sound like you boys knew what to do, how to do it, or when to do it, for that matter."

Arch was dejected. "You're right, Dingus. But I swear that I did just what you would have done. About noon everything was lookin' mighty fine and it looked right easy, until that old coot started shooting. That was the whole damn problem."

Arch felt bad enough for one day so I changed the subject by telling him, "I'm sorry, Arch, for all of you. But how is everything else coming?"

A smile played around his lips. It seemed I'd finally hit upon what he really wanted to say. "Most of the boys have used up a lot of their share from the Liberty bank. What we need is another Liberty. What do you think Dingus?"

I turned it over in my mind. And I was of two minds about it. I knew that with such a large group as we had used at Liberty there was the chance of problems. Probably more problems that we'd want to live with. We just didn't need eleven men to rob a bank. On the other hand, the guys at Liberty were close guerrilla comrades.

The loyalty side of my internal argument won and I told Arch, "All right, Arch. Let's all meet just as we did before in the brush outside of my parents' farm on May 22. And let's make it the same eleven as we had at Liberty."

Arch seemed pleased as I told him to do the contacting and to tell all the boys when he saw them to just be there, same as before.

"Where we going and who we going to rob?" he wanted to know with a spark in his eyes.

I wasn't ready to answer that question yet. "That's what I'll determine by the meeting date. And nobody but me will know until then. But remember the rules must be strictly complied with by all. I'll give them the details on May 22. Be sure and tell each man when we meet it'll be 'boots and saddles' time once again. We'll do all right – not like what happens when we're *not* together."

As Arch left to carry out the commands I had given him I allowed to myself that I was truly beginning to get the hang of being a leader and commander of men. There wasn't the slightest question as to who was in charge. Actually, I didn't have the least notion as to what bank we were going to rob, in spite of my bravado. But by May 22 I would.

I knew I would need help if I had to scout out a bank and make all the detailed plans for our next assault on Northern money. Also, I had stirrings that I wanted to seriously discuss some long-range plans for the outfit. As the leader, I wanted my lieutenants beside me, Frank and Cole Younger.

Three weeks later Frank James and Cole Younger arrived and were passed off as just friends of the sick man who was visiting his Kentucky cousins. We three entered into some long and serious discussions. Cole wanted to rob the Hughes and Wasson bank in Richmond, Missouri while I favored a bank in Russelville, Kentucky that my cousins had mentioned as a Northern bank with large deposits and an equally large vault.

We decided to investigate both. Frank would look over the bank in Richmond by posing as a cattle buyer to the bank people and I would mosey around Russelville. After that we'd make our decision.

With that, Cole became defensive and wanted to know why the decision should be made by Frank and me – why it couldn't be made by the three of us.

Again, I had to act decisively. These little challenges to my right to lead were coming thick and fast. So I just smiled good-naturedly (which I wasn't feeling, I was damn annoyed) and told him, "You know Cole, if Moses had been a committee, the Jews would still be searching for the promised land."

Cole had to laugh and that took some of the sting out of the point I'd made. Thus was Cole's antagonism overcome. Yes, I had learned the lesson of fast-talking well.

Frank and I met just one week before May 22 when the entire outfit would gather. He was convinced that Richmond was the bank to rob, based upon his observations as a "cattle buyer."

Russelville wouldn't take eleven men to rob so Russelville, I told him, would be put on the back burner until some later date.

With our target determined, Frank and I talked the afternoon away about plans and aspirations for the future, about our loves, and about our innermost feelings. Frank felt that we should be thinking about leaving Missouri to scout on what might be available to us elsewhere where we wouldn't be hounded by the redlegs and the Drake convention.

We talked of California and our uncle Drury Woodson James who ran a hotel out there with mineral springs nearby where people took hot baths. Frank thought that this might be good for our health, and perhaps we oughtta ride out and take a look.

Our talk turned from California to wives and families. Each felt we were entitled to have our own family and the idea was an important one to us. Our upbringing in the bosom of a large, loving church-going family had been so strong that having my own family was uppermost in my mind. Frank said he was lukewarm towards the Church, which I was not, but about a family he felt as strong as I did. That's when I told him that Zee and I had plighted our troth, and Frank understood and was happy to hear it.

"It is stated in Genesis 2:18, *'It is not good for a man to be alone; I will make him a helper suitable for him,'*" I told him.

Frank smiled, "Or," he said, "As the great bard stated in Hamlet, *'Man and wife is one flesh.'*"

I came right back at him with a grin. "Or I could quote Proverbs 31:10, *'An excellent wife, who can find: Her worth is far above jewels.'*"

We were having fun like two schoolboys with our verbal duel. Not to be outdone in any way Frank showed off his knowledge of his beloved Shakespeare by coming right back at me with *"or as it is said in Henry V, 'Man and wife, being two, are one in love.'"*

As we strutted our stuff for each other, showing off our erudition, I thought of how things might have been if it hadn't been for the war – I, a preacher and Frank a professor of English. But this was not to be. We were already embarked on another trail. This afternoon's discussion was probably the most intimate we had ever had. We had never really confided in each other to this degree ever before. The last subject we discussed was my recurring dream. I admitted to Frank that I still had it and that I was more convinced than ever that when I died it would be from a shot in the back. I also told him I believed that it would not be soon. Frank was genuinely happy to hear me say that and said he was looking forward to being an uncle to Zee and my kids.

Last of all, our discussion turned back to our planned robbery and what alibis we might establish.

Frank's alibi, we figured out, would be that he would make sure he was seen leaving Kansas City on May 18 with other men in a position to supply affidavits that he was 200 miles from Richmond on the day of the robbery.

I worked out an alibi which would be that I'd be seen in a hotel 100 miles from the scene on the evening before the robbery.

After all, no man could travel that far in that short a period of time, especially in my physical condition, now could he?

Richmond, Missouri Bank Robbery

On May 22, 1867 I was in the barn changing my saddle from one horse to another when Frank arrived. He had been riding for 12 hours and he and his horse looked spent. He quickly dismounted and removed the saddle from the horse he had ridden to a fresh mount. We said nothing to each other.

A few minutes later we joined the other nine men in the brush outside Ma's farm just as we had done 15 months before. As I inspected the group I noted with satisfaction that all nine were riding the finest horseflesh that money could buy and each was equipped with the newest type of revolver available on the market. It was a professional looking group, which gratified me. They all exchanged warm greetings with Frank and me as we entered the meeting place.

In all, the meeting was almost exactly as it had been when we were planning our first assault on the bank at Liberty, Missouri, with a slight, subtle difference which I immediately noted. As the talk escalated there was no mention of the words guerrilla or irregular but more and more the men kept referring to the "the outfit." No name was given to the "outfit" but it soon became apparent that all of them were identifying themselves with the group. The continued remarks about the "outfit" left no doubt in anyone's mind that this time we were not meeting to fight for a cause, but merely to rob a bank for personal gain.

I was sensitive to other slight differences in the men's talk and wondered if I would have to re-establish myself, again, as their leader, deflecting small challenges and reproaches as I had done in the past. But Arch Clements resolved that matter once and for all when he asked, "Dingus, where is the bank and what is your plan?"

I inwardly felt a deep swell of satisfaction. I hunched down on my knees, picked up a stick from the underbrush, and began drawing the diagram of the bank and the position of each man in the dirt.

The bank was in Richmond, just 25 miles away. My plan was that we would all ride into town from different directions, screaming out the old guerrilla yell, ride up to the bank, and enter. For this attack, I explained, only five men would actually enter the bank. I am sure the men were surprised, although they didn't exhibit any outward evidence of it, when I announced the names of the five who would enter the bank, and neither Frank nor I were included. Cole Younger was designated the carrier of the grain sack. Four men were given detailed and highly specific instructions as to how they were to ride up and down in front of the bank shooting to keep the townspeople at bay. Frank and I were to dismount and take up what I considered highly strategic positions from a defense point of view outside the bank. I had placed myself in the most vulnerable position in the event the townspeople decided to fight back and attack.

From the position that I had pre-selected I would be able to see in all directions. In the event there was any opposition, I would undoubtedly be the first to be shot at. After all, I still considered myself and was considered to be by all the others the best shot in the outfit, including Frank. Frank was positioned to cover my backside. No one else knew why, but Frank did. He was, however, in a vulnerable position as well should there be a counter-attack.

I explained to the men that the bank's split would be equal, but that neither Frank nor I would return to Ma's farm for the split, but that Cole Younger would hold our shares.

Once all the details and particulars of our raid were out of the way, the men rested for about two hours, much as we had done before any important guerrilla raid. But before we mounted and I gave the familiar "boots and saddles" order I called the men around me to lay down one other highly important directive. I gave an order that no one was to fire a shot at any person unless he were fired upon first, or I was fired upon. In other words we could retaliate – but only in self-defense.

Red Monkers quickly spoke up, "O.K., Jesse, but if I'm fired on directly or you're fired upon, then what?"

"If that occurs, then do what the good Book gives us permission to do – an eye for an eye – and shoot back. But don't miss!"

With that I announced "boots and saddles" and we mounted and started for Richmond.

As our outfit leisurely rode the 25 miles to Richmond my thoughts were mixed and somewhat apprehensive. I knew that I was operating with too many men. This was too large a group. My next thought was that I couldn't have left a one out. Actually, it was important to have the type of camaraderie and kinship we had established as a group than to execute the robbery with a smaller and probably more efficient outfit.

I had outlined our plan of operation and tactics very carefully, but with 11 men riding, all kinds of unforeseen events could occur. Also, I was worried about the order I had given for shooting. I had no assurance that everyone would comply and I didn't want another Jolly Wymore incident, which preyed heavily on my mind and conscience. I finally rationalized that if the townspeople did fight back, by shooting first, that they deserved whatever my outfit could dish out because we would only be returning their fire in self-defense. Gradually, the distinctions between a guerrilla raid and a bank robbery began to blur. When you're shot at during war you quickly return the fire, otherwise the person shooting at you will kill you – dead.

Richmond, Missouri Bank Robbery

When we hit Richmond, as planned, we rode into town from different directions giving the blood-curdling rebel guerrilla yell, and riding in at a furious gallop, firing left and right just as though it were a guerrilla raid. Five men dismounted at the Hughes and Mason Bank to find that the doors were locked!

These five men, led by Cole Younger who was the biggest, quickly charged the door until it gave way and entered the bank. Outside, four of my men were riding up and down in front of the bank shooting into the sky, hooting and hollering to frighten the townspeople and keep them inside. Frank and I took our pre-designated positions. I was directly in front of the bank for all to see.

Inside the bank there was no resistance. The money from the cash drawers was quickly crammed into the grainsack which Cole held. However, to Cole's frustration, there was very little cash on hand inside the vault. It was almost bare. The little found in the vault brought the grainsack up to only half full.

Outside, things were different. As I had anticipated, if there was going to be trouble it would come from outside. The Mayor of Richmond, of all people, was running up and down the street attempting to rally the men of the town. Finally, he leveled his six shooter at me and fired.

His aim was poor. But the signal had been given. Instantly four bullets entered his body almost simultaneously. One was mine, one was Frank's, and the other two came from our riders. The town of Richmond had a mayoral election coming up in their future. They no longer had a live one.

Next, I noticed a young lad running out of the town's jail, shooting wildly at the riders. An older man was fast behind him. I later learned that the young man was only a fifteen-year-old and the man behind him was his father, the town jailer. The son was the first to bite the dust. His father fell over him, both dead.

I did not see which of the men fired the shots that killed the jailer and his son but I knew that as the outfit's leader, I was responsible. And it hurt. Again, I once more rationalized to ease my internal ache, that their deaths were different than Jolly Wymore's death, because they had come at us first, and fired their guns at us first. That's the way it is in war, I said to myself, kill or be killed. The jailer and his son had fired first and missed. No one gets a second chance.

Of course we were *not* at war and this was *not* a guerrilla raid. It was a bank robbery. But no one pointed that out to me – least of all myself – and if they had I wonder if I would have listened.

Our escape went off as planned with all 11 men leaving town as a group, then quickly dividing into batches of one or two horseman, all going in different directions.

Later, I was told that the meeting back in the brush near Ma's farm took place as scheduled shortly after the robbery. Cole Younger divided the money into 11 equal shares. Cole kept our share. There were no bonds this time. As soon as the financial division took place, nine men quickly left the farm to wait eagerly for the next call to "boots and saddles."

Frank left just as fast as he could to re-join a group he'd been riding with earlier who were headed for California. His alibi was an excellent one. While Frank had been riding with them the California-bound convoy had stopped about 10 miles outside of a town on the Kansas trail. Frank had already planned to have his horse throw a shoe at this spot. When his horse began limping slightly Frank allowed as how he had to ride into town to get his horse the attention of a blacksmith. When Frank returned to the western-bound party in only one-and-a-half days with a new horse, he aroused absolutely no suspicions. Months later when his group learned about the Richmond robbery, nobody was able to remember on what particular day Frank James had rode into town to trade his old horse for a new one. What an alibi!

As for me, I rode the 100 miles back to Kentucky where I was supposed to be and have stayed during the robbery, in record time. Where the strength came from, I don't know. But I did it. I was back in the hotel in Chaplin, Kentucky, before I was missed. Nobody realized I hadn't been there all the time.

As I rode, though, I was attacked by the voice of conscience, that still, small voice within. I was feeling good, on one hand, that the bank robbery and our escape had gone so well. On the other hand, there were several deaths that I felt I was responsible for. I went to feeling high to feeling mighty low and blue almost in minutes. What was I, I asked myself. Was I a Southern hero as I sometimes like to think I was? Or was I just a lowly brigand who robbed and killed for pleasure? Was I doing this for pure ego? The two parts of my soul fought for mastery, the Lord and the Devil. I thought of Matthew 4:1-11 and the temptation that had been given to Christ by Satan. The difference was that the Lord had been strong enough to defy and defeat those temptations. But I was not Christ and had not overcome the temptations of the flesh. What I really wanted to be, a man of Christ like my minister father, the Drake convention forbade. *". . . no ex-Confederate soldier, whether regular or irregular, can become a member of any profession or a deacon of any church."*

If it had not been for the Civil War I would have been a preacher. But now what was I? I did my best to talk to God but I received no answer. The only constructive thought I did have was that I, myself, could never use the funds from this robbery for any personal gain. I must give it away to others for their good. (After expenses, of course!).

This melancholy meditation and decision somewhat quieted my conscience and I rode into Chaplin, Kentucky with renewed peace of mind.

AFTERMATH. Not one of the 11 men who took part in the Richmond robbery was ever charged with the crime. However, eight warrants were issued for alleged members of the gang. All of the eight were ex-guerrillas who had served under either Quantrill, Anderson or Todd. These former guerrillas were James White, John White, Payne Jones, Richard Burns, Isaac Flannery, Andrew McGuire, Thomas Little and Allen H. Parmer.

Some had alibis. Those without alibis were hung on trees without benefit of any trial. They included Richard Burns, Andrew McGuire and Thomas Little. The other four so accused were never arrested nor were their names ever heard of again in Missouri. This was a time when it was common for men to change their names and identities and it is most probable that the four never arrested left the state and changed their names. Only Jim White was to ride with me in the future.

Hanging without benefit of a trial was common in Missouri in those days and "guerrilla Hunting," especially if the tiniest of excuses could be found, was rife. Whether the men who took part in the lynchings had the correct information or not was unimportant. After all, the North had won the war. That seemed to automatically put "right" on their side, in their opinion, and many an innocent man lost his life in these unlawful times.

Although it was painful to hear that three of my ex-comrades had been hung, it seemed to justify the killing of the jailer and his son. Because if I and my men had not shot our way out of Richmond on that night of February 18, surely we would have met the exact same fate.

Again, my conscience eased.

Back in Kentucky

After I was back in Kentucky, Nelson County to be exact, at the hotel for about a week, I returned to "kinfolk" at the Donny Pence home. When I arrived, I was firmly told that Donny's brother Bud Pence had arrived about two weeks prior to my visit.

Now that Bud could have arrived at the Pence homestead two weeks before and still been present with me at the Richmond bank robbery, seemed mighty magical. But this was typical of kinfolk. It sure did establish a good alibi for Bud, especially since his brother Donny was the sheriff of Nelson County. After all, if the sheriff said that his brother had been there two weeks, who was going to dispute him? Only a mighty foolish man, I had to figure. The whole situation gave me a much-needed laugh because I had found somebody who had an even better alibi than I did.

I received a letter from Frank. In it, he explained how he had rejoined his friends and ridden to California and how he had established his own alibi with his lame-horse tale. He wrote that the group had gone first to San Francisco, then south to Monterey. At Monterey he had separated from the party and ridden to Placerville for the express purpose of trying to find the grave of our father, the Reverend Robert S. James.

This he was unable to do, although he hunted everywhere. It was a serious disappointment to him, and to me, also. He went on to say that he'd left Placerville with a very heavy heart and gone south to the farm of our uncle Drury Woodson James, who with his partner J. D. Thompson, owned the La Ponsa Ranch about 50 miles southwest of Paso Robles in San Luis Obispo County.

Frank was fascinated with the sulphur hot springs at the ranch and strongly urged that I come to California and join him. He felt that at the ranch I might finally have a chance for a full recovery from my wounds, especially my lung wound, which still plagued me.

I finished the letter, carefully folded it, and stowed it away in my belongings. California sounded interesting and the idea of going there to recover had a certain allure. I knew I would give it serious consideration, but at the moment I had other things on my mind.

Bud Pence had decided to return to Missouri. After all, he pointed out, over two months had elapsed since the Richmond robbery and it should be safe. No sooner did Bud leave the Pence residence than Jim White arrived. He carefully refrained from using his real name. No one was told that Jim White had arrived. Instead, the neighborhood learned that a "cousin" of mine had arrived for a visit. The full story of what had happened to those who had been indicted for the Richmond robbery was told to me by Jim White. I had heard rumors, but Jim's was the first full and factual report I'd received.

At first I didn't know why Jim had decided on a Kentucky visit. I reasoned that it was just to hide out for a spell. But that was not his real purpose at all. His "hiding out," he told me, was going to be done in Tennessee at a real cousin's house. His visit to Kentucky was for the purpose of discussing future plans with me. He wanted to know if I was going to be doing any further "business" like at Richmond, because if I was, he wanted to be counted in. His reason was much like mine when I had decided to become a bandit. He said that if he was going to be hung for being an ex-guerrilla he might as well take the chances on being hung for being a bank robber. And if he took the chances on being hung, he might as well have the rewards of bank robbery, as well.

Convoluted thinking, no doubt. But that's the way our minds ran in those uncivil days following the Civil War.

There was no doubt in my mind as to Jim's sincerity even as I questioned the purity of his thinking, as I did my own. I had full and complete trust in Jim, knowing of his services to the Confederacy as a guerrilla. I assured him that he would be included in the next venture and obtained his address in Tennessee so that when I was ready he could be easily contacted.

For the next six months I went from one kinfolk to another. Again, I was in considerable pain from my lung wound. I had to drain the pus every few hours. In fact the wound got so that that I sought out the attention of Dr. Paul F. Eve of Nashville, Tennessee. I became so sick that it was difficult to ride my horse. Often, I had to be taken to the doctor by wagon. Frequently he came to see me at the house in which I was staying.

Just about the time that I was showing some evidence of recovery, partial at least, I had another letter from Frank. It convinced me that complete recovery lay in a trip to California. I knew there was no way I could ride that far, but I figured that I could go to New York by train, then by boat to Panama, across the isthmus, and then again by boat to San Francisco.

But there was one more thing to do before I left. Some time back I had scouted out the bank at Russelville and because Richmond seemed like an easier bank to rob at the time, I'd put it on the back burner. Now it was time to take out my previous thoughts about Russelville and to look at them again. The bank was not located in Nelson County, Kentucky and therefore there would be no conflict with my cousin Sheriff Donny Pence.

I had already promised Jim White that he would be included in any of my future plans and through other channels I contacted Cole Younger. Cole told me that his brother Jim Younger would not be available as he had migrated to Texas and become, of all things, a deputy sheriff. Cole also told me John Jarrette was available. Besides Jim White, Cole and Jarrette, I decided to include George and Ol Shepard. That would make a total of six of us. Just the right amount of men, I concluded.

We had our meeting the next day. Even though it had been over a year since I had scouted out the Russelville bank I was pleased to find that I remembered every exact detail about the place. (God bless my photographic mind!).

I caused a definite stir among the men when I told Jim White to bring a grey horse to the rendezvous point in the brush when he arrived. I gave him the money to buy a good one. It was Cole who voiced what the others were thinking. "What the hell, Jesse, we ain't never had extra horses, what is the deal?" I explained that I would be riding one horse to the meeting, and then would change to the grey horse for the robbery itself. I explained further that it was part of a careful alibi I was laying down in advance. The guys listened intently but they all shook their heads at my explanation, as if to say, "it's too much for me!" Cole did remark that he couldn't see the reason for all this alibi stuff, because when anybody saw him he was easily recognized due to his size. Laughingly, Jim White said,

"O.K. Little John, we all know who *you* are, but Robin here wants everybody to think he's *not* there. As for me, I could care less. I'm already under indictment."

After our meeting, my cousin near Champlain and I bought two horses. I paid, but we purchased the horses as though it was one for each of us. In that day and age everybody recognized others more by their horses than anything else. So I had good and calculated reason for doing this.

I left the black horse at my cousin's and rode the rust on to the Marshall house where I was going for their local baths under the recommendation of my doctor. The one thing I insisted on doing was letting everyone at the Marshall House and everyone in the town of Champlain know all about my fine, new rust horse. I showed her off to everyone with ill-disguised pride. "Isn't she a beauty?" I asked enthusiastically, showing off her fine legs and well-bred head and they all oo'ed and ah'ed about her.

As I marked time before the robbery took place at Russelville my only reservation was that Frank would not be at my side. It would be the first time. As time grew near I began to really worry that he would not be there. Obviously, I couldn't tell the others about my recurring dream. Frank would have understood in an instant.

Another reason for apprehension and a slur on my ability to lead occurred, but I only learned about it later, after the fact. Had I known at the time, I would have been really nervous. Cole Younger had gone to the bank in Russelville posing as a cattle buyer just to check out that everything that I had said had been correct. Apparently he had not had 100% confidence in my well-known photographic memory. However, I learned that he discovered every little detail I had spelled out for the men had been accurate. After that he never again questioned my memory. But at the time it was a slap in the face. I had to confess that my ego twinged. It would still be necessary to establish and re-establish my right to be the leader of the "outfit."

The Russelville, Kentucky Bank Robbery

On the first day of Spring most young men's fancies turn to thoughts of love, or so say the poets. But those whose business it is to rob banks had better keep their minds on practical matters. So on March 20 and 21, 1868 I was concentrating on the upcoming assault on the Russelville bank.

On the night of March 20 I let it be known to everyone at Marshall House, where I was staying, that I felt a lot better. I allowed as how I was going to take a short ride the next day on my new rust horse, of which I was so proud. After all it was the first day of Spring, I nattered on, and the fresh Spring air would probably do me some good.

Artist's impression of the Russellville Kentucky Bank Robbery 1868.

"You better not ride too far, Jesse."

"Dang it all, son, you're not ready to get up on the back of that there horse."

"Take it easy, boy, there's plenty of time."

So went the many cautionings I received. Even the stable master where I mounted my rust threw in some warnings.

With everyone primed to recognize that I was not well, and couldn't really ride far, I mounted my rust horse and rode her out of town.

However, as soon as I was out of town and out of sight I sped up, rode the five miles to my cousin's house hard, changed to the black horse and rode hell bent for leather to the pre-arranged spot just outside of Russelville where I would meet up with the others. They were all there, including Jim White with my extra horse, the grey.

We six then immediately took to our pre-assigned routes into town and the well rehearsed mode of operation went into effect. I took up my position just outside the bank. Jim White gathered the reins of the horses of the three who sauntered into the bank.

However, Cole Younger had been inside earlier when he had posed as a cattle buyer in order to check out my memory of the bank's layout, and he didn't want to be recognized. So the Shepard boys, Ol and George, brandished their guns and attracted the attention of the bank tellers, while Cole remained in the background. As a result, the president of the bank was able to slip out the bank door, even as the grainsack was being filled with $20,000. Had Cole been in the forefront of the action, he never would have allowed the president to escape.

Unfortunately for the banker, John Jarrette was stationed outside the bank and as soon as the president opened the back door, Jarrette shot him. The gunshot alerted the town. Shooting began. By this time the Shepard boys were running out of the front of the bank with their well-filled grain-sack. With a few shots in the direction of the townspeople who were starting to descend en masse on their financial institution, we rode hard out of town. As we left, we split and dispersed into ones and twos – our normal manner of retreating.

The grey horse was fresh and rested. We rode hard and fast for 75 miles until I reached my cousin's farm. In the brush outside the farm I had tethered my rust horse. I put the grey horse to sleep with a quick and merciful shot and quickly mounted the rust horse. Then I rode calmly back into town, greeting one and all, especially the stable master. He could plainly see that my horse had not been ridden very much that day. It was obvious the rust had only gone a few miles, and even that very slow. It wasn't hard to establish this alibi because it was true. The rust had only been ridden about ten miles that day. Nobody, and I mean nobody, could have ridden that rust horse from Chaplin to Russelville and back in that short of a time, much less rob a bank.

I felt quite safe and secure, my alibi established. However, this bank robbery was not to be as lucky as the others. One of the greatest and noted detectives of that era was assigned to the case, Yankee Bligh of Louisville. Before his investigation was over, two of our six would be either dead or captured.

Yankee Bligh, who had a first-rate reputation, took to the trail the very next day. With his posse he followed the trail out of town made by two horses. He didn't bother following the trail of the single rider.

Unfortunately the trail Yankee Bligh followed led straight to the house of George Shepard of Nelson County, Mo. George was returned to Russelville, identified, and spent three years in the Kentucky State Penitentiary. True to the outfit's rules, which I had set down before the event, he refused to identify any of his accomplices.

George's brother Ol was not so lucky. His arrest was assigned to vigilantes by the government officials. As the posse of vigilantes descended upon Ol and asked him to surrender, Ol spat in their face, yelled out that he was a rebel and would not surrender to "any God damned Yankee federals." He took his stand against the posse with his back against a tree. They shot it out. Ol finally dropped with seven bullets in him. But, by God, he never did surrender to any federal!

Yankee Bligh knew that the Shepard boys and Jesse James had a close relationship. So he made a thorough investigation of me and my whereabouts on the day of the bank robbery. He soon became convinced that I could not have been at Russelville.

During the investigation he did ask for warrants for arrest to be issued for Cole Younger, John Jarrette and Jim White, but because he had little evidence on those three and no eye-witness descriptions were able to be obtained, the matter petered out.

I stayed at Marshall House about a week after the robbery, long enough to hear about the Shepard boys. Then as soon as I felt that there would be no suspicion aroused by me leaving, I returned to Nelson County and the home of my cousin Sheriff Donny Pence. About three weeks after I arrived at the Pence farm a large man arrived who was described to the neighbors as just a "friend of my cousin's who's a-visiting for a spell."

When Cole Younger and I had a chance to be alone he told me that Ol Shepard's share of the robbery had been given to his widow and that George's share had gone to George's family.

After I received my share of the Russelville raid I decided now was the time to discuss with Cole what had been festering in the back of my mind for a long time.

"You know, Cole, before Russelville and right after Liberty our original plan was to establish a 'pot' for our outfit so we could get into other things. A cattle ranch, for example. But so far we haven't done anything about it.

Cole beamed his pleasure.

"I can tell by the tone of your voice Jesse, that *now* is the time we do something about it, before it all drips through our fingers, right?"

"Absolutely. In fact now is the time to try to cash those bonds. And since I've written to Frank that I'm coming to California, I'll go and talk it over with him. Maybe together we'll come up with something, maybe Frank and I will have some thoughts as to what we should do – and where."

"Sounds good to me, Dingus," Cole concurred. "Do you think we actually can cash those bonds? I know that in the banks we've been into I haven't seen any posted notices about stolen bonds. Have you?

"Well, most of the banks we've been into and out of pretty fast," I chuckled, "But the ones I've just scouted for possible future visits haven't had any posted notices. But don't forget, these are bearer bonds."

"What do you think, Dingus, about us going to New York? We can pose as cattle buyers, see the sights, and cash the bonds at the same time?"

"Sounds good, Cole. Let's do it."

Obviously I couldn't travel my horse for any great distance. So one early morning in late March, our spirits high, Cole and I boarded the train in Nelson County for the big city. We readily slipped into our roles as cattle buyers from Texas and no one found any reason to dispute us. We spent a few days seeing the sights, dining at fine restuarants, and talking cattle business. When the time was ripe we found a bank, explained that we had a good cattle buy in Texas but the transaction had to be handled in cash, and readily exchanged the bearer bonds for dollars. It was accomplished so easily that we felt that for a couple of farm boys we had done all right with the city slickers.

The day we obtained the cash Cole left by train for Texas, de-trained in Missouri, and disappeared into the landscape.

I also left the same day, having previously booked passage for Panama under my real name. The boat ride to Panama was pleasant but I discovered that I had no sea-legs, despite the relative calmness of the waters. The ride across Panama was accomplished, then back to San Francisco by ship.

A small nagging thought kept at me. Had the serial numbers of the bonds been distributed to New York bankers? Could this blow our cover? Could the bonds be traced back to me and Cole? We were never to learn if they were or were not because neither Cole nor I ever heard anything about those bonds ever again.

The trip to California was doing me some good already. I was beginning to relax. Not the least of my benefits was that my recurring dream about being shot in the back did not occur. Things were looking up. Or were they?

5

By the time I arrived at Uncle Drury Woodson James' farm near Paso Robles in California, travel-weary but somehow inwardly relaxed, Frank had already been there for almost six months. I was received warmly and hospitably as the "kinfolk" that I was. No pretense at kin was necessary here. Uncle Drury was a blood relative. In fact, we three were very close.

As for me and Uncle Drury, our middle names were the same. And it was from Drury that I again heard the legend of the two bastards which Ma had told Frank and me over and over again when we were little. Drury kiddingly stated that he didn't think *he* would fulfill the legend, but maybe Frank or I would, since we had become quite well known as guerrilla fighters during the Civil War.

"Actually," Drury said, "It'll probably be you, Jesse, since you were the 'hero of the battle of Centralia'." Here, Drury was referring to the battle when I killed Major Johnson.

Little did I realize when I arrived that I was to stay in California for almost one year. Throughout the fall and winter I used the mineral baths. At this time they had become quite famous and visitors came from far and wide to use them. Both Frank and I became quite robust. In fact, I felt that my lung wound was completely healed and this made me quite happy, to say the least.

We did not always stay on the ranch. We made one trip to Placerville and several to San Francisco. Our trip to Placerville was a disappointment. Once again we could find no trace of our father's grave.

The trips to San Francisco were different. I wasn't looking for something, but I found something. Uncle Drury had a lot of friends in San Francisco and one of his friends had a beautiful daughter. Her name was Marguerite. And I was smitten with her. She gave me a small picture of herself to carry in my wallet, and I consulted it often. Frank kidded me a lot about how this girl had fallen for the young, tall, dashing Confederate war hero.

During the past few years I had added three inches to my height and I

now stood 5′ 11″. I didn't think this height qualified as "tall" but Frank did. I was glad I had grown from the 5′ 8″ I was when I was a guerrilla fighter, but a bit disappointed that I wasn't going to be taller than Ma, who, of course, stood over 6′.

Ah, luscious Marguerite – she of the dark brown curls and wide green-blue eyes. I was fast becoming very involved with this beautiful damsel. And then one night when Marguerite and I were alone, it happened. I had been passionately kissing her and every muscle in my body was tight and strained with passion. As I lovingly unbuttoned her blouse in preparation to caress one of those lovely breasts of hers I saw a vision of my father. His voice clearly stated, "No my son. She is not your betrothed."

I stopped dead in my tracks, as the saying goes, just as though someone had thrown a pitcher of ice cold water in my face. I stopped what I was so happily engaged in at once. That beautiful girl must have thought that I'd been shot because I immediately pulled back and buttoned her blouse.

I was visibly shaken. I took her home, returned to Paso Robles and the ranch and never saw or wrote to Marguerite again. But I did keep her picture for the rest of my life. Whenever I looked at it, memories of California returned and the sweet interlude with Marguerite flashed before my eyes. I frequently pondered over a life that "might have been" with Marguerite. But then what man can truthfully say that he does not have one spot in his heart for a forgotten love . . . a love that "might have been" but in my case was destined not to be. There were fond memories of Marguerite, always, but my life was to take a different track.

When we returned to the ranch, the three of us – Uncle Drury, Frank and I had many discussions, most of them centering on our future. I think it was Uncle Drury who convinced us in his calm and clear manner, that a person cannot run from his destiny. Uncle Drury felt that we were too involved in the history of and the love for Clay County to ever set down roots and be happy anywhere else. He felt we should return.

Perhaps he was right. There was no doubt that Frank and I were home-sick for our loved ones. And after all the only crimes we had actually committed, as far as the authorities were concerned, were crimes that we committed during the Civil War. It might be true that the James boys could return and live within the rules and be ultimately forgiven for our guerrilla days.

That night Frank sat down and wrote a somber letter to Cole Younger. He suggested that maybe Cole, together with his brother Jim Younger, could also settle in Jackson County, their home. After all, we now had the "nest egg" that the bonds had provided. When divided they could provide all of us with a good life.

While these discussions were taking place I was doing some serious thinking of my own. I kept returning to the vision of my father and what he had said to make me back away from Marguerite. And I realized that there was only one woman for me, and that was Zee. This finally became a resolution. I must return to Missouri.

When Cole's answer came, we were all very pleased. He said he'd been thinking along the same line – that all four of us could settle down and make a go of it. He was willing to set a date to divide the nest egg.

Frank and I had known but forgotten, but Cole's letter reminded us, that Jim Younger had migrated to Texas and become a deputy sheriff there.

"Well, Jesse, if Missouri doesn't work out maybe we could head for Texas. Or after we divide the nest egg and see our friends and folks we can always come back to California if we want."

It seemed as though life with all its possibilities was opening up before us. With my lung wound healed, with my mind made up that Zee would be an important part of my future, things looked mighty good.

Return to Missouri

It was an optimistic pair of young fellows who started back to Missouri in the Spring of 1869. I was 19 years old and Frank was four years older, making him 23. Our future was secure (those bonds!) and looked mighty bright, for change.

I was impatient to get back home. I knew that once we divided the nest egg we could establish the James/Samuel farm as one of the leading farms in Clay County. The farm could be expanded. I could marry Zee and we could have our own house on the farm property.

I knew that Zee was still waiting for me as her letters had arrived in California on a regular basis. They had been as affectionate as ever. I'd written to her and told her everything about my experiences on the West Coast with one exception. Of course I had not told her anything about Marguerite. Needless to say, some things are better left unsaid. I had no guilt about Marguerite at all, because I had stopped before any serious love-making got underway. If I had not, I would have felt guilty inside but I believed with all my heart that my real father had known and come to me at the right time.

Yes, if matters proceeded as well as we anticipated there was no reason I could not claim Zee for my wife within the next year.

As we rode towards Missouri Frank and I talked a great deal. We decided that with the security of the nest egg there would be no need to leave Missouri to make a new start in Texas, or even California. We talked of family and how all would benefit from the sale of the bonds, Ma, Dr. Samuel, our sister Susan, and our half brothers and sisters. We were going to be a real "family" at last! I'll admit that I've never been shy about expressing my thoughts and I did most of the talking with Frank finally coming around to my way of thinking – that happiness for all of us lay in one direction and one direction only – Clay County.

The only disquieting experience we had on our journey was that one night I had the dream. When Frank awoke me from my out-loud protestations and mumblings I told him that I had been having the old nightmare. Frank calmed me down but said nothing more. Frank was always better at keeping his thoughts to himself than I was.

The next morning I felt fine and was just as optimistic about our futures. To reassure Frank I told him, "You'll see, Frank, there will be just friends at home. And nobody will get behind me to shoot me. Better yet, nobody will want to shoot us, Frank, as there won't be any reason to. For we are "forgiven" just like the prodigal son. You'll see."

"Yeah, Jesse. As Shakespeare put it in I Henry IV, "We may boldly spend upon the hope of what is to come in." Just like Frank to be quoting from Shakespeare after I had talked of the Bible!

I looked steadily at Frank and said, "Buck, I think we should both get down on our knees and pray that what we find is an atmosphere of "let bygones be bygones" when we get back.

"I don't know about praying, but I sure hope within my heart that you are correct, because that's what we all want."

"I just hope that all our planning of those alibis will pay off" I replied. Then we were both silent with our own thoughts for a spell.

Our welcome home exceeded our imaginations. It was a warm one and the house was full of bustle with Aunt Charlotte and her son Ambrose scurrying around killing and plucking the fattest chickens for the feast. The good feeling of abundant Missouri/Kentucky hospitality imbued the farm house. Relatives and friends had come from as far away as Kansas City to welcome us home. What was of major importance to me was that Zee was there, pink and blushing, aflutter in spring muslins and a poke bonnet edged with lace. She had never looked more beautiful.

Old neighbors came to greet the returning travellers and to hear about California. Old guerrilla comrades, although scattered all over the landscape, came to talk politics and to discuss the economic condition of the countryside.

One guerrilla, Allen Parmer, came clear from Texas. During his stay, however, I noticed he paid more attention to my sister, Susan, than to Frank and me, his old comrades. The one consensus among all – which meant most to us – was that Frank and I had a chance to be at peace and to establish ourselves as a part of the community.

After the excitment of our return subsided we settled down to the immediate problems of the farm. I had always loved farming and I enjoyed putting in the crops and plowing the fields.

This was the first plowing I had done since that time five years ago when I had been lashed by whips and prodded by bayonets by the Federal militia, who were searching for information about my brother Frank and Quantrill.

This time when I plowed I took precautions. At all times when I worked in the fields I kept two revolvers strapped to my side and a rifle within easy reach. I thought what a lot of things had happened during the past five years. I was not yet 20 years old but I'll bet that I had more adventures and experiences in fighting than an average person has in three lifetimes. Even so, I was truly happy doing farm work and although I was ever watchful, I was also ready to live and let live.

After a few months I began to attend church and then I did what I've always wanted to. I professed my conversion and belief and was baptized in front of a large group of church members at a spot along the river not far from where I'd been baptized as a baby. Ma had often told me how she had held me proudly aloft as my father baptized sixty converts with the Baptist ritual of immersion.

After this I was a regular and fervent church member. I prayed long and intensely for Frank's conversion. Buck, however, enjoyed playing cards and liked a convivial drink now and then. But there was none of this in me. At this time I was so straight-laced I believed religiously in "look not on the wine when it is red" and believed deeply that there was a devil in a deck of cards.

I once asked Frank about the playing of cards and the drinking of liquor. And he, as might have been expected, answered in the words of his favorite bard. This time he cited what the Dauphin had to say to King James, *"Have I not here the best cards for the game, to win this easy match play'd for a crown"* and then he half-smiled as he reminded me of how he had got the best men available for the bank robbery at Liberty. I saw his point and shut up.

As for drinking, Frank reminded that Jesus, Himself, had changed water to wine and to illustrate his position quoted Shakepeare, citing the Hostess in II Henry IV. *"I'll drink no more than will do me good, for no man's pleasure I."*

From this discussion I was assured that Frank would never allow himself to overindulge in liquor and that he would always stay alert and ready for whatever came his way. I had never seen him drunk, nor ever heard of him being intoxicated, even after a battle during the Civil War when the majority of the guerrillas would drink themselves blind, if they could.

I also realized that to attempt to push my brother any harder to convert to the Baptist faith was useless. When Frank made up his mind on anything he was as stubborn as any Missouri mule. Stubborner.

Summer came and then autumn when the crops were gathered and I was gratified to find that the farm had yielded in full measure the fruits of our Spring planting. I felt that our bountiful harvest was due, in part, to my conversion and I felt I was reaping the blessings of a life lived in security and peace.

Living as we did so quiet, retired lives so to speak, we attracted little notice of a public sort. From time to time, rumors that since the James boys were home again old war animosities were being revived came my way, but I ignored them.

I thought, "Oh, don't they know that the war must end and that life is too short to harbor these tales and reawaken gossip?" At the time I was soaked in virtue. That I had been a participant and planner in three major bank robberies wasn't a part of my thinking at the time. In fact, the memory of the robberies was just a dim blur.

Just before Thanksgiving, which was to be a big family celebration and to which we were all looking forward, Frank and I received word that we had been indicted and were to be arrested for crimes that had occurred when we were guerrillas under Anderson and Quantrill. That damned Drake convention again, which pardoned all Union soldiers but persecuted and prosecuted all Confederates.

Frank didn't seem at all surprised that he'd been charged with atrocities while serving under Quantrill, including the raid at Lawrence. I was charged with the "murder" of Major Johnson during the battle of Centralia. All of these were considered "crimes" under the law of Missouri as provided for in the Drake Convention and affirmed in January 1868, still in force and effect.

The big blow came less than a week later. Certain members of the Mount Olive congregation, hearing of the charges against me for "murder" prevailed upon me to resign and although Brothers Major and Henderson visited me, and attempted to change my mind I felt for the good of the congregation that my withdrawal remain. I had done nothing to warrant this action and I was devastated. My old war record, and my old war record only (they knew nothing of my other activities) now branded me a murderer.

After the announcement of my name being excluded from the rolls of the church on the 1st Saturday of November, 1869 a great depression descended over me, a depression so deep that I went to Ma and told her I felt it was God's will that I die. With the help of Frank, who had been too wary, too circumspect to lay himself open to this type of rebuff, Ma convinced me that it was not "God's will" at all, but merely the circumstances of the times.

It was at this time I realized that Frank had had a point when he stayed aloof from joining the church, being too suspicious of human nature and all too aware of human frailty. Frank was very kind to me when he reminded me that even though my name had been stricken from the rolls of the church, I was still baptized and a son of God in His eyes. Also he felt keenly the unhappiness that I was going through and did his best to alleviate this. All of this made me feel even closer to my brother.

The depression began to wear off a little and was replaced with anger. I became infuriated that as a Southern soldier I was not allowed to live and let live. The indictment had resurrected the past and when I thought about the past I realized that therein lay some unfinished business.

From the recesses of my mind where it had laid dormant but never dead I recalled my vow to kill Captain S. P. Cox, or was he really Captain Sheets? I had sworn to revenge Bloody Bill. I knew Cox/Sheets lived in Galatin, Daviess County, Missouri just 40 miles away from our farm. I also knew that he worked in the bank as a cashier.

The thought crystalized in my mind. What better way to kill Sheets/Cox than while robbing a bank?

I decided to rob the Davies County Bank. That's all I told Frank. I didn't mention Sheets/Cox originally. Cole Younger readily fell in with my plan. Cole had also been indicted for "crimes" while he was a guerrilla.

The problem was that I didn't want to tell either Cole or Frank that the bank robbery had a dual purpose. Since I had already established the policy of being outside the bank, this was going to be ticklish. As we three discussed the job, it was Frank who made the suggestions that if it only took three of us to rob the bank, then I should change my position and be the one inside. Thus, my problem was solved. Unknown to Frank, this was exactly what I was hoping for. And when he made the suggestion that I should be inside, and that Frank should take up the sentry position outside, I heartily agreed.

I was ready to proceed.

The Gallatin Bank Robbery

On December 7, 1869, Cole Younger, Frank and I mounted our horses and with a casual air of unconcern rode leisurely into Gallatin.

Frank stayed outside with the horses in a position of lookout while Cole and I entered the bank. Cole handed the cashier a $100 bill and asked for change. While the cashier was concentrating on counting out the change I thrust my revolver towards him and demanded the keys to the inner doors of the safe. The outer door already stood open.

While Cole held his revolver aimed at the cashier I went behind the counter and removed about $700 from the safe. As I did, I kept studying the cashier. He looked damned familiar.

As I stuffed the money into our grainsack I walked over to Cole and whispered to him, "that sure looks like Captain Cox to me, does it to you?"

Cole answered in another whisper. "It sure does. But I'd like to be sure."

Hearing this answer, I called out to the man, "Captain Cox, remember the head of Bill Anderson?"

The cashier's head jerked and his eyes turned to granite. "Damned right I'm glad I . . ."

The rest of the sentence was never completed. Now that I was sure the cashier was Captain Cox I shot him right through the head. Blood spurted everywhere, but not on me thank goodness, as his body slumped to the floor.

In my own way I had kept my vow to my God and I felt an intense satisfaction as he expired.

Outside, Frank was beginning to have trouble. At last he understood my contention that when trouble comes it will come from the outside, rather than inside the bank. He had deterred several of the local citizens from entering the bank but when they left they quickly raised the alarm that "something strange" was going on inside. Just as Cole and I were leaving the bank we heard Frank yell for us to put some steam into our exit and hurry it up.

Shots were being fired outside but they were sporadic and seemed to be coming from a great distance. I wasn't too concerned until I started to mount my horse. Just as I did, she bolted and my leg got caught in the stirrup. She began to drag me in the dusty street. I got free, but my horse bolted for the town's livery stable.

Frank saw my plight and as he waved Cole ahead to keep going with the precious grainsack, he turned around and came back and scooped me up behind him onto his horse.

A single rider was approaching the town as we were leaving. He was riding a nice looking gelding. Frank asked the rider to rein up. With Frank's revolver aimed at his head, he immediately complied. I asked him his name, where he lived, and the rental value of the horse he was riding. He quickly answered all three questions. I told Mr. Smoot that I was renting his horse and that the horse would be returned to him in a few days.

Mr. Smoot quickly dismounted, and Frank and I galloped off in pursuit of Cole. When we reached him we put our guerrilla procedures into effect. Cole went in one direction. Frank and I rode in an entirely different direction, towards the town of Kidder.

Almost immediately we heard hoofbeats approaching and another rider came into view. He looked like an ordinary cowpoke except he was riding a beautiful chestnut mare and over his rough plaid shirt he was wearing a black waistcoat. He was about 35 years old with black hair and an unkempt black beard in which a few hairs of gray were beginning to show. Frank and I were concerned that word of the robbery might have already reached the town of Kidder so we wanted to avoid going right through the borough. We hoped to go around the town but we were unfamiliar with the roads.

Frank and I pulled the rider over.

"Greetings, stranger, do you know a way we can ride around Kidder? We don't want to go through the town."

The stranger scratched the side of his nose and peered at us curiously.

"Why the hell not?" he spat out somewhat challengingly.

Frank's patience was on a short string. So was mine. The aftermath of a robbery was always a nervous time because we got so fired up before-hand and kept ourselves on such a tight rein while the robbery was in progress. Frank pointed his revolver right at the man's head. I pulled out my gun, too.

"None of your business, buster," Frank growled.

The stranger reined his horse back a few paces, held up his hand and said, "Whoa. I'm a Methodist minister. You certainly can't shoot a man of God in cold blood!"

He was genuinely affrighted and with good reason. Frank and I were a formidable duo, especially with six-shooters in our hands.

As he told us he was a minister, the devil within me tapped me on the shoulder and made a sneaky suggestion. Here was a good chance, the devil said, to establish a good alibi with the man of God about the killing of Captain Cox.

After we had successfully navigated the outside of Kidder, with the minister sheepishly and obsequiously leading the way, we magnanimously told him he could go. But not until I told him, "I'm Bill Anderson's brother. I've just killed S. P. Cox. Cox killed my brother and now I've taken his life for vengeance. Been after him for five years. Goodbye, parson!"

So far, so good. But there was still an unpleasant thought nagging at me.

Sooner or later my horse would be identified as mine. Although there were no brands on horses, when a stray was found riderless three for four people would be able to identify it. And they would be correct. A man and his horse were inseparable. I didn't know how long it would take the detectives to identify the horse but I knew it would happen. I needed an alibi!

The robberies were big news. The more I read about them in the papers the more threatened I became and the more I realized I needed an iron-clad alibi. The leading journalist in our area was the editor of the Kansas City Times, John Newman Edwards. When I first knew Major Edwards he had been the adjutant to General Shelby. I knew him to be a Confederate – through and through. I then made a decision that I was to be thankful for the rest of my life. I decided to go and see Major Edwards.

I met with Major Edwards and we talked for many hours. I held nothing back. I confessed that I had planned the death of Captain Cox. Even though I was convinced of the rightness of my actions, it felt good to share this knowledge with someone else. Even Frank did not know that Cox's death had been a planned act, although I think he suspected it. But he never said a word. When he wanted to be, Frank could be very close mouthed. This was one of those times.

During our conversation Major Edwards spoke often of his respect for the guerrillas. He told me over and over again how much he admired and esteemed them. In fact, in his well-known Civil War reminiscences, "Shelby and His Men" he had described them as "like gladiators under Spartacus."

He also said he completely understood my vow to kill Captain Cox, which was reassuring, and reiterated his great admiration for Bloody Bill and the contempt and disgust he had always felt for Captain Cox and the manner in which he had beheaded Bill Anderson and displayed his head on a stake in a carnival atmosphere.

After all of this I asked him if he would help me. He fixed me with a stern and unfaltering eye as he stated, "As long as I live I will." Here again was an intense feeling of kinship as the losers of war joined together for mutual benefit. But Major Edwards had something even more powerful with which to aid me and that was commonly called "the power of the press." I was to experience this power in the days and years to come many, many times.

It wasn't long before the detectives assigned to solve the Gallatin bank robbery established that the stray horse belonged to Jesse James.

True to his word Major Edwards and the Kansas City Times printed the story, together with a letter from me *admitting* that yes, indeed, the horse was mine. But my letter also included the completely erroneous information that I had sold the horse to Bloody Bill's brother, Jim Anderson, just a few days before the bank was robbed. The newspaper also printed affidavits that Frank and I were in the area of Kearney between the 6th and 8th of December, and sworn statements from our family that we were both home the entire day of December 7th. Obviously, we could not have been at Gallatin.

Frank and I then put on a performance in Kearney which received a great deal of attention from the press. We rode into Kearney, showed our incense at being thought of as robbers, and offered to give ourselves up if we could get a fair trial. The trial could take place anywhere but Gallatin, we said.

Things seemed to be working in our favor. The Methodist preacher who had shown us around the outskirts of Kidder had come forth and testified he had met a man who said he was Bloody Bill's brother and who had killed Captain Cox on the day of the robbery. His testimony, together with the newsprint, appeared to be having the effect we wanted.

However, the Governor of Missouri kept urging Sheriff Thomason to bring the James boys into Liberty for questioning. Sheriff Thomason, who had been a well-liked and respected Confederate soldier, came to the farm with three others, including his son Oscar, to bring Frank and me in for questioning.

Frank and I were convinced we would be fairly treated by the sheriff. The townspeople of Liberty were an entirely different matter. We knew many guerrilla comrades who had been taken in for questioning and who had suffered the fate of dangling from the end of a rope when town vigilantes stormed the jail. We would not allow this to happen to us.

When the sheriff and his deputies advanced on the farm, we were ready. The barn door flew open and we galloped down the road and over the fence. Shots were fired but nobody was hit. The posse rode hard after us but only Sheriff Thomason on his fine war steed took the fence. More shots were fired but they all missed their targets. Finally, I had had enough of this chase. I turned in my saddle, took careful aim, and shot the sheriff's horse in the head, killing him instantly.

Ma later told us that Sheriff Thomason was embarrassed at being reduced to borrowing a horse from her in order to get back to Liberty.

Borrowing a horse from Ma was very humiliating to the sheriff. It was bad enough to have to beg for a steed, but the tongue-lashing that went with it was even worse. Everyone knew Ma had a tongue that could make anyone cringe, even the constabulary. Ma told the Sheriff in a commanding voice, looking down at the man from her over 6′ height, "You know dang well that if he had wanted to Jesse could have shot *you* through the head, instead of your horse. Stop your bellyaching. You also know that if you had been a Northerner your horse would be looking at a dead man."

As Sheriff Thomason was meekly hitching up the borrowed horse, he said, "You're right Zerelda. But gosh darn it, do you have to make me look so bad in front of my son and the other deputies?"

Ma suppressed a giggle when she told us this and added, "Darn it all, Jesse, if I didn't very nearly feel a bit sorry for the man at that point!"

Despite the Sheriff Thomason episode, eventually the governor finally stated in print in the Kansas City Star that in his opinion Jesse and Frank James had nothing to do with the robbery and murder at Gallatin. The affidavits, and more importantly the newspaper stories and my letter, had convinced him.

When this statement was published, I gave a long sigh of relief. And I fully realized that the biggest ally I now had, a most powerful friend indeed, was Major Edwards – the spokesman for the Confederacy and the champion of the guerrillas!

The Widow Benton

After the brouhaha about the Gallatin robbery died down and we were exonerated, Frank and I decided to pay a visit to our kinfolk in Kentucky and Tennessee.

The Widow Benton

As we were riding through the snow-clad hills of Tennessee we came upon a farm house about supper time. Supper time for farming people was the noon hour and was always the big meal of the day. It was common practice for travelling riders to stop at a farmhouse, request a meal, for which, of course, the riders paid.

On this particular day, although it was still winter, the air was fairly mild and bespoke of the Spring to come. We stopped at a farmhouse and when the lady came to the door, asked for meal. At first she seemed reluctant until we assured her we could pay. Finally, she said she would prepare the meal but that we must stay outside until it was ready.

While we waited we had a chance to observe the farm. We both remarked to each other how shabby and rundown it was. We wondered where the man of the house was. If he was fit and able, he sure wasn't keeping his farm up. As we were discussing this, the lady called us to supper. She had prepared a big and good meal. We ate it with the family which consisted of the lady herself, and her five children. The oldest was a thirteen-year-old boy who sat with us and his mother at the large dining table while the four smaller children ate nearby at a children's table. It seemed to be a real nice family.

While we ate, Frank, in his usual smooth manner, gracefully asked as to the man of the house. We learned that the thirteen-year-old was the man of the house since the lady's husband had been killed during the war serving in the Confederate army.

As the meal was being finished, Widow Benton, for that was her name, began to cry. As Frank quietly explained there was nothing to cry about, because we'd enjoyed the meal and were going to pay for it, she cried even harder. Between her sobs we learned that the farm was all she and her family had. She had been working very hard to hold onto the farm in order that the children would have something, but now everything looked hopeless.

It seemed the farm was mortgaged. The sheriff, a Northern carpet-bagger, was coming that very afternoon to foreclose on the mortgage because she had less than $50 to her name.

She sobbed. "So gentlemen, you've joined us in our last meal in the Benton household. Because there is no way I can hold off that man any longer."

Up until now I had been pretty quiet, but I'd been observing the widow and the family very carefully. So I broke into the conversation with, "How much is the mortgage – what would it cost to pay off the entire amount?" I knew this was good farming country and with work, the Widow Benton's farm could be a profitable one. Her fate seemed an ignoble one for the widow of a good Confederate soldier.

She was shocked at my quesion. Her upper lip trembled as she told me, "It's $800 – and that kind of money we could never get!"

Neither Frank nor I looked like we had ever come into nodding acquaintance with that kind of money, either, but at the moment she spoke I knew what we had to do. I pulled myself up with dignity to my full 5′ 11″ and declaimed importantly, "Well, I've been looking for an investment. And I just happen to have $800. And I'll give it to you for your mortgage payment. However, my friend here is the scholar. He'll draw up papers for the sheriff to sign so you will have a complete release and full title to your mortgage. The next time we're in the area we'll stop by and get a note from you."

With that Frank began to write out a paper for her to give the sheriff/money lender to sign.

As we were doing this and after the widow recovered her shock and surprise at our offer she asked, "But don't you want a note now?"

I replied, "No, it wouldn't be legal as we have to wait 30 days," which was complete nonsense but it seemed to satisfy her. "After 30 days we'll stop by and to be sure it's legal, you know. By the way just tell the sheriff that you got the money from kinfolk who raised it for you. Don't mention us at all.

That poor lady would have done anything we asked her to do at the time, so she solemnly promised. When Frank was through writing the papers we took our leave. As we left, the Widow Benton asked us anxiously, "But what if you don't make it back?"

I gave her my most gracious smile. "Then just figure it was payment for a wonderful meal from kinfolk." I graciously swept off my hat and made her a deep, polite bow.

What happened next is something I enjoyed remembering and chuckling over for the rest of my life. In the years ahead, the memory of this incident never failed to raise a warm glow around my heart.

About two miles from the Benton farm we met a lone rider also coming from the direction of the farm. We were fairly positive who it must be but to make sure Frank asked, "Are you the sheriff hereabouts?"

The big, taciturn man with a glowering, red face, answered tersely. "That I am."

I replied, "Well, in that case put your hands up" and Frank chimed in with "And hand over your money, including anything in your saddlebag."

At first I didn't think the big man was going to reply until he took a good look into my eyes. I got the impression that he saw something there that quickly convinced him because before we knew it that man had handed over his total stash, which not surprisingly turned out to amount to $800.

Frank and I had to laugh when we saw the money and I had to state that I didn't realize a sheriff made that much money. Maybe I should become a sheriff, I teased him.

He was in no mood for jocularity. He didn't reply.

We ordered the sheriff to dismount. His horse was sent on his way and Frank and I retained his saddle. We then profusely thanked the sheriff for his cooperation. Frank, who was having a very hard time concealing his mirth, said something which tickled my funny bone as well. He smiled broadly and told him, "By the way, my name is Dick Turpin." I knew Dick Turpin was the name of a legendary British highwayman. Just like Frank – his knowledge of Merrie Olde England was gargantuan.

I wasn't to be outdone, however, so I chimed in with, Oh yes, and I'm Robin Hood."

We were laughing like two schoolboys as we galloped off into that safe realm of trees and brush that Dick Turpin, Robin Hood and of course the members of the equally legendary James-Younger outfit were to do so well.

I have to admit that I never did receive any documents for my investment in the Widow Benton's farm, nor did we ever return to pick up our promised note, but what the heck, I doubt if Robin Hood ever did either.

The James Boys with Their Pants Down & Their Hands Up!

We had been riding for hours and the sun was hot on my back. It was late Spring, 1870, and if the day was any indication, we were facing a mighty hot summer to come.

Frank and I had been visiting Cole in Jackson County and we were on our way back to Clay. We were both mighty dusty and sweaty when we came across a nice spot in the Little Blue River. We both looked at each other, and at the invitingly cool water, and almost as one, tethered our horses and stripped. A nice, cool bath seemed very appealing.

We were diving and cavorting like a couple of ten-year-olds when suddenly from the bank came the alarming command, "Throw up your hands."

Startled, I looked toward the bank.

I immediately put up my hands and so did Frank. It looked as though the James' boys career had come to a decided halt. Thoughts zipped through my mind with the speed of lightning. True, we were not actually wanted for any crime in either Jackson or Clay County, but who knows? This hombre might shoot and ask questions later. Or he could be a federal. I could only think what a complete dummy I was to be caught in such a position – naked as a jaybird and as wet behind the ears as a newborn babe.

Stupidity, the name is Jesse James.

I didn't dare look at Frank. I began to wade to the shore complaining vociferously as to why two gentlemen should be disturbed while taking a bath.

As I got to within four feet of the man with the shotgun, Frank, who was farther out in the river, stared ululating the guerrilla yell. This so startled and disconcerted the guy with the gun that he turned his head.

That was all the chance I needed. I grabbed both him and his shotgun. We went on grappling with each other for a few minutes, with me getting the upperhand one minute, and him winning the next. Then I heard Frank say in a clear, steady voice, "Mister, if you want to live, stop that wrestling with my brother. Or this revolver in my hand will go off and you'll be dead!"

The wrestling ceased.

Frank and I grabbed the shotgun and threw it in the river. Next, we heaved the man, himself, in after it, with all his clothes on. The dunking seemed to cool him down, for he immediately launched into a justification for his actions. He told us he was a constable and having come upon two excellent examples of horseflesh, he just assumed the men in the water were horsethieves.

He did not know us from Adam.

I figured I'd give him something to think over when he was in a calmer mood, maybe back at his farmhouse with his wife having supper.

"Yes," I agreed amiably, "these are excellent horses. Mine is named 'Stonewall'."

He turned a little paler than he already was when I told him the name of my horse. Maybe he wasn't as dumb as he looked. During the war, when I rode with "Bloody Bill" Anderson, that had been the name of Jesse James' horse and it was well-known throughout Missouri.

Well, he'd have something to tell the wife and kids when he got home, all right!

Not much was said after this pronouncement and our ambusher looked mighty anxious to forget the whole thing and just ride on out.

Now there was a wise man.

As Frank and I were riding away from out little encounter he asked me, "Did you think this was the time?"

"Nope," I answered truthfully, "I sure didn't. This man was facing me." Frank looked solemnly at me. "You still having those dreams, little brother?"

"Yes, Buck, I have the same one. I'll die someday, but it will come from the back. This I know and it's as sure as the fact that we're riding along together."

We both rode in silence. The encounter with the constable had given us both something to think about.

When we were nearly in sight of the farm, our thoughts turned back to our discussions with Cole. We three had decided that our "pot" or "nest egg" would now be used for a definite purpose. We had decided to establish a ranch in Texas.

Cole had pointed out that Jim Younger was a sheriff in Texas, and the two junior Younger boys were getting old enough to be out on their own. So it seemed not only a logical choice but one which would benefit all of us.

I had been all for the decision, telling Cole and Frank, "We've just got to have other things going for us than robbing banks. We really need a place where we can have some peace and quiet and not be looking over our shoulder each and every day."

I'd hoped all along that we could establish our centre of activities in Clay County, because Clay would always be home to me and Frank, but it seemed as though it just wasn't meant to be.

As for the encounter with the constable, Frank said, "Aw, it's just another strand in the rich tapestry of life."

"Did old Will say that?" I queried.

"No," Frank guffawed. "Old Frank James."

6

During the next one and one half years, we worked hard to establish the ranch. We spent many hours discussing its location, poring over maps, and comparing different sites. Finally, we all agreed on the Pecos River Country.

We bought a good-sized parcel of land in this country and set to work building a modest but comfortable ranch house. Working with my muscles instead of my head felt good. I had always enjoyed working the land and building the farmhouse took the same kind of exhausting but satisfying physical effort. Frank and Cole felt the same way.

Next, of course, we had to stock the ranch with cattle. And we soon found that "talking" and "doing" were two different things. While our impersonations as cattle buyers had been great when we were dealing with the bankers to either scout out a possible robbery location or to turn in the bonds, our actual performance was not so good.

We soon realized that what we really needed was a man experienced with cattle, who would ramrod the outfit and act as foreman. We also intended to give such a man a percentage of ownership in the ranch.

We were lucky. We found such a man whom we could all respect. In fact as the days went by we grew to respect him more and more. His name was Tom Howard. He became the front man in all the ranch operations.

As the ranch began to take shape, Tom Howard suggested that a name be established as it would be necessary to brand the cattle and horses.

We had a meeting after supper to name the ranch. Everyone who was there threw out some outlandish names such as "The Last Hurrah," "Gone, But Not Forgotten." "Here Today, Gone Tomorrow" and "Guerrillas Never Die."

Frank, in his quiet and scholarly manner, turned – as ever – to his beloved Bard, quoting from II Henry IV. *"Not to break peace or any branch of it. But to establish here a peace indeed. Concurring both in name and quality."*

Cole scratched his head and asked, "What the hell are you saying,

Frank? Say it in English!"

"Obviously, what we all wanted when we came here to Texas is peace. Therefore, the name should be 'Peace Ranch'."

Everybody just looked at each other and since there were no objections, that became the name of the ranch. The brand was a simple "PR."

Cole had two younger brothers, Bob and John, and they both took to being cowboys and ranching like it was second nature. So did we all. Both of them learned to ride and to shoot under their older brother's tutelage and John Younger, who was 19-years-old, 6' tall, and a bit of a bully to boot, got really good at both.

As the days went by I noticed that John Younger was chafing at the bit, a little, anxious to be as good or better than his older brother and a bit surly. I couldn't really fault his attitude because as a younger brother to Frank, I'd often felt the same way, myself.

In January, 1871, a cold and bitter winter month which I'll never forget, John took matters into his own hands. He decided he would show the world just how big a man he was in his own right, never mind his older brother, Cole, and he rode off.

Not two weeks after leaving the ranch, John got drunk, was arrested, killed the sheriff who arrested him with the sure shooting eye and hand he'd learned from Cole, and escaped. Yep, there was no doubt now in anyone's mind that little John Younger had "become a man."

John returned to the ranch a-strutting and bragging about his big doings. But I felt somewhat differently about his escapade. I listened patiently to his long and involved saga but then told him in tones of an older brother, or father, "The trouble is when you drink, your guard is down and you take the chance of being arrested. Next time you may not be as fortunate to escape. So stay off the liquor, or at least as long as you're part of this outfit."

When he heard me chastising his brother, Cole exploded. In a tone of voice I'd never heard him use before he said, "You're not his brother. I'll make the decisions whenever it refers to my brothers. *You-stay out of it!*"

This was the first time Cole and I had ever openly clashed. Although he had tested my memory by going behind my back and checking out the Russelville bank on his own, he'd never contradicted me in front of others. Maybe it riled him to be taking orders from a younger man such as myself when we were mapping out the bank robberies. There was no doubt that it agitated him to have me giving orders to a younger member of his family.

I decided that when it came to blood loyalty, Cole was probably right in that he would make the decisions for his family. I backed down. Something I rarely did. Something I never did when it came to mapping out our bank raids.

I looked directly into Cole's eyes. "Your're right, Cole," I told him. "John is your responsibility and your brother. You make the decisions for the Youngers."

I don't know what transpired between Cole and John, but within the month John saddled up and left, returning to Missouri.

As has been observed before, and will be again, Texas is a large state. No connection was ever made between John's escapades and Peace Ranch. Also, what seemed mighty peculiar to me was the fact that although John had killed a sheriff in Texas, there didn't seem to be any link between his actions and another sheriff in another Texas county – James Younger. I put two and two together and figured out that Texas was definitely not "kinfolk" country at all.

While homesteading at Peace Ranch, I daydreamed a lot about Zee, fantasizing that Zee and I were married and living in the ranch house, where I was the undisputed boss.

Letters came from Zee, but somewhat erratically, and I always answered promptly, avowing my affection and steadfastness. In the day I drew fancy castles in the air. At night, I often was troubled by my recurring nightmare about being shot in the back. The day-time dreams were a lot nicer.

Peace Ranch soon became a haven for those former guerrillas who were passing through, or who just needed to hole up for a little of what we had plenty – peace – for a time.

Some of those "kinfolk" from our lost cause stated they'd like to be included should we decide to do some other business besides ranching.

I carefully studied those who showed any interest for the purpose of perhaps including them in some extra-curricular activities in the future.

My health was 100 percent. My muscles were smooth and hard from all the physical labor we'd done around the place, and I was getting restless. Life at the ranch was peaceful, all right, but a certain tension, a certain thrill, was missing.

Jesse James Rides Again

Corydon, Iowa, was a pokey old town, just a few miles from the Missouri border. It boasted a general store, a saloon, a blacksmith shop, and wonder of wonders – its very own fire station – in a day when most towns were still getting by with a voluntary bucket brigade. Most importantly, it was the banking center for all the farmers in a several-hundred-mile radius. It was quite a nice little bank too, architecturally speaking. And I should know. Because I studied it quite diligently before I rode into town with five of my best men.

Attached to the fire station were two big black and white dogs, Dalmatians, I think they're called, and I was amused to discover on my scouting trips that these two dogs made the center of the main street of Corydon their undisputed favorite spot in which to sunbathe – or just laze around.

So on the day when the James-Younger outfit hit town, as was our custom riding in groups of two from different directions, and coincidentally meeting in the vicinity of the bank at the same time, these two Dalmatians were smack in the middle of the road – totally oblivious to the riders coming and going beside them.

As we rode up to the bank, I swept low off my horse and couldn't resist petting one of the two hounds on the head. He gave a kind of satisfied grunt and flopped back into the dust. I chuckled.

While the dogs amused me I had a cold and clinical eye on two new members of my outfit, Clell Miller and James Koughman. Besides me, Frank and Cole, the sixth member of the outfit was Jim White. He, of course, knew what to do as he had ridden with me before.

I stationed myself in my usual position, outside the bank in the position of a sentry. I could see if anyone approached the bank from either direction. The robbery proceeded as it was rehearsed. There was no activity whatsoever near the vicinity of the bank.

Inside, I later learned, there was only one cashier. He quickly complied by putting $40,000 from the cash drawer and the vault into our grainsack. The men inside leisurely tied up the cashier and ensconced him in the vault. They had plenty of time. There were no outcries or interruptions. The cashier said that help would have come to him before this, except that all the townspeople were attending a political meeting where a famous orator by the name of Henry Clay Dean was speaking in front of the Methodist church.

When Frank and Cole came out of the bank and told the rest of us about the famous orator, I couldn't resist. Call me a show-off if you like – there was a bit of that in me – but I was only 23-years-old and never could pass up a bit of fun.

"I'm sure that our fellow Missourian would like us to stop by at his political meeting," I told the boys with a glint of mischief in my eye. "And, of course, we should let him know what we've been doing today while he's been talking."

I swooped down and patted the Dalmatian as the six of us rode slowly towards the church. When we came abreast of the crowd I interrupted the speaker by calling out, "Mr. Dean, I rise to a point of order, sir."

Being the accomplished orator that he was, he quickly answered, "What is it friend and fellow citizen? If anything of paramount importance, I yield to the gentleman on horseback."

All of the Iowans in the crowd turned and studied us closely and with interest.

"Well, sir, I reckon it's important enough." I drawled lazily. "The fact is, Mr. Dean, some fellows have been over to the bank and tied up the cashier. And if you all ain't too busy, you might ride over and untie him. I've got to be going." With this, I tipped my hat in a gentlemanly way, and we slowly rode away.

The good orator, believing that I was merely trying to disrupt his speech, began to reknit his address. It was a few minutes before one of the crowd got to thinking there might be some truth in what I'd said. When they investigated the matter, they found the cashier bound hand and foot and $40,000 missing.

We learned later that a posse was formed, but the James-Younger outfit did its usual split up and the posse never made contact with any of us. I rode with Clell Miller and James Koughman rode off paired with Frank. Being alone with Clell, I got to know him better. Although he had not been tested under fire I got a good feeling from him. He was a good man. He would follow my rules and eventually become an excellent member of the team.

The posse did follow our trails into the counties of Jackson and Clay, but there we disappeared into the scenery, just like Robin Hood and his Merry Men did years ago. Of course the fact that the posse was mounted on workhorses and we were astride some of the finest horseflesh in the state, was very helpful.

A robbery of this magnitude in a Northern state caused repercussions. Not only were the papers full of it, but the bankers in the state had a meeting and decided to no longer limit the investigation and pursuit to sheriffs. The Pinkertons were called in.

The Pinkerton Agency, the first in the United States, had a formidable reputation. They had gained national prominence by solving the Adams Express robberies, guarded Abraham Lincoln on his trip to Washington for the inauguration, and during the Civil War, organized and conducted secret service activities for General McClellan. No less a personage than Robert Pinkerton, brother to founder Allan, followed our trails until he became convinced that further inquiry was fruitless. He deduced that the James and Youngers had so many friends that would protect them and falsify alibis for us if necessary, that further inquiry along those lines was non-productive.

But just when everything looked hopeless for the Pinkertons they got an anonymous tip that one of the robbers had been a young Kearney lad by the name of Clell Miller. This new recruit to our outfit did not have so many friends, nor was he an ex-guerrilla.

Clell was arrested. And although he was threatened, bribed and cajoled to implicate the rest of the outfit, and was even promised immunity before the trial if he would talk, Clell maintained his innocence and kept his mouth firmly shut. He did obtain affidavits and lined up witnesses to swear that he was in Missouri on the date of the robbery, and not in Iowa, but nevertheless he was taken to Iowa and tried for the robbery.

He was acquitted.

Even though Clell had not been tested by gunfire during the robbery, he had withstood a more insistent fire, and had maintained – the most important rule as far as I was concerned. He had not talked, regardless of all the pressure put upon him by both the Iowa authorities and the Pinkertons. Thereafter he was to remain in my strictest confidence for the rest of his life.

As I thought of Clell, I also thought of Proverbs 17:17, *"A true friend is always loyal, and a brother is born for adversity."*

The score was now: James-Younger outfit – 1, Pinkertons – 0. The Pinkerton had lost this round in what was to become a continuous battle of Pinkerton vs. James-Younger. But what the heck, I always enjoyed a good fight!

Taking from the Rich and Giving to the Poor

One day in the early fall of 1871, Frank returned from a brief trip to Kansas City. We were staying at the James/Samuel farm for a while before leaving once again for Peace Ranch.

While in Kansas City, Frank had run into one of our old guerrilla pals, Harrison Trow, who had changed his name to Thomas (in order to shake off the dust of his past) and homesteaded near Salina, Kansas.

Harrison Trow/Thomas had built a sod house, good out-buildings and was on his way to a stable and prosperous life. Unfortunately, when things looked rosy, Harrison had been induced to buy an adjoining section of land and had given a mortgage on the entire property for security. The rate of interest was 2 percent per month.

Mortgaged up to his armpits, Lady Fate turned her back on Harrison. He suffered a crop failure. He came down with typhoid fever, and a Kansas twister put the icing on the cake by devastating his house and barn.

Naturally, he asked his banker for more time to make good on his mortgage. It was refused. The Salina bankers foreclosed on the loan, took his entire section away from him, and turned Harrison and his family out on the highway, penniless.

Somehow, the indigent family had managed to get back to Kansas City, where Frank had run into him. Frank told me he'd managed to talk Thomas into accepting a loan of about $100, which would see the family through the winter.

This kind of story was so common in those post-Civil War days that it almost didn't bear giving one's attention to. But Trow/Thomas was an ex-guerrilla. That made a difference.

I listened carefully to Frank's story, and my dander and ire rose. I suggested that Frank and I and perhaps Cole should go and visit the loan shark to see if maybe he'd like to make a loan to us – on somewhat better terms.

Frank carefully explained that the lending institution in Salina was not a bank after all, but simply what we called a "three ball" loan office, where the cash purchase of mortgages, county warrants, bearer bonds (mostly at 25 cents on the dollar, and no questions asked) were transacted.

Four riders, itching for action and aching to right wrongs against their kinfolk, fully equipped for a long, long ride if necessary, left for Salina, Kansas the very next morning. The ride was only 200 miles, but the return trip – depending upon whether or not we were pursued – could turn out to longer if circuitous routes needed to be taken. The four were myself, Frank, Cole Younger, and – for the first time – Robert Younger, a lad of 18 years.

After four days of moderately hard riding, we made camp on the Saline River, a few miles north of Salina. Frank and young Robert Younger rode into town to look things over and pick up a few supplies. From the description and location that Harrison Trow had given him, Frank readily located the loan office. It was outside the main part of the town and an easy mark.

The loan shark had advertisements all over the front of his building that denoted considerable cash was kept inside for "instant deals." Frank also noted that heavy iron swing shutters were at every window and on both entrance doors for use at night when the office was closed. These iron shutters were expensive and weren't generally used unless something mighty precious needed to be protected. Things looked good.

After discussing it with Cole and me it was decided that Frank should go into town, put up at a nearby boarding house, pose as a landowner and buyer, and seek out more information from the loan shark. In his scouting trip and visits to the lending office he hoped to discover such vital matters as the exact location of the safe, where the rear door was placed and where it led to, etc. All important details which would make our robbery go smoother.

Frank entered into discussions with the loan shark about farms in Kansas, his prospects of either trading or purchasing a section of land in the vicinity, and like matters. In this way he found out that our ex-guerrilla friend's section of land could be purchased for just a little over four times the amount of its value when it was foreclosed. A real "bargain."

By merely asking to change a $20 bill, Frank learned that the cash was kept in a large, iron safe. It was a combination safe but as the loan shark converted Frank's money he unwisely explained that they didn't use the combination "in the daytime."

Back at camp that evening we discussed what route to take after the robbery. In Kansas, especially during the fall, it was necessary to parallel a river so the horses could be watered.

While Frank had been exploring the town and its environs, Cole and I had ridden south of Salina. Twelve to fifteen miles directly south of the town was the bend of the Smokey River. A good half-day's ride from the bend would bring a rider to the upper Arkansas.

This seemed like our best bet for getting out of Salina, fast, if we were pursued.

My second choice, which was much shorter, would be north – following the Solomon River about 20 miles, then veering east to Kansas, back by Leavenworth. But although a quicker route to get out of Kansas it was more hazardous since we would have little time to shake off a posse before we reached the outskirts of Clay County.

The actual robbery followed our usual pattern. Frank and Cole entered the loan office, Bob Younger and I stayed outside to deflect any attacks from the citizenry. Just after Frank and Cole crossed the loan shark's threshold, a red-headed, freckle-faced bare-foot boy of about 12-years-of-age came up to me and said, "What's going on in there?"

If I had been a swearing man, which I'm not, I would have let loose a string of invectives. Instead, I bit my tongue and said, "Nothing. Just two friends are trying to buy a farm. Why don't you go get yourself a treat? Here's two bits to do just that."

I had made a mistake. The young freckle-faced lad knew immediately that two bits was way too much for a stranger to be giving away, so he grabbed the money, skipped back to the center of town and apparently began to spread the word that something peculiar was going on at the loan office. I sure did learn a *BIG* lesson. When you're attempting to bribe somebody it's sometimes wiser to give too little, than too much. Too much makes them suspicious that you have an ulterior motive, which of course I did.

As Frank and Cole emerged from the office, quite an audience had collected. However, whether there was a lack of firearms in the town or just a lack of nerve, I couldn't guess. But there was no shooting.

With the gape-mouthed assembly looking on with great interest we calmly mounted our horses and rode north through the town in a cloud of dust. Calm had given way to urgency. There might have been no firing on our immediate exit but who could tell how long that would last? About a half mile north, we turned east on a by-road and thence back south again. We were being pursued. With this fast change in direction we managed to lose most of them, but three or four seemed to be on very good horses and stuck with us.

Just before we reached Wichita, where it could be assumed our followers would pick up a larger posse, our outfit split into two groups. Frank and Cole headed for Indian territory. Bob and I crossed the river a little below Wichita. In this way Bob and I arrived first at the James/Samuel farm and Frank and Cole rode in two days later. Again, our old guerrilla tactics saved the day.

We spent a few uneasy days at the farm before we were totally assured that no one had followed us to our home. We quickly reached an agreement that all the money, except for expenses for the trip, would go to Harrison Trow/Thomas.

Along with the money we gave Harrison some cogent advice. It was to take the money from his former lender, go back down to Cass County, buy a little farm, and stay out of Kansas – forever.

Trow/Thomas was suitably grateful and agreed to do just that.

The Columbia, Kentucky Bank Robbery

We were back at Peace Rance in Texas for the winter. Jim Younger promptly joined us. While being a Texas sheriff might have carried some authority and prestige, Jim explained that his $10.00 a month salary, plus room and board, left a little to be desired. Especially when out of that magnificent amount he was expected to buy his own ammunition.

Everyone seemed to be a little short of cash so at the beginning of the new year, 1872, we began to talk haphazardly about another robbery – this one, we decided, would be strictly for us.

At about 2:30 on that afternoon of April 29, 1872, we five rode into the small town of Columbia, Kentucky from different routes. There was in Columbia, of course, a bank. I was getting to be quite an authority on bank architecture. Columbia's wasn't much to look at – being not more than a white-washed wooden storefront with a black door and black shutters for decoration. The deposit bank was entered by Cole and Frank. I took up my usual position directly outside with Jim Younger (the sheriff), and John Younger who had joined us from Missouri.

I wanted to keep a vigil on John, in particular. I wasn't too happy about him being part of the outfit, after his hot-headed actions in Texas, but both Cole and Jim had insisted so that was the way it was. But I sure was going to be watching him with a wary eye. And of course his older brother, Jim, was there to keep an eye on him as well.

All was calm and serene outside the bank. But there was a problem within. A cashier, whom I later learned was named R.A.C. Martin, took one look at the colt leveled at him and hollered "robbers!" He steadfastly refused to hand over the key to the vault. When the cashier began his outcry, four customers inside the bank started screaming "robbers, the bank is being robbed" at the top of their voices.

Despite the guns leveled at them, the customers headed for the exit door like bewildered sheep. Jim Younger and I began to sound the rebel guerrilla yell, but that seemed to cause more confusion. We started shooting. Chaos reigned.

The boys inside were only able to get the money from the cash drawers. That amounted to only $1,500 – not much to split between three Youngers and two James boys.

In any event, amidst all the confusion, we managed to get on our horses and galloped along the pre-scheduled route to the south. As we turned up a creek and through a pasture to access the road we wanted, a man and a boy closed the pasture gate.

I yelled, "Open the gate."

The man, a Kentuckian with a stubborn streak named William Conover, got his back up.

"Who the hell do you think you all are, ordering people around? If you want to open the gate, you can just get down off that critter and open it yourself."

The three Younger men and Frank guffawed at his reply but I didn't think it was so darn funny. I drew my trusty Smith & Wesson and leveled it right at his eyes.

"Either you open the gate right now or I'll blow that empty head off your shoulders."

The farmer's eyes and mine locked. I've been told that at times like this my blue eyes get steely and anyone looking into them would realize that he'd better do what I say. This was one time when I really was angry and in no mood for jokes.

In any event, the farmer retreated and quickly opened the gate.

His parting statement was very contrite. "Why, shore, gentlemen. I was only fooling. No hard feelings."

We were to learn much later that for the rest of his life he became known as "Open the gate, Conover." In such ways are nicknames coined.

As we rode together in a group before our usual split-up Cole remarked, "I should've killed that cashier when he yelled."

Automatically, I contradicted him. "No, Cole, the objective is to get the money first. Only time you need to shoot a man is after he pulls a gun."

Looking back, I guess my remark sounded condescending. Cole's face got red and he exploded at me. "That's a hell of a statement for a man that shoots a cashier at Gallatin who hasn't done anything to you!"

This was about the third or fourth time Cole had challenged my leadership. And for one of the few times in my life I swore at a man when I replied, "Damn it, Cole, you know that was entirely different. We already had the money. And that particular cashier was Captain Cox who I had vowed to kill for his beheading of Bill Anderson."

Cole smirked. Dang-bang it the man was beginning to get my goat. "I thought his name was Sheets."

I was getting angrier and angrier by the minute, a state I rarely allowed myself to reach.

"Cole, you know that was just a ploy. Cox and Sheets are the same person, no matter what the newspapers say. It was him, all right. Anyway, he admitted as much."

Some kind of signal got through to Cole – maybe my vexation, because he changed his tone and attitude completely.

"Yeah, I heard him when you called him on it. And you were right to kill that son-of-a-bitch. But damn it, Dingus, we got to make decisions, too. And sometimes inside the bank it's not as easy as you try to make it out."

Cole's about-face cooled me down and I realized that we all had our separate problems, but the main thing was we had to stick together, so I told him, "I'll never second-guess you again, Cole. Do whatever you have to do. But let's all remember that getting the money is our first consideration."

Jim Younger chimed in with, "Amen to that, especially after trying to live on $10.00 a month – and that before you buy the bullets for your own protection."

It might have not been the best joke ever told but it came at the right time and we all laughed, easing our tensions.

Shortly thereafter we did our usual splitting up. By now we had ridden into the Cumberland mountains of Tennessee. We were being pursued by the diligent and trenchant Yankee Bligh of the mighty Pinkertons.

As far as I knew the Younger boys didn't have any investment in Tennessee. Not so Jesse and Frank James. We had a prior investment in a farm owned by a widow by the name of Benton. This seemed like as good a time as any to collect.

When we arrived at the Benton farm we found the widow and her children in good shape. The kids had all grown up a lot in two years. That boy we'd met when he was thirteen was truly the man of the house now, even though he was only fifteen-years-of-age. The farm was doing well, and widow Benton looked as though she had added some sorely needed pounds. It was good farming country.

The widow came to her door as she had before when we'd asked her to cook us supper. I explained that we were on a long trip and that people who were "not our friends" might be stopping by and looking for us. I asked her to make no mention that anyone was at her farm.

The Widow Benton, who was so enormously in our debt, would have done anything we asked and she readily agreed. All the kids nodded their heads solemnly and we were ushered into the farm house.

For three weeks while the manhunt was on we had a pleasant time with the Bentons. The entire family kept their ears and eyes open and gave us all reports from the outside on a daily basis. How that investment was paying off!

After this time passed I felt secure that our pursuers had left the area, so Frank and I made plans to leave. The widow was very insistent that she wanted to make out a mortgage or a note in our favor. I carefully explained that the investment we had made was of a different kind. Our investment was to assure good tried-and-true friends like the Benton family. It was the second time I had seen that good lady cry – but this time she shed tears of joy.

As we were leaving the oldest son, Andrew, gently told us, "Anytime Robin, you and Friar Tuck here, or any members of your band from Sherwood Forest need a place to hide, this place will be yours as long as any of us live."

This so touched me that I had to wipe away a tear from my eye. It was not many who ever saw Jesse James cry. But as I explained, it seemed as though I had caught an early Spring chill.

Frank and Cole Make Plans to attend a Fair

After we left the home of the Widow Benton and her children, we returned to the James/Samuel farm in Clay County.

There was a lot of gossip in the area about us. The James boys were considered somewhat wild. But there was nothing, absolutely nothing in the way of proof to link Frank or me, or any of the Youngers, to the bank robberies. My careful planning and strict attention to detail had paid off.

The Drake Convention was still the law of the land in the state but the Missouri legislature was considering changing the state constitution and the enforcement of the Drake Convention, which punished Southern soldiers for their acts during the war, seemed to be waning.

Although the best detectives from Louisville, Kentucky and Nashville, Tennessee were still actively working on the Columbia Bank robbery, no results were forthcoming. There was not a shred of evidence to implicate anyone – least of all the James boys. Whoever the robbers were, they seemed to have just vanished into thin air.

The summer of 1872 was a difficult farming year in Clay County. Dr. Samuel was in extreme poor health, and although there were several farmhands to do the work, someone needed to be in charge. That lot fell to Frank and me and we remained in Clay County for the entire summer.

As the hot, long days of summer were drawing to a close, Frank and I discussed going to the fair in Kansas City in the autumn. The advertisements in the paper were mighty tempting. But it wasn't the rides, the food, and the midway attractions which tempted me. It was the fact that 20,000 people were expected to attend – *in one day* – at an admission price of 50 cents per person. Those figures translated into a pretty nice piece of change, to my mind.

Frank wrote to our close and good friend Cole Younger who he knew enjoyed a spot of diversion now and then. We asked him if he might enjoy riding down and joining us for a nice, relaxing day at the fair. In his letter, Frank spelled out all the facts and figures that so attracted us. Cole got the point.

His return letter was very cordial. Cole allowed as how he would be delighted to attend, and ever alert to entertain the younger generation, would bring his brother John, to visit the fair with us. After all, it might be fun to see what could occur when four young adventuresome men got together to have a bit of fun on a beautiful fall afternoon.

The Kansas City Fair Robbery

On a beautiful September afternoon, Frank James, wearing a new blue shirt with a red bandana tied around his neck Western-style rode leisurely and nonchalantly up to the box office at the Kansas City Fair.

He was alone. He reined in his horse at the gate to chat with Mr. Ford, the box office attendant, an acquaintance from some years past.

A short but friendly chat ensued in which Frank determined that the day's receipts were in the tin box which his friend kept a proprietary arm on, that they would be counted later in the day, then transferred to the bank for deposit.

During the conversation Frank jokingly asked the man what would happen if some robbers, such as the famous Jesse James, were to come up and rob the till. Would Mr. Ford put up a fight to defend the box? Mr. Ford said vociferously that he dang sure would.

Frank tipped his hat to his friend in a gentlemanly way and told him, "Well, don't worry. Nobody in their right mind would attempt a robbery in front of all these people. Why I'd guess there's at least 20,000 people at the fair today."

Mr. Ford laughed and told Frank that was for sure. It would be just too dangerous. Frank graciously thanked him for his time and attention and sauntered into the fairgrounds.

About three hours later three desperate-looking men rode up to the gate. I got off my horse and told Mr. Ford, "What if I told you that I was Jesse James and for you to hand over that money in the tin box. What would you say?"

"I'd say that you can go to hell" was the acidic reply.

"Well, that's who I am. If you don't hand it over pretty quick, I think you may get to hell a lot faster than I will."

I made this emphatic statement at the same time as I drew the colt.

At the same time the other two grim looking riders drew their guns. Mr. Ford thought things over, and figured he wasn't ready to go to hell or heaven yet. The tin box was duly handed over.

With that accomplished I swiftly mounted my horse and the three of us wheeled our mounts around and rode off. Yes, it was quite an entertaining excursion – that day at the fair – even if I, Cole and John Younger never did go inside. But as someone once said, sometimes work must come before pleasure.

There were banner headlines in the Kansas City Times the next day. The front page story, written by John N. Edwards, was curiously laudatory. It described our daring feat like this:

"A deed so high handed, so diabolically daring and so utterly in contempt of fear that we are bound to admire and revere its perpetrators." It went on to praise the principals as *"Men who can so coolly and calmly plan and execute*

a scheme . . . in the light of day, in the face of authorities, and in the very teeth of the most immense multitude of people that was ever in our city deserve at least admiration for their bravery and nerve."

After the article appeared some four days elapsed before a letter ran in the Kansas City Times on September 20, 1872, from me, claiming that I was not there. That someone had used my name to throw suspicion on me and away from the actual perpetrators of the crime. I stated in the letter that I would gladly give myself up if I could get a "fair trial." All I asked was that the jury be composed of Southern sympathizers and that at least two of them be former guerrillas who had fought for the South in the late war. If, and only if, these conditions were met, I would give myself up.

For some reason my offer was never accepted. However, my letter and agreement to surrender did engender good propaganda and publicity.

Two days after my letter was published in the Times, an editorial appeared which read, in part, as follows:

"There are men in Jackson, Cass and Clay a few there are left who learned to dare when there was no such word as "quarter" in the dictionary of the border. Men who have carried their lives in their hands so long that they do not know how to commit them over into the keeping of the laws and regulations that exist now, and these men of the border sometimes rob. But it is always in the glare of day and in the teeth of the multitude.

With them booty is but the second thought, the wild drama of the adventure first. These men never go up the highway in lonesome places to plunder the pilgrim. That they leave to the inobler pack of jacals. But they ride at mid-day into the County seat, while court is sitting, take the cash out of the vault and put the cashier in and ride out of town to the music of cracking pistols. These men are bad citizens, but they are bad because they live out of their time. The nineteenth century with its Sybaritic civilization is not the social spoil for men who might have sat with Arthur at the Round Table, ridden at tourney with Sir Lancelot or won the colors of Quinevere; men who might have shattered the Casque of Brian de Bois Guilbert; shivered a lance with Ivanhoe or won the smile of the Hebrew maiden; and the men who could have met Turpin and Duval and robbed them of their ill gotten booty on Hounslow Heath.

Such as these are they who awed the multitude on Thursday . . . What they did we condemn. But the way they did it we cannot help admiring . . . It was as though three bandits had come to us from the storied Odenwald, with the halo of medieval chivalry upon their garments and shown us how the things were done that poets sing of. Nowhere else in the United States or in the civilized world, probably, could this thing have been done. It was done here, not because the protectors of person and property were less efficient, but because the bandits were more dashing and skillful; not because honest Missourians have less nerve, but because freebooting Missourians have more."

At the time of publication and my letter and this editorial none of us were in the neighbourhood to read it at the time it appeared and to discuss it with the family. We received copies of the Kansas City Times quite a long while after they first ran. Of course my family and other "kinfolk" in Missouri kept them for us. But the James-Younger outfit was long gone – right after the fair robbery we headed for the place that was, at least for the time being, safe and unknown: Peace Ranch.

However, John Edwards' poetic prose was obtaining not only sympathy for us, but was establishing the beginnings of a legend for the James boys which was to serve us well. Our guerrilla kinfolk were impressed. Those were heady names with which to be linked – Arthur at the Round Table, Sir Lancelot, Brian de Bois Guilbert and the others. I loved his saying that the "wild drama of the adventure" came first – because that was how I truly felt. The money was important, after all it was our primary objective, but the chase and thrill of the escapade was *all*.

I looked back on the day I had decided to tell my story without reservation to Major Edwards and thanked my lucky stars. Once in a while, Jesse, I grinned to myself, you do something right!

7

The fair had been a profitable venture. Not long after, Cole, Bob and John Younger and Jim White and I started for Peace Ranch.

As we were nearing the border where Arkansas and Missouri touch, in the area commonly known as the Ozarks, Jim White's horse started to act up badly. The horse was what we called a "bad actor." He bucked and reared and "spooked" at any little critter we met on the trail and did his best to disobey any signal Jim gave him through the reins. Jim felt it would be better to try to buy another horse, or to trade him as we proceeded to Texas.

It was late September. At night there was a slight chill in the air which foreshadowed autumn. We came upon an isolated settlement in the road which contained a small dry goods store, a general store, and across the road an old water mill.

Cole mentioned that he had been here once before and that the place was run by a disagreeable fellow by the name of Tucker. But Cole thought Tucker might have a horse or two, and it was worth a try to rid Jim White of his uppity mount.

Tucker was not in the store, so Jim White dismounted and started across the road to the mill. Just as he was going up the steps, a young boy about twelve years old came out the door followed by a big man holding a long buggy whip. It was the kind of whip usually loaded in the end with a butt of lead.

Without a warning the whip struck the boy across his back. As the large man drew back his arm for a second lashing Jim White protested, "Hey, there! Isn't he a little small to be whipped with such a big whip?"

Without saying one word this Tucker turned viciously upon Jim, hitting him with the butt of the whip. The full force of the impact landed across Jim's head, splitting the skull open. Jim dropped like an ox in his tracks. He was instantly dead.

At the same second as Jim hit the ground, Tucker's legs crumbled and

he dropped – with a bullet through his heart. He fell within three feet of the boy who looked at the smoke coming out of my revolver with terror.

We immediately mounted our horses and rode over to the mill. I took the forty-five colt from Jim White's holster and put my revolver near Jim's already stiffening hand. I also put the empty shell next to the revolver.

I studied the scene of the two sudden deaths carefully. To a casual observer it would appear that Jim White and Tucker had drawn on each other and both had lost. Things happened so swiftly that there wasn't any time to think – just to act. I would grieve for Jim White later.

There only remained one problem. The young boy. He was a witness. That's one thing I didn't want. So I told him to get up behind me on my horse.

We got out of there quick, although no one had appeared from the stores or the mill at the sound of the gunshots.

As we rode along, somewhat shaken by the events, I asked the boy what had happened to bring about his beating. He told me that he had run away from home to escape a violent stepfather who had beaten him regularly. He had arrived at the mill, entered, and was watching a black man trimming a pair of stone bars, when Tucker came in and ordered the boy out. He told me he was obeying Tucker's orders, ambling his way out, when the big man grabbed him yelling he wasn't moving fast enough, pushed him out the door and struck him with the whip. He said he was twelve years old. He hadn't known Tucker's name or anything else about the place.

I was riding a black gelding that was, in my opinion, one of the finest horses I'd ever possessed. The gelding had no trouble carrying the extra load. Not much was said in the way of conversation as we headed for Texas. There were a few desultory remarks about what a fine member of the outfit Jim White had been, and Cole remarked that he'd also been an upstanding guerrilla. Robert Younger mumbled that maybe we should have given Jim White a decent burial, instead of just leaving him the way he did.

Dang, it all, did no one have their head on straight but me? It didn't take a genius to realize that it was more important to leave the scene just the way we did than to risk an investigation. As usual, it fell to my lot to straighten them out. I was a bit annoyed but I merely stated in a low but authoritative tone of voice why, since we were carrying the loot from the robbery at the fair, it was prudent not to bring the long arm of the law down on our heads.

I asked the kid riding behind me if he wanted to get involved in such an investigation and he quickly replied "NO!" He was fast to realize that if there was a murder investigation he would have to go back to his stepfather, and that was a risk he didn't want to take.

As we rode along the two younger Younger boys, Bob and John, called "Jesse." That's the way we referred to *them* – the younger Youngers. It had became a kind of a joke. The boys hadn't been in the Civil War so they didn't call me "Dingus."

Billy, the kid behind me, all of a sudden looked wide-eyed and exclaimed, "Hey, by any chance are you *Jesse James* the man I've been reading about in the dime novels?"

I was taken aback. I'd heard that some journalist back East had turned out a couple of books about the James-Younger outfit, but I'd never seen any. Later I was to see many of these novels, by the New York Detective Library and others, none of them had one ounce of truth, but that I guess is one of those things that a legend in his own time must suffer.

I got a kick out of his reaction. When I told him that yes, my name was Jesse James, all he said was, "Leaping Lizards!" he exclaimed, "You're supposed to be mean as hell, but you sure don't act like it."

His reaction broke our solemn and doleful mood and the Younger boys began to kid me calling me "mean old Jesse James." I decided to scare the boy with my cold and baleful eye, so I turned in my saddle and fixed him with my icy stare. He was completely flustered.

Maybe he really was scared because the next thing he said was "I'm getting pretty shook up back here. I hanker to ride the dead man's horse." We had Jim White's horse on a lead and he was riderless, following behind us.

"I think we could all make better time if you'd allow me to ride that horse."

I told the kid that the horse was a bad actor, and that the reason we'd stopped at the mill was to try to trade him off.

This didn't deter Billy at all and he boasted, "I can ride anything on four legs." He said it with a great deal of gusto and loud enough for the other men to hear.

This made me smile. "Well, kid, you just may have your chance to prove it. We might as well find out right now if you can ride, or if you're just a talker."

We stopped a few hundreds yards farther on where the trailed widened a bit. Billy and I got off the black gelding. I untied the stirrups secured over the saddle of Jim White's bronc. Then I turned to the boy and said, "Let's see now what you can do."

With the confidence and brashness of youth the boy adjusted the stirrups and vaulted onto the horse's back. As he hit the saddle the bronc began to buck and rear and twist sideaways – anything to rid himself of the burden on top of him.

However, Billy kept his seat and kept a tight hold on his reins. His jaw was jutted out in a grimace of determination and his brown eyes sparkled with pleasure at the challenge. The horse soon stopped bucking, and when he did, we all gave Billy a rousing cheer. I told him, "Where we're headed, you've got yourself a job. Anybody who can ride like you can deserves a good job on the ranch." I reached over and rumpled his unruly, long grown hair with affection. "You're a good talker, too," I added.

Robbing is one Thing, Stealing is Another

As we five rode through the Choctaw Nation Territory, Billy keeping up with us manfully on the now docile Bronc, we came across a small farmhouse. We were horse-weary, dusty and dirty and it had been two days since we'd eaten anything except dried beef jerky and a handful of the chicory plant which we mixed with water to make a drink which passed for coffee. Our saddlebags were almost bare of food.

As we approached the house, Billy got off his Bronc and just naturally took over the holding of all the horses. The rest of us approached the house. I was leading, so that anyone watching from within would spot me first. The rest spread out in such a way that the entire area was covered.

A lady emerged. Cole inquired, "Where's your husband."

The lady sighed. "Oh, he's off preaching to the Indians, trying to make Christians out of them. I'm Mrs. Lloyd. Can I help you?"

Cole told her, "Yep, we're powerful hungry and we'd like a good supper. We're cattlemen on our way to Texas."

I was watching the woman closely and sensed immediately that something was making her hesitate. Our request for supper was a normal one. I thought maybe her hesitation was because Cole had not added the obvious, so I chimed in with, "Ma'am, we're willing pay handsomely for the meal. But we sure need a good one."

Mrs. Lloyd looked directly into my eyes and seemed to see something there which made up her mind.

"Of course. I'll get you gentlemen a good chicken dinner."

"Sure thing." said John Younger. "Show us your fowls."

With that she took us to the chicken yard and pointed out two plump, good-looking chickens.

I decided to have a little fun at the same time. I smiled at Bob and told him, "Bob, you've been talking a good shooting game for a long time, now. Let's see which one of us can shoot the head off that chicken first. You can have the first shot."

Bob smiled back, drew a revolver from under his duster, took aim and missed.

As the shots began to fly, a small boy ran out of the house, grasped his mother around her apron waist and asked anxiously, "Are they after the gold?"

Mrs. Lloyd looked panic-stricken. She shot a beseeching look at me. At first I thought she was going to lie, but she didn't. She explained in a trembling voice that she and her husband, the Reverend Lloyd, had agreed to keep $10,000 in gold for Wilson N. Jones, the chief of the Choctaw nation. Jones, it seemed, was the caretaker for the money the government paid to the Choctaws. Jones, she said, was afraid of both the outlaws and the Choctaw braves so he had entrusted the money to them for safekeeping.

The poor lady thought both she and the gold were goners. But when she added that her husband had made a solemn promise as a preacher of the Lord to keep the gold safe, everything tipped in her favor.

The others had heard the conversation and they all looked at me for a decision. I motioned them to one side and we all withdrew out of Mrs. Lloyd's range of hearing. I told the men that there was no way we could rob a preacher who had promised to do something in the name of the Lord. Each of the "baby" Youngers made a faint objection, but they weren't very vehement about it. They all knew how I felt about the Lord and his preachers. After all, my father had been one.

I returned to Mrs. Lloyd and told her, "We're not going to disturb your gold because your husband is a preacher and has given our Lord's word. We don't rob preachers."

There was no further mention of the subject. She cooked the meal, we ate an excellent chicken dinner, paid for it, mounted our horses and rode away.

As we continued on to Texas I thought to myself, "Well, Billy has sure learned a lot about me in the short span of a few days. He's seen me react quickly, be gentle of tongue, decisive, full of deviltry, and most important of all – God fearing. Young minds are impressionable and it's up to the older generation to set a good example.

The Ste. Genevieve Savings Bank

When we rode into Peace Ranch, the last of our jerky and chicory consumed two days before, Frank James was there to greet us. I was mighty happy to see him. Clell Miller rode in two days later and was greeted like the hero he was. Throughout his entire ordeal, his arrest and trial, he had never given any information to the authorities about the robbery or the outfit. He had conducted himself like a hero and we told him he was one which made him swagger and stand just a little bit taller.

We stayed at the ranch throughout the winter, which was fairly mild. Each person on the ranch worked hard. In addition, there was a lot of target practice. Billy became quite a good wrangler but his shooting proficiency was slow.

I patiently schooled Billy, Clell and Bill Chadwell, another newcomer to the outfit, in the art of shooting well – and often, if necessary. I also drilled into them that they had to shoot to attempt to wound the other party rather than killing him. All three became quite proficient before the winter was over.

In the Spring I had a very long and serious talk with Clell Miller, whom I trusted implicitly. Clell's duties were to be in charge of the horses but he was also to always assume a position behind me. When Frank rode with us he always protected my backside. Now I could also feel confident when Frank stayed at home.

Clell never asked me why I was so concerned with my rear and I didn't tell him. Yes, I was having the dream of being shot in the back almost every week. Sometimes the shot came during a robbery, sometimes while we were just riding and other times when I was inside an enclosure such as a house, store or stable. But the dream persisted no matter what.

One day I announced that it was time for the James-Younger gang to strike again. I consulted with each member in order to make the final determination as to who would ride with me. It wasn't necessary to include everyone.

Everyone accepted my decisions except Billy. Billy was upset. He said he couldn't understand why he'd been trained so well to shoot – only to be left behind at the ranch.

I was inwardly chuckling to myself as I told him in a very serious tone, "Gosh, Billy, I have to leave some good men at home to come and rescue us if we're caught. You *would* be ready to break into a jail or prison just to rescue us, wouldn't you?"

Billy's eyes widened with surprise and pleasure. "Oh, I understand. You want to leave the cream of the crop here so when the real big job of breaking into a prison comes, we'll be ready, right?"

My smile got even larger as I answered, "That's right, Billy. So keep thinking how you can break into a jail to get us out, if you have to."

The final group was made up of Cole and Bob Younger, Clell and Bill Chadwell and myself. Our first stop in Missouri was in the hill country south of Springfield, known as the "Queen City of the Ozarks." After this stop we rode eastward into the rugged Ozark ridges to Bismark, a town on the Iron Mountain, about 75 miles south of St. Louis. We then rode through St. Francois and Ste. Genevieve Counties to Ste. Genevieve itself, arriving on the morning of May 27, 1873.

Before entering the town itself, three of us rode in from the north and the other two entered from the south.

I took a watchful position outside the bank and Clell took his pre-arranged stance at my back.

Cole and Bob Younger entered the bank, where they pointed their guns at O. D. Harris, the cashier and Firmin A. Razier, Jr., son of the president of the bank.

As they aimed, they yelled, "Surrender!"

Mr. Harris surrendered immediately. Junior, being young and indiscreet, ran hysterically out towards the street waving his arms above his head and screaming that the bank was being robbed.

I took careful aim at Junior and fired. The bullet went right through his coat, scaring him, but otherwise leaving him unharmed.

Inside, things were proceeding right on schedule. Mr. Harris willingly and meekly surrendered the keys to the safe and deposited the money from it and the cash drawers into our grainsack. Bob Younger also grabbed another sack, which was full of gold coins.

Because Junior had left the bank maybe to alert the citizens of the town, Cole and Bob decided on a little insurance. They exited the bank with the trembling cashier, Mr. Harris, between them as a hostage. If any shooting started, Mr. Harris would be in the direct line of fire.

However, it appeared that the citizens of this town wanted nothing to do with challenging bank robbers. As we mounted our horses without interference Bob Younger took the sack of gold and handed it to the newest man of the outfit, Bill Chadwell, who was riding with us for the first time. "Thought you might like a first-hand look at what our outfit accomplishes," he bragged. Bill looked duly impressed.

As we five started out of town we all yelled, "Hurrah for Sam Hildebrand." This was part of my plan for Sam Hildebrand had a small, local reputation as a bank robber and I felt that this misdirection might do us some good.

Just as we reached the edge of town Bill Chadwell's horse stumbled and Bill dropped the sack of gold he was carrying. The entire party stopped while Bill got off to pick up the now scattered treasure. After he got it all carefully back in the sack and started to remount, his horse reared up and took off minus both treasure and rider.

By this time we all were laughing, all except Bill. Bill gazed after his fast-disappearing horse in a forlorn and wretched manner. A farmer was riding into town, heading in our direction. As he came abreast of us, Bill looked up and commanded, "Hey you, ride after that horse and catch him and bring him back here quick."

The farmer, who appeared to be one of the many Dutchmen of the area replied, "And vot do I get?"

Bill's temper snapped. He pulled his colt.

"You get the horse and damn your Dutch hide. If you don't, you get a bullet right out of this nice little Colt."

The Dutchman, after examining the muzzle of the sixshooter, turned and rode after the horse. Some distance down the path he caught the animal and delivered it back to the unmounted Bill Chadwell, who, in the meantime, had turned over the sack of gold to Clell Miller as though it contained a snapping turtle. Bill had had enough.

The farmer, having delivered the horse, set his horse solidly in the middle of the road and naively inquired, "Yah, I catch der horse, now, vot do I got for dot?"

By this time, although I was bent almost double in laughter, I managed to get out, "You get away with your life, you dumb Dutchman. Vot else you 'spect, hey, already yet?"

Everybody was now laughing, even Bill Chadwell.

Just before we five did our usual split up after riding away from town, I said, "Well, Cole you'll have to admit this wasn't our most artistic robbery, but Bill Chadwell sure adds a lot of fun to the outfit."

Cole's reply was sobering. "Well, for the little we got in loot I'm glad the robbery at least produced a few laughs for some of us."

Actually, the haul had been fair – and Cole was right. It had not been our most financially-rewarding robbery.

It was Bob Younger who now reminded us that Frank was working on something more remunerative for us. "Let's hope Frank and Jim find out something about the gold shipment that's being transported by train next month."

When Bob Younger said this, our new member, Bill Chadwell looked stunned.

"A *train* robbery? What's a train robbery? Nobody has ever robbed a train before!"

"That's right," Clell told him. "And nobody had ever robbed a bank, before Jesse did. If anybody can rob a train, Jesse will."

The First Train Robbery

The time had come to tackle bigger things than banks. It was time to expand the business!

After the bank robbery at Ste. Genevieve we returned to Missouri, to Clay and Jackson Counties.

Frank and Jim Younger had been busy. With the silver tongue that Frank possessed and with Jim Younger's affinity for making judicious friendships, the two had ferreted out the information that I sought. On July 21, 1873 the eastbound train of the Chicago, Rock Island and Pacific Railroad would be carrying between $75,000 and $100,000 *in gold* in its express car as it crossed Iowa.

That would sure be a pretty sight to see – all that money in gold – and I wanted to have a look.

On July 12, 1873, seven of us, mounted on fresh and spirited horses, left Jackson County and headed for Council Bluffs, Iowa where we headquartered. Our group consisted of the five who had taken part in the Ste. Genevieve robbery with the addition of Frank and Jim Younger.

Our confederate in Denver, Stan Little, sent us a coded message confirming the shipment. The first train robbery was about to take place.

Just two counties west of Council Bluffs was the small town of Adair, in the county of the same name. I rode the railroad lines many hours until I discovered just the site I was looking for. It was several miles west of Adair where the line made a sharp curve. My plan was to halt the train by pulling out the curved rail. Obviously if there is no rail, the train must stop.

About 100 yards eastward of the end of the curve we pulled the spikes from the rail and tied a long rope around it. At 6′ 3″ and 200 pounds Cole Younger was the perfect person to hold the other end of the rope. Together with Frank, he concealed himself in the shrubbery and grass some yards from the track. The rest of us, covered in long white robes and white hoods

with slits for our eyes, hid in the brush breathlessly and excitedly awaiting the train. It was right on schedule. At 8.30 p.m., it came around the curve and Cole put his 200 pounds to the test and yanked the rope. The rail moved slowly out of position to the outside of the track. The train kept coming . . . nearer and nearer . . . it kept coming on . . . and I panicked within. It had to stop! It had to stop! But it appeared the engineer either hadn't seen the break in his rail or was ignoring it. Suddenly, the train began to reverse. However, what frantic efforts the engineer was making came too late. When the locomotive hit the displaced track, there was a sickening crunch of metal against metal, screams and cries from the passengers within, and the locomotive turned over on its side, looking like some giant insect which had turned over and died. Frank and Cole were the first to rush over to the locomotive. They were greeted by the ugly sight of the engineer, who had been crushed to death in the debacle.

Frank looked with dismay at the dead man, and as was his way at all times, quoted from Shakespeare's *"The Passionate Pilgrim."*

I had a brief moment of disorientation as I heard Frank say, *"Fair creature, killed too many by death's sharp sting! Like a green plum that hangs upon a tree, and falls, through wind, before the fall should be."*

What's Frank doing quoting Shakespeare? I remember thinking briefly, before the scene – and my mind righted itself – and I sprang into action.

Jim Younger and I swiftly boarded the express car, pointed our guns at the train messenger and compelled him to open the safe. We were doomed to disappointment. Instead of the huge amount of gold we expected, we found only $4,000 in paper money. Later, we learned that our informants had been correct about the time of 8.30, but they had the wrong day. Just 12 hours later on July 22, the $75,000 was to pass over the tracks safely on reconstructed rail.

When the others learned about the loot there was a great deal of unhappiness. I tried to explain that neither Stan Little, our Denver informant nor Jim Younger or Frank deserved any blame. It was just a miscalculation. The complaining and grievances continued. Everybody was in a foul mood. The warm white robes and hoods we were wearing – in an attempt to disguise us as members of the Ku Klux Klan – didn't help anyone's disposition. It was Bill Chadwell, in attempt to save the day, who piped up and yelled that we could recoup some of our losses by robbing the passengers. I had my qualms. On the other hand, I was responsible, as the leader, for the futility of our endeavor so I quickly acquiesced.

We strode among the bruised and frightened passengers, brandishing our guns and taking a gold watch here, a wallet there, and a few signet rings. Our take was discouraging. We only obtained about $600 – which hardly made up for the $75,000 in gold we had expected!

There were seven of us at the robbery site. This meant there would be only $4,600 to divide eight ways – the eighth man being Stan Little, our inside man in Denver. The men were in a murderous mood and I had to assure them over and over again that the misinformation had been no one's fault. And since we'd be needing Stan Little in the future I asked them to accept their losses as good naturedly as possible. We'd all live to work together another day! They all eventually agreed.

The robbery made big news! It was the front-page story in the newspapers in Europe as well as this country and was considered a disgraceful outrage. Passionate editorials called for a stop to the lawlessness which was "rampant in the country" and equally impassioned news stories called for a "halt to the nefarious James-Younger gang." No one came right out and said the train robbery had been a deed perpetuated by Jesse James, but the implications were clear.

It had been a terrible day all around. "Nothing like being in the *right* place at the wrong time," I told myself. And then there was the matter of the engineer's death, which concerned me deeply. I just had not calculated that he would not be watching carefully as he came around the curve and see the misplaced rail and that he would not be able to stop in time. I never wanted to be responsible for taking a life – except in self defense.

I sent my share of the robbery plus one-fifth additional to his widow, anonymously. Not that money could make up for the loss of her husband (who I later learned was named John Rafferty), but I had been the one to make the miscalculation and I could not profit from my deeds.

At the age of 25 I was still somewhat naive and unworldly because with this act I firmly believed that I was complying with God's word in both Numbers 5:5-7 and Leviticus 6:1-5 by making restitution, plus contributing the one-fifth required in the Bible.

Fun at the Fair

The year had passed so swiftly that I could hardly believe where all the time had gone. It was equally hard to believe that the time had rolled around once again for the Kansas City Fair. During the last year, despite all my letters of protest to the newspapers and my establishing of intricate alibis it was only too apparent that when the fair had been robbed last year, Jesse James had been involved. It hadn't been proved but it was fairly well accepted that the James-Younger gang had been in on it.

There was also a good deal of talk and innuendo after the train robbery and for the first time a reward of $500 was offered for my capture and arrest. A similar amount was offered for Frank James.

Dime novels, purporting to be the "only true story" of the James-Younger gang were rolling off the presses in New York City and other metropolitan centers, and were becoming popular with the young male readers in Missouri and environs. Frank and I were becoming too well known for our own good, I thought, but I saw no way to put a stop to the purple prose which filled these books. We would just have to live with them.

And as usual when things started turning against me I felt like putting something over on the authorities. Frank had gone to the fair last year, but drat it all, I'd been denied any of its pleasures.

I proposed a return trip to Frank but he was dead set against it.

"Dingus, you're out of your mind if you do something to call attention to us at the fair!" he ranted, a stern look on his face.

That is, until I came up with the craziest, zaniest idea yet.

The newspaper had published a list of the fair's scheduled events and I read with interest that a prize would be given for the "best lady's saddle horse." In the last nine years since I had led those guerrilla charges with "Bloody Bill" Anderson, my horse, Stonewall, had matured and tamed down a great deal. In fact, he had become one of the calmest mounts imaginable. We decided to enter that beautiful horse in the contest!

Then a snag arose. Who would be his mount? At first I thought of Zee, but Frank and Ma argued, and rightly so, that this would be disastrous since everyone knew that Zee and I were engaged to be married.

Ma, who always admired her boys' "spark" as she called it (some others called it "devilry") came up with a suggestion: Annie Ralston.

I knew what Ma was up to, and I expect, so did Frank. Annie was a friend of Zee's. She was a small girl, brown-haired and brown-eyed and Frank had taken her out on two dates. Ma wanted to give Frank an additional shove in the direction of the altar. After all, he was 29 years old. But apart from Ma's romantic notions, Annie was a good idea because she sat a horse extremely well. I was all for it.

At first Frank didn't take to the idea as he didn't wish to put his cherished Annie in any danger. But Ma prevailed (as she usually did) pointing out that few knew of Frank and Annie's courtship and no one would make the connection between Annie and the James family.

Annie accepted the challenge. She would ride Stonewall at the fair. Frank determined not to allow her to attend the fair alone so sure enough on the day of the competition Frank and I entered "Stonewall" under his real name and listed ourselves as owners. Of course we weren't so dumb as to list our real names.

In jubilant spirits – off we went to the fair. Annie gave her correct name as the rider and it was announced over the bullhorn that the winner of the trophy for the "best lady's saddle horse" was Annie Ralston, mounted on Stonewall, owned by two Kentucky horse buyers and traders named Woodson and Alexander. Frank and I, wearing huge grins, stepped to graciously accept the prize.

I'll tell you that this prize in 1873 meant more to me than the cash-box prize we had captured in 1872. Right there in the records, under the prize for the best Lady's Saddle Horse, was the name "Stonewall" ridden by Annie Ralston and owned by Mr. Woodson and Mr. Alexander of Kentucky.

I felt as though I'd done a fair job of tweaking the authorities' noses. And right in the spotlight of the center ring at the biggest amusement event taking place in the state! Talk about nerve! Talk about gall! Talk about guts! I did – and others would!

That was one time the James boys were *on the record* – even though we had to use assumed names to do so.

What was really fun about the names is that I used Frank's first name and he used my middle name. It was a way of proving – if we had to – to doubters that this event had really and truly occurred. It was for real. So, for a brief moment, one warm, exciting day at the Kansas City Fair, were we.

The bad feelings I had about being responsible for the train engineer's death receded – just a little bit.

A Job for Billy

After the Kansas City Fair in 1873, Frank and I returned to Peace Ranch in Texas. Several of the outfit had preceded us, including Clell Miller.

It didn't take a genius to observe that something was eating at Clell. He had a long face and dispirited air. At first I thought he was homesick, and might want to return home. When I got him aside and suggested this to him, I found I was completely wrong.

Clell's problem as he confessed it to me, surprised me. It had never occurred to me. His unhappiness stemmed not from being away from home, but the fact that the outfit – and especially me, he said – treated him like a "kid." He owned up that he realized he had not served time as a guerrilla, like the rest of us, but he felt that the job of holding the horses and protecting my backside, was beneath him. He longed to prove his competency, his manhood and his loyalty. He felt he'd gone a long way to proving his

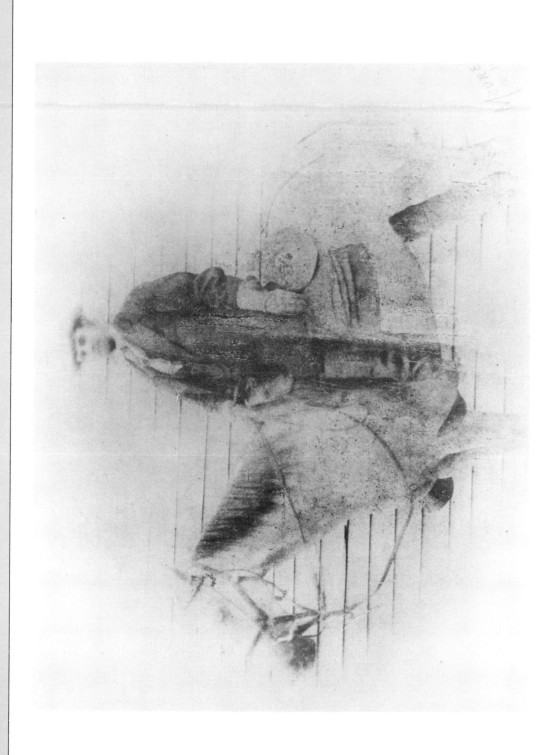

Jesse James mounted on 'Stonewall'. Appears to be a badly faded photograph re-touched with a soft lead pencil. Signed 'Moore Kansas City'.

loyalty – and the fact that he should be entrusted with more important assignments – when he was arrested. He had kept his mouth shut. Valiantly.

When I heard his complaints, I realized that he was right, and I told him there and then that from now on he would be considered a full member of the outfit, able to take on the most risky and difficult chores, and that he would no longer be consigned to just "holding the horses."

That solved Clell's problem, but created a new one for me. I needed a replacement. And since the job of guarding "my backside" was kinda important to me, since I still had my recurring dream of being shot in the back, I cast around for a replacement.

My eyes immediately fell on Billy. As I watched him work with the horses and watched his marksmanship improve day-by-day, especially when shooting from a horse, I realized that I'd found my answer. True, Billy was only 14 years old, but then I had been only 15 when I became a guerrilla.

When I broached the subject with Billy he reacted with wild enthusiasm. He fell all over himself telling me that working with the outfit had been his most precious dream. And if possible, he was even more excited about being assigned to guard my rear.

Billy had been a runaway boy just two years ago without any shape or direction to his life. Now he was embarking upon an adventure that most boys his age only daydreamed about. Why wouldn't he be excited?

While my outfit was at Peace Ranch my old friend John Edwards published an article in the St. Louis Dispatch, a paper he had joined in late 1873. It was headlined "A Terrible Quintette" and it purported to be the result of personal interviews with Frank and Jesse James, Arthur McCoy, Cole and Jim Younger.

The article went on to belie its headline. It stated that the James and Youngers had been driven from their homes into guerrilla bands by Northern persecution of their families. It provided an alibi, in cold print, for all five of us for every robbery – starting with Russelville through the train robbery in Iowa. More importantly, the article graphically described specific incidents during the Civil War in which all members of the "terrible quintette had served the Confederacy with valor, either in the regular army or in the guerrillas." It all described, in words guaranteed to arouse sympathy, the hanging of Dr. Samuel by the Northern militia and my mistreatment in the corn fields when the militia had whipped my back into red-flowing ribbons of blood and gore.

John Edwards made his final point by stating unequivocally that the five men he was writing about "are eminently creatures of the war, four of them lived upon the border and were tried in the savage crucible of border warfare.

When we first received copies which were sent to us by our relatives I felt – as did the others – that our side had finally found a champion. For the first time, our story was being told. For the first time in many months I began to have thoughts of marrying Zee and settling down, once and for all, as a family man. Perhaps the right time had arrived.

But all that took money. And as we were branded criminals and forbidden from taking regular jobs in profession or ministry by the Drake convention, I knew only one way to get it. So there in the calmness and solitude of Peace Ranch I spent some valuable hours making plans. I laid plans for robbing a train once again – in January, 1874. With a twig in a dusty hollow I drew and re-drew the plans – showing where each man would be positioned – and then I wiped out the tell-tale squiggles in the dust with my boot. Family man or no, lover or not, I was first and foremost a man of action.

I'd always prided myself on being a good judge of character. But in order to judge a man – or a boy – you had to observe him. So for this reason I left Peace Ranch with Billy in time to arrive home for Christmas. I was particularly anxious to study Billy in his new role.

The plan was that if there was the slightest indication that there was anyone at all in the vicinity behind me, Billy was to immediately take a position to my rear and from that position to keep a close lookout to protect my backside.

Billy did a good job, and long before we arrived at the James/Samuel farm I was congratulating myself on making a good choice. The ride was a long one, especially in winter, but it was rewarding in that Billy proved himself so well.

We arrived in plenty of time for the Christmas celebration and Billy was readily accepted into the family with warmth and affection, except by my younger brother Archie. At first I couldn't fathom why, until I realized that Archie was jealous. Here was Billy, just a little bit older than he was, and he was already being treated like a man by his big brother – me.

After that realization I bent over backwards to include Archie in on everything that Billy and I did and soon "we three men" went everywhere together and were inseparable. In fact, Archie and Billy became life-long friends.

I completely relaxed at home, even though there was now a price on my head. It was wonderful to be back in the bosom of my family, all of them watching out for my benefit. Yes, I was truly at home in what the newspapers called "Jesse James Country." Here in Clay, I was among "kinfolk" and could be assured of being informed of any small matter which might intrude on my security or happiness.

Of course I immediately called upon Zee, but when I did I felt a slight chill in the air from my Aunt and Uncle, her parents. Zee was as affectionate and loving as always but there was no doubt that her parents were not quite as welcoming as they had been in the past. I put it down to just a sadness and reluctance at losing their lovely daughter. I didn't stop to think that in the years since I had been courting Zee my name had appeared in the newspapers with an alarming frequency, when viewed by settled people such as Zee's folks, and my notoriety and fame – or infamy if you like – had spread from the Atlantic Ocean to the Pacific. No, those matters did not occur to me at all. I was so smitten by Zee's beauty that it's a wonder I detected the chill in the air at all. But I did.

The only thing I did while at home that Christmas season that could be construed as "work" was to make the short ride to Gads Hill to check out very carefully my plan for robbing a train. My photographic memory had not let me down at all. I only had to make minor changes in the plan that I had initially drawn in the dust back at Peace Ranch.

The Arkansas Stage Robbery

I wished I could have been there to observe Cole Younger in his role of gentleman and gallant. But I wasn't. I was back on the farm and I had to be content with a second-hand description.

On January 23, 1874 five men arrived at the farm. The five were Frank, Cole, Jim and Bob Younger and Clell Miller. Clell, apparently over his self-pity and sulks, swaggering a bit since he was to be included as a full partner in our planned train robbery. Every time I saw the Younger brothers in a group I had to remark to myself on how good looking they were. They all had the same well-modeled faces, straight noses, dark brown eyes which had a habit of boring into whomsoever they were looking at, and a seriousness of mien and purpose which gave them power. I assumed they got that look from their father who was three times elected to the Missouri legislature and was for eight years judge of the Jackson County Court. He was a good man until the Jayhawkers killed him.

The war had ruined the Younger family, all right, financially and morally.

And here they all were today, anxious to tell me what had happened to them on the way to the farm.

It seems as though Frank and Cole had "interrupted" a stage coach on its way to visit the well known Arkansas hot springs. As I heard the story, it was Frank who called for the driver to halt. As Frank explained, "Why I felt as if I was right there on the highway of merrie olde England. Of course unlike Dick Turpin, who worked alone, I did have four others there with guns ready. It was fun!"

So Frank halted the stage and Jim Younger and Clell Miller began taking the loot from the passengers. One of the passengers remarked, with an obvious Southern drawl, that he wished he had his guns because he would not have surrendered. Hearing this, Cole stepped forward.

"Were you in the Confederate Army."

"I was."

"Name your regiment, company and colonel," Cole commanded.

The passenger, a slim young man of about 35 years of age, immediately did so.

Cole told him "I was a captain under General Jo Shelby of Missouri." With an elegant flourish, Cole handed the Southerner his watch and chain and wallet.

Cole said he felt like a judge's son for the first time in many years when he told his nice-looking passenger, "We never rob Southerners, especially Confederate soldiers. We consider them exempt." With that Cole said he removed his hat from his impressive 6′ 3″ frame, bowed low and declaimed, "Me and my friends here, who have had the honor to relieve you gentlemen of your extra goods do so because we need it more than you do. Because as old Confederates we are forced to indulge in this irregular business due to the fact that we have been persecuted in our homes, our families outraged, some of our loved ones murdered, solely because of the wartime sympathies we hold, and because of our wartime activities."

Cole said he was feeling mighty magnanimous about this time, puffed up with chivalry and valor. That is, until he looked at the wallet of the next man in line during the stage coach robbery. This man's wallet showed that he was the honorable (?) ex-governor of South Dakota. When Cole got a look at this chap's identification he changed his tune. "However, ex-governors of Union states are not on our exemption list," he explained, as he quickly extricated the bills within.

The robbery was over. With an air of knightly courtesy Cole told the beleagured passengers, "Now you may proceed to the beautiful little city of Hot Springs and its healing waters . . . that is, if you can afford it now."

Frank was grinning happily as the story was told. "That's how it happened, Jesse," he said. "First we have Jesse acting like Robin Hood. Now Cole becomes Little John. And I've been referred to as Friar Tuck."

I couldn't help interjecting, "Well, I can see that the power of the press is having its effect. A couple more articles by Major John Edwards and we'll all start wearing Sherwood Green."

Jim Younger summed up our genial mood, "I don't know how to shoot a bow and arrow, Jesse. Can I at least keep my Colts?"

By this time we were all in a silly, rollicking mood. We sat down to one of Ma's ample and delicious meals. And after that we got more serious. We entered into our final discussion regarding the next "Robin Hood and his train robbery."

Building a Church

We seven were riding across the state of Missouri, heading toward the east and a rendezvous with the Iron Mountain Railroad at Gads Hill, Missouri.

After a rough day's ride we came upon a beautiful stream, a branch of the Meramex River which bordered the South and the East of a little valley. We forded the stream and made a camp in a bend of the river under the trees that spread their branches over us and up to the water's edge, the heavy timber extending east along the river.

Each of us had the same thought. It was one of the most ideal camping spots we'd ever seen, more like a park than the wild mountain timber country we thought it to be. Both Cole and I wondered and commented aloud on the fact that it was so clean and free from underbrush. We wondered about it all right, but we decided that it was safe and who were we to quarrel with nature?

We ate, settled down to sleep, not dreaming that the morning would bring us to a situation that would make us all laugh at its incongruousness.

When this rampaging, looting, marauding group of guys woke to a sparkling morning we heard a commotion just above us, and noted with surprise that several rigs and horses were tied up – quite near to our camp. My first thought was how in the world did I lead my outfit into such a trap! However, on inspecting the horses and wagons more closely I deduced it looked more like some kind of picnic party then lynching party. My fears subsided.

After our usual cold breakfast of hard tack and beef jerky we sauntered over to size up the intruders. The first thing we noted was a goodly array of dishes, lunch baskets and coffee pots spread out on the grass.

Clell Miller, with his usual reliable nose, sniffed out a rich picnic dinner. The group turned out to be composed of Missouri mountaineers and backwoodsmen. Good, solid folk. A half-completed log church stood in the open spot near the river, the hewed logs ready for its completion piled on skids nearby.

The ever-friendly Clell, now joined by the rest of us once we realized there was no danger from this group, soon had the full story. In fact, it appeared that the intrusive group regarded my outfit as active members of the volunteers, coming here for the express purpose of assisting in the completion of the church.

We were having a laugh or two realizing that we had been mistaken for church members. Then Clell put his foot firmly into his mouth by assuring several of the group that he, himself, was a past master in building log houses. The fact of the matter was he didn't know the difference between a notch-end and a door jamb. Clell was anxious to endear himself to this group, having his eyes firmly on the supper the good church sisters had supplied. The good church members told Clell that laborers were in short supply and they were desperately in need of a competent carpenter, or two, who would go ahead with the notching and placing of the logs.

After Clell's bragging, the good citizens said that they would be mighty pleased if Clell acted as foreman on the job. Clell knew an emergency when he met one head-on. The only way to get out of this tight situation, he decided, was to get someone else into it. He modestly allowed as how though he was good at constructing log houses, his friend here – indicating me – was better. And that probably I should act as foreman.

I smiled. After all, I did have my sweet side, although not everyone thought so. I remember that Clell had abided by my rules implicitly when he'd been arrested, had kept his mouth shut, and always diligently protected my backside when that was his job. I bowed to the ladies and gallantly accepted the job – on behalf of myself and the entire outfit.

The rest of my outlaw gang were "drafted" before they had a chance to put it to a vote.

Clell had absolutely no idea whether I understood this work, or not. But he had gotten out of his pickle. The surprise was that I not only thoroughly understood how to build a log house but was more than competent in notching and laying up a log building.

All of the outfit stacked their guns, holsters and dusters alongside the wagons and began to work on the church. What the sight of the Jesse James' gang of roughnecks working on a church would have done to any person who knew our identity was only to be guessed at. No doubt we were an incongruous spectacle. I wondered what some of those dime-novel writers would make of the James-Younger gang building a church. I grinned to myself.

Everyone worked like a proverbial dog until it was time for supper. What my outfit did to that sumptuous supper of roast turkey, chicken, venison, cakes and pies would have astonished even a starving man. It was an overwhelming bonanza to an outfit which had been subsisting on jerky and other dried food for days. Clell ate so much that after he filled his plate with a third helping, he took one look at it, turned a bit green and set it back down without touching it.

By late afternoon the church was almost complete, with all the top logs laid. The head man of the church group solemnly said a prayer, blessed all who had helped in the erection of the church, and generously left the balance of the food with us for our evening meal. They departed.

It was Clell who piped up, later that night, after eating his delicious evening meal, that he rather liked their brand of religion (or cooking?) and thought he might join the group as an "onarary" member. Frank replied dourly with a hint of humor that "ornery was more like it!"

As the outfit rolled into their sleeping bags I called out loud enough for everyone to hear, especially Frank, "This is one night we can all go to bed with a full stomach and the thought that we have done something positive for our Lord!"

It was a good feeling. I rarely admitted it to myself but I had quite a conflict between the reality of the life I was leading and the internal life within. Before falling asleep I thought of 1 Kings 6:37, 38, *"The foundation of the Temple was laid in the month of May in the fourth year of Solomon's reign, and the entire building was completed in every detail in November of the eleventh year of his reign. So it took seven years to build."*

The log church we had constructed that day was not Solomon's Temple but was a church, and I had been the foreman carpenter. Yes, a carpenter, as was my Lord Jesus Christ.

I went to sleep and I did not dream.

8

Expectations were high and nerves were tense as seven of us approached the small hamlet of Gads Hill, Missouri, about one hundred miles south of St. Louis.

Gads Hill wasn't much – just a train station and two other buildings, but it was perfect for what I had in mind.

As carefully planned beforehand, Jim Younger split off from the rest of us and rode to the north where he could observe the train pass some twenty miles of track before arriving at the station.

From his vantage point, Jim would study the train to determine if a contingent of guards or a military platoon was on board. If so, he was instructed to ride fast and furiously to Gads Hill to warn us. This was a matter of about seven miles cross-country ride and we knew Jim had ample time in which to make it.

Jim saw nothing. Meanwhile the train rolled on towards its destiny with disaster.

We left two men with the horses, including Billy. They hid in the nearby bush. Billy was also keeping a careful observation of my backside and was alerted to warn us if any one approached from that direction.

The Gads Hill station manager must have wondered at the popularity of his station that afternoon as five men strode out of nowhere.

The Little Rock Express was not scheduled to stop. But after we five arrived, all respectably attired in dusters, Clell Miller placed a red flag in the middle of the track. This was the signal to the engineer that passengers were waiting to be picked up. As Clell did this, we turned the switch to a siding, so that the train would be compelled to come to a halt – if for some reason the red flag was not heeded.

I had laid my plans well. I had purposely chosen Gads Hill because the train always stopped for passengers on a red signal, and because the station had a siding. I had learned my lesson well and I did not want another engineer's death. Once was enough.

Artist's impression of the Gad's Hill train robbery, 1874.

The Iron Mountain Express Hold-Up

The express came roaring into the station on time, bells clanging and black smoke rising from the engine. The engineer obeyed our signal and stopped when he saw the red flag. When the conductor stepped to the ground alongside the station to assist the prospective passengers with baggage and with entraining, he found himself looking directly into the muzzle of a pistol held by Frank James.

Simultaneously, I climbed aboard the cab and pointed my revolver at the engineer and fireman. The three trainmen were ordered to walk into the woods a short distance, where they were immediately detained at gunpoint by Bob Younger.

Cole Younger and Clell Miller, wearing their calico masks with eye holes cut out, as did the rest of us, entered the coaches and sleepers, compelling the passengers to turn over their valuables. At the same time, Frank and I entered the express and mail cars, easily subdued the clerk/guard, cut open the mail bags and took out the express box. We ordered the guard to open it.

The guard was quite convincing when he told us he didn't carry the key. I called out, "bring the dynamite," which the men did immediately. We had learned that express cars were different from vaults, so we were prepared. We used the dynamite and the top and side of the express box was blown off easily. We scooped up the contents.

The trainmen, a little pale looking, were brought back to the train and ordered to proceed on to Little Rock. Just before they left I handed the conductor a note, which read:

"The most daring train robbery on record – the southbound train on the Iron Mountain was stopped here this evening by five heavily armed men and robbed of $_____. The bandits arrived at the

station a few minutes before the train's arrival and arrested the station agent and put him under guard. Then they threw the train on the switch. The robbers were all large men, none under six feet tall. They were all masked. After they robbed the train they rode off in a southerly direction. They were all mounted on fine blooded horses. There is a hell of an excitement in this part of the country."

It's true, I just couldn't resist a joke. Though the train was headed in a southerly direction, we seven men mounted our horses after the train left and headed westerly. I fudged a little in saying we were all over six feet. I had grown to 5 feet 11 inches and stayed at that height. But what they didn't know . . .

We learned later that the train conductor stopped at Piedmont, seven miles down the track, and notified the telegraph operator. He sent the note exactly as I had written it and it can be assumed that diligent posses set off *southerly* while the James-Younger outfit galloped *westerly*.

Clell Miller added an additional spot of humor to the day's events when just before the train was to pull out of Gads Hill, he yelled at the engineer and waved his sixshooter at him. The engineer blanched and the train stopped. The engineer probably thought he was going to be shot, but Clell reassured him by saying, "Dont' worry, I just want to get my duster off the track before you run over it!" Clell had left this fashionable item of men's wear folded on the track before he had climbed on board to rob the passengers.

Cole got a particular kick out of Clell's worry about his duster and called out, "Holding up a train is hot work, even on a cold night, Clell. You ought to know that by this time!"

After the news hit the wires and the papers, few doubted that the train robbery had been our work. In an article published on February 10, 1874, the St. Louis Dispatch carried an article condemning the attack and connecting my outfit with it, and with other robberies clear back to the one at Liberty.

I was to learn later that when Major John Edwards read the article, he wired the city editor, "put in nothing more about Gads Hill. The report of yesterday was remarkable for two things, utter stupidity and total untruth." Edwards had been out of town on another assignment when the paper ran its diatribe.

What was interesting was that in the same issue of the St. Louis Dispatch was an editorial, previously prepared by John Edwards, which stated that the crime at Gads Hill had "Neither produced more reverence for the criminal and less respect for the law than the rest." Edwards had also stated that the Western highwayman was superior to the Eastern "for he has more prowess, more qualities that attract admiration and win respect; but this comes from locality . . . which breeds strong, hardy men who risk much, who have friends in high places, and who go riding over the land, taking all chances that come in the way, and spending lavishly tomorrow what is won today at the muzzle of a revolver." He appended a long and bitter denunciation of the practices of the Union party during the war and during reconstruction.

We had certainly found a champion in John Edwards. We could use more.

The Pinkertons

As my outfit rode away from the Gads Hill train robbery, we made our usual split up. Cole and Frank proceeded to Texas by way of Oklahoma. John and Bob Younger took off for Jefferson County, and Clell and Billy and I headed back to Clay County.

Cole and Frank broke up the routine Texas trip by robbing a stage-coach at San Antonio with the help of Art McCoy, Jim Greenwood and Jim Reed, who was married to a pretty well-known Western gal at the time by the name of Belle Starr. They told me it had been a profitable amusement.

Robbing a bank in a small town was apt to raise a hue and cry and a thirst for vengeance within the town itself, and perhaps in a few, scattered neighbor towns who also felt threatened. But robbing the railroad turned out to be an entirely different matter. The railroads were the property of the very rich. The railroad barons had made millions of dollars by obtaining large, mostly free land grants from the government. They charged whatever they wished for passenger fares and freight. Obtaining wealth by subterfuge, corruption, coercion and graft was a routine affair for these railroad millionaires, but that someone had profited from the railroads at the end of a gun was a national outrage!

There was a huge hue and outcry as the railroads banded together and let it be known to anyone who could read that anyone who robbed a train would have to pay dearly – with his life. A few thousand dollars lost in such a reprehensible and ungentlemanly manner was an act too disgusting to go unpunished.

The railroad millionaires turned to the highest priced and most effective detective agency in the country – The Pinkertons. They had been hired in the past on an individual basis to try to hunt down or capture the James boys and the Youngers without success.

But now the heads of the major railroads met with the head of the agency, Allen Pinkerton and his brother William, in Chicago, where an all out attempt to capture – dead or alive – those men who would dare to hold up one of their trains was mounted.

"Results," the railroad scions shouted, were what they wanted.

John W. Whitcher, a younger Pinkerton operative, fervently asked to be the one to bring in Jesse and Frank James and he outlined his plan. After listening thoughtfully to the eager young man, it was agreed that he should make the attempt. He would work alone, turning to the local authorities in Liberty, Missouri, should he need to call for assistance.

Whitcher's simple, but somewhat naive plan, was that he would garb himself as a farm laborer, walk to the Samuel/James farmhouse, get work, gain the confidence of the family, and "at the appropriate time" either capture or kill Jesse and Frank. What could be simpler?

When apprised of Whitcher's plan, our local banker told him, "I'd advise against you trying it. It won't be safe for you. You do not know the James boys as we know them here in Clay County."

This did not deter Whitcher one bit. He next met with Colonel O. P. Moss, a former sheriff of the county, and a Pinkerton friend. After revealing his identity and his plan he was advised by Colonel Moss to forget the under-taking. "You don't know at all what you are up against. I do. I know the resources of these James boys; they are not ordinary criminals. You are not going after a pair of city crooks, mind you. No, you are about to undertake the capture of two of the keenest minds in America. Those boys are not asleep, I warn you! They never sleep, in the sense of becoming overly con-fident and secure. It is even rumored that Jesse has a dream that he will be shot in the back and he is continually aware of who may be behind him. If they're home, one or either one of them, your life won't be worth fifteen cents if you go out there disguised as a farmhand. They'll see clean through you. I repeat, you can't fool Jesse or Frank James."

Whitcher paid no attention. After all, he had worked for many years for the top detective agency in the country and he thought he knew his stuff. He checked into a local hotel, exchanged his city clothes for a farm outfit, and concealed a Smith and Wesson revolver in his bosom. Then he boarded the afternoon train for Kearney, ten miles from Liberty and about four miles from the Samuel/James farm.

At all times he was under observation by one of my "kinfolk" ever alert to any unusual behavior. He couldn't help wondering why a young fellow would meet with a bank president, a former sheriff, then check into a local hotel to change from city clothes to farm clothes. It seemed mighty peculiar behavior to my friend and as soon as he observed the city slicker buying a ticket to Kearney, this "country bumpkin" friend of mine mounted a fast horse and rode straight to the Samuel/James farm to report on the doings in person. It was March 10, 1884 – just a little over five weeks after the Gads Hill train robbery.

Leaving the train at Kearney, Whitcher started down the dusty road leading to the farm, lulled into a sense of security at how nicely his plan was progressing so far. It was almost dusk when suddenly out of the brush at the side of the road, a man loomed over him, holding a great big sixshooter.

"Who are you, and where you be bound for?" I demanded.

"I'm looking for work on a farm," Whitcher replied. "Can you tell me where I might be able to find a job in these parts."

I gave him a sickly, sardonic grin. "You don't want a job. You've already got one – with good old Pinkerton."

"I don't know what you are talking about," the detective said in a last ditch effort to keep up his charade, "I'm a poor man out of work and . . ."

I didn't let him finish the sentence.

"And you're looking for the James boys, eh? Well, here take a look at one of 'em – I'm Jesse James."

At this point, Clell stepped into the road and immediately began to search the detective. As Clell extracted the weapon from its place of concealment, I glared menacingly into Whitcher's eyes. "Oh, a farmhand with a concealed weapon. Now let's see your hands!"

I felt one of his palms which was soft and smooth. "A heck of a farmhand you are! Well, Mr. Pinkerton is just going to have to wait a while longer to try to capture the James boys!"

Clell and I consulted briefly. "Let's finish him right here," Clell said. Whitcher began to plead for his life, stating that he had a young wife at home. The appeal softened me and I finally said,

"Well, let's not do it here anyhow – not on my side." (Meaning the Clay County side of the Missouri River).

Later that same night, Clell and I awakened the Captain of the Blue Hills Ferry. It was about 2:00 a.m. We asked him to be ready to take four men across the river from Clay to Jackson County. When we boarded the ferry, the captain saw that one of us four was bound and gagged. I carefully explained that me and my two friends were taking a captured horse thief across the river. We were heavily armed which the ferry captain noticed immediately. He did not question us or argue with us but obligingly took us four across the river. In addition to the terrified Whitcher, there was myself, Jim Anderson (the younger brother of my former leader, Captain

"Bloody Bill" Anderson, a man to be reckoned with), and young Billy, again assigned to watch my rear.

After we arrived on the other side of the river, the captain watched as the horse thief was put into the middle of two of the men, while the third took up a position in the background. Whitcher only made it down the road a short piece. His dead body was discovered later that morning, riddled with bullets through the head and heart. As we three horsemen rode away from the body, I was the first to put all our thoughts into words. "Just how dumb does Pinkerton think we Missourians are?" I wondered. "They must think us just dumb country bumpkins."

"I wonder," said Jim Anderson. "This was a clear case of it being either him or you – Jesse, and after you avenged my brother's death by killing his murderer, it was my pleasure to return the compliment!"

A man's death was something I never took lightly, whether justified or not. I consoled myself by saying, "It may be a Pinkerton who writes 'finish' to my days but it will have to be a Pinkerton who is a whole lot smarter than this one – and of course he'll shoot me in the back."

Jim Anderson stated, "Billy sure was doing a good job covering your back this time. With Billy on the job you won't have to worry about a Pinkerton sneaking up on you."

I looked back over my shoulder at 14-year-old Billy and raised my voice so he could be sure to hear me. "Billy's doing a fine job. With him around, I sure don't worry about my backside anymore."

At just about the same time as we were dispatching the Pinkerton's top detective, this impressive body was meeting once again with the railroad executives discussing the Younger brothers. They were to meet the same fate as the James boys. They were to be hunted down, captured, – and this was preferred, two-to-one, killed on sight.

The fact that no one had identified anyone who had taken part in the Gads Hill train robbery or that a trial had been held didn't bother either the railroad men or the Pinkertons. They were anxious to sound a loud and clear warning to anyone who would listen and that was that anyone who was even *suspected* of a train robbery, would meet a terrible and swift retribution.

After this meeting Allen Pinkerton called in Captain Louis Lull and John Boyle, two of his top men. They were to spearhead the drive to capture and kill the Younger brothers. Allen Pinkerton bragged to them. "We're going to accomplish what the entire Union troops could not – we're going to kill those irregular confederates."

Aliases were assumed. Captain Lull chose the cover name of Captain J. W. Allen and John Boyle elected to use the pseudonym of James Wright.

The two men, strutting a bit under their new names, were ordered to proceed to St. Clair and to meet with another Pinkerton undercover agent, former Deputy Sheriff Edwin B. Daniel, who boasted he knew the Younger family well, knew their habits, knew their territory.

The meeting of the three Pinkertons took place at, of all places for an ex-guerrilla to remember, the town of Osceola, Missouri. It was here that Boyle confessed to Lull that he also knew the Youngers by sight, having known them during his service in the Confederate Army. When Lull asked why he hadn't admitted it before, Boyle explained that he knew Allen Pinkerton didn't like Confederate soldiers and therefore, he thought it best not to endanger his job by acknowledging his past.

Daniels told the other two that a rural watering place called Monegaw Springs had been known as an occasional refuge and hiding place for the Youngers. Daniels said he knew the area thoroughly so on March 18, 1874, the three met, took up temporary residence in the Monegaw Springs neighborhood.

Near the Springs lived a farmer bearing the odd name of Theodoric Snuffer. He was a distant cousin to the Youngers. Beyond the Snuffer farm lay the home of a widow named Simms.

As the three Pinkerton men approached the Snuffer farmhouse, Boyle pointed out that since he knew the Youngers, they might recognize him. If, by chance, the Youngers did happen to be visiting at the Snuffer farm, he reasoned, he should stay behind the other two so as not to be recognized. This sounded sensible to Daniel and Lull, who allowed him to trail behind while they stopped at the Snuffer house with the excuse of needing directions to the Widow Simms.

By chance, John and Jim Younger *were* inside the Snuffer farmhouse, eating their noon supper. But always alert at the approach of strangers, they immediately left the table and hid.

During the friendly conversation between Lull and Daniels and the farmer Snuffer, somehow or the other the talk got around to the Youngers and the farmer was asked if he still saw them, etc. This was just aimless conversation, or so Daniels and Lull (using their aliases of Allen and Boyle, of course), deduced. But inside the farmhouse the Youngers were watching the strangers with a cold and wary eye.

As Daniels and Lull rode away, Farmer Snuffer and his cousins noted that they did not follow Snuffer's directions to the Widow Simms house. Their suspicions were sharpened when Boyle, who had lagged behind, passed the house and joined the other two. This peculiar action prompted John and Jim, as usual heavily armed, to investigate.

About a mile beyond Snuffer's house, the Youngers caught up with the Pinkerton trio. It was Jim who asked, "Hey, you all, I understand you're looking for the Youngers. Well, I'm Jim Younger and this here is my little brother, John."

As soon as he spoke, a badly frightened Lull pulled his gun and shot John straight through the neck. But before John went down (never to rise again), he was able to unload his shotgun into Lull's face. Jim immediately levelled his own gun and shot Daniels. When the firing began, Boyle showed his true character, spurred his horse, and got the hell out of there.

We had lost a good man in John Younger and we all mourned. Looking back, it was John's death which really escalated the war between the Pinkertons and my outfit. And many more good men – on both sides – would be lost before the final score was in.

Zee

The killing of John Younger coming so soon after our killing of Whitcher made me extremely depressed. I knew that I could now never stay for long in Clay County. The Pinkertons would never give up; we were a blot on their record. Their purpose was to kill Jesse James, along with Frank and the Youngers, and they wouldn't rest until they did. What was worse, was the realization that I would never be able to have a wife and children. All I could think of was Zee.

Since we had pledged our troth to each other in 1865, there had been six years of off-and-on wooing on my part. There was no other woman in my life with the exception of Marguerite in California, and that had ended with the vision of my father reminding me of my betrothal to Zee. Yes, Zee was too young in 1865 and I was too sick. I had wooed Zee while she was away at school and in her home in Kansas City, at least for a spell. Later as Zee's parents heard of the suspicions and of actual acts of mine the wooing at her home was greatly curtailed.

Zee had three older sisters, all of whom were married. Nan was married to Charles McBride, a wealthy contractor in Kansas City; Lucy was married to Bowlen Browder, an ex-guerrilla, who lived in Kearney; and Sally was married to John Sullivan, a carpenter in Kansas City. All three sisters and their husbands were very fond of Zee and me as well and sympathized with our problem. All would allow me to woo Zee in their homes when she was present.

Bowlen Browder, Lucy's husband, had not been as well known as either Frank or I during his guerrilla service, and his family had not been as outspoken as Ma and therefore his post war difficulties had not been as

Zerelda James (Née Mimms). Daughter of John Mimms of Kentucky, a staunch suppor-ter of the Southern cause. Nursed her cousin Jesse Woodson James back to health after he was gravely wounded in the chest at the close of the civil war, and became engaged to him. Married April 1874 in Kearney Missouri. From a tintype 3" × 3½" mounted in a small leather carrying case.

great as Frank's or mine. This had been a haven for Zee as it was close to our farm. Also we met many times at the home of the McBrides in Kansas City when Zee's parents curtailed our meeting at their home.

We had one other ally. This was an aunt of both of ours; Mrs. Tillman West, who was married to a very wealthy man in Kansas City and moved in the highest society circle of the City. She helped us throughout that period of six years. It never occurred to anyone to question who called on Mrs. West's pretty niece, for in truth Zee had many callers amongst the young men of Kansas City.

Zee

I was not alone in observing that Miss Zerelda Mimms was pretty, sweet-natured, and utterly charming.

As time passed and conditions did not improve for the James Boys and as the series of charges and suspicions piled up against me, Zee's parents finally told Zee that she was not to see me anymore. True, I was blood kin and I was to be trusted, and although they had no objection to me as a man, I was an outlaw, had no sure means of making a living, my future was indefinite to say the least. I could not offer Zee a settled home, nor ever safety in public. Such a man could not be a husband for their daughter. It was what any parents would have said under the same circumstances.

When I heard of Zee's parents' decision I felt powerless to do anything about the situation. Too much water had passed under the bridge. I did meet for one last meeting with Zee and talked everything over with her. I felt in fairness to her, that although my love was as great as ever, that her youth was flittering by, and I released her from her troth.

We both cried, but agreed to part.

For two long years we did not see each other, nor did we communicate in writing. I heard that she had gotten thinner and paler, but I consoled myself by knowing that we had done the correct thing. I certainly was in no position to think or do otherwise. Oh, certainly I dreamed of Zee, both day and night!

I heard, while I was despondent after the killing of John Younger, of the wealthy and very respected suitor who called upon Zee regularly and had offered marriage. I learned also that Zee's parents were very much in favor of this marriage, and although it hurt me deeply inside I knew that it was best for Zee and I prayed for her happiness, although I still hoped that some miracle would occur that would allow Zee and me to be thrown together and become man and wife.

For some inexplicable reason and full of my noble resolutions and reflections I looked at Zee's picture in my wallet and decided that before I left for Peace Ranch, I would go to see Bow and Lucy Browder and hear the final news, that the date for Zee's wedding had been set and that my beloved Zee would be gone forever.

I'll never forget that day. I left my horse with the colored boy at the door and entered the Browder's home, and there in the middle of the parlor stood Zee. Oh my God, I realized that her picture did not show how pretty she really was, or was it that she had grown even prettier in the last two years? I looked at her and couldn't speak, and Zee looked at me and she did not speak either.

Fortunately for both of us Bow began the conversation, and both Zee and I collected ourselves to the best of our abilities and attempted to join in the conversation. The situation was too tense for anyone to misinterpret. Finally it was Lucy who said, "It's a beautiful day for riding and you haven't been out of the house Zee, why not take a ride with Jesse, I'm sure he'll take good care of you." That was all I needed and Zee appeared relieved and we left.

After we had ridden for a spell and attempted to make small talk, we halted alongside the stream where we had stopped when I was making my recovery lo those 8 years before. It was then that I finally knew that I had to break the spell. I asked about her approaching marriage to Tom and quickly stated that I wished her all the happiness in the world.

Zee was never one to engage in coquetry nor subterfuge. She faced me squarely and looking in my eyes she almost shouted, "I can't marry Tom. I sent him away. I love you and always will. I've tried to forget you, I have kept my word, I have never spoken of you nor tried to contact you or have news of you. I tried my best to be interested in Tom – it was useless. I knew that if I should hear that you were wounded, if you were ill, I would have to leave him and come to you. I would bring disgrace on myself and on Tom. I love you Jesse."

What could I do? It was the answer I had longed and secretly hoped for. I took Zee in my arms and told her that I loved her, that I would never forget her, but that I could not marry her and condemn her to share my fate.

With this Zee burst into expostulation. "Being married to you would be better than this. We could be together sometimes. As things are, I live in fear; I do not know where you are, I have no claim on you, I cannot help you if you are in trouble. As things are I cannot even see you except through arrangements with other people." The tears were beginning to well in Zee's eyes.

As I looked at that beautiful young girl, no, she was now a woman, I could see her pent-up love and longing which matched my feelings exactly. There was nothing else I could say, my feelings had overcome those lofty honorable thoughts which I held when I first entered the Browder's home, and which I had tried to put forceably to Zee. There was only one answer, and I said it, almost crying myself, "I love you Zee, and we'll be man and wife."

As we rode back we talked of our plans for the future. We would go to another state, away from the pressing problems of Missouri. We would make new friends in our new home. The old friends would come to visit. It would be near enough so that I could keep in touch with Ma. Texas was too far, but Tennessee was not. I had never committed a crime in Tennessee, and I had liked the area when I had been there. We agreed that Tennessee would be the place where we could start anew and have our family, although we would undoubtedly have to use an assumed name.

Our announcement, when we returned to the Browder's home surprised neither Bow nor Lucy, and to our delight neither of them had any objection. They said that it was obvious to both of them that we belonged together, and they both opined that we should live for today and let the future take care of itself. Bow put it into perfect perspective when he said, "At least you'll be together, and you'll always be welcome here as long as either of us live."

Everyone seemed to be in a philosophical and rather melancholy mood until . . . Zee announced, "I want a wedding. I've waited nine years for Jesse and I don't expect to be married but once. I know Pa and Ma won't approve and give me a wedding and I know that I may not be able to have a normal house of my own to entertain friends after we are married, but someplace I am going to have a wedding."

I knew that having a wedding would be dangerous, but what Zee wanted, Zee would have, and I replied, "You'll have a wedding" but before I could utter more it was Lucy who said, "And it'll be right here." After more discussion the date was set, but it was to be a closely held secret until the final preparations were made.

Zee returned to Kansas City to break the news to her parents. They were heartbroken, they had hoped that she had at least begun to forget me. They pleaded with her but it was useless. Zee had become a woman and had made her choice. Zee went to Aunt Tilly West and asked her to intercede with her parents. Aunt Tilly was sympathetic and tried to intercede, but Zee's parents were adamant. They looked into the future and saw no promise for our marriage.

Zee however told me that she believed that in time all would pass, that people could forget and that in our new home in Tennessee all would be well, that our lives could be built anew.

The wedding was planned and the invitations sent. The date was April 23, 1874 and each invitation so stated. Of course the invitations were hardly engraved, no they were by word of mouth. The wedding was at the Browder's in Kearney. There was a wedding dinner and reception.

If there was any doubt by the bride it certainly did not show on her face, she was radiantly happy in her bridal veil and gown. Zee was attended by her sisters Nan and Sally, with Lucy as matron of honor. Since her parents were opposed to the wedding and were not there she was given away by her brother, Thomas Mimms. Also present was her brother Robert Mimms and his wife. I knew she missed having her parents present, but the Mimms family was sure represented, and for that I was very pleased and thankful.

Our uncle William James, a pastor of the Methodist Church in Kansas City officiated and pronounced us man and wife.

After the wedding there was laughing, feasting and gaiety. I did overhear some of the ladies talking of how plucky Zee was, and how it tugged at their heartstrings as to what might lie ahead for her, this girl who had chosen to snatch her happiness from the very midst of the encircling dangers that surrounded her groom by day and by night. I am sure that many of the prayers of that gathering were that the heartache predicted for us would be spared, or at least softened, for Zee.

On the day of the wedding, I had come through the main streets of Kearney, dressed in my wedding clothes, riding *Queen*, the best Kentucky thoroughbred there was. I was happy and I'm sure it showed on my face. Neighbors came to their doors as I passed and shouted their good wishes to me. The wedding was no secret anymore. But I was optimistic, these were kinfolk, this was my hometown, there would be no enemies on this my wedding day.

I was wrong.

The ceremony was over, the feasting done, the bouquet thrown, and the bride dressed in her travelling suit to start on her honeymoon (however her destination was unknown to her, as I had planned it for a surprise and besides, using utmost caution I knew if Zee did not know, she couldn't let it slip) when the warning came. A posse of old militiamen was riding into Kearney straight for the Browders.

I knew that it would be wiser to go alone and return for Zee. A heck of a way to start a marriage, so it was a kiss and a parting. As I mounted *Queen*, I was flanked by two of my outfit who had also always kept their steeds ready. I had mingled thoughts. I was bitter that I had to be a hunted man even before my marriage could be consummated, but thankful because of my loyal comrades ready to ride with me.

Zee evidenced to all present that she was ready for what lay ahead as she shouted, "I must hide. If they don't find me, they'll think I've gone with Jesse and they won't come back here."

As everybody started to think of where to hide Zee, it was Lucy who thought of the best place of all – the big feather bed – just the place. The bride was hastily pushed in between its smothering folds, riding boots and all, and the spreads re-arranged in a twinkling.

The wedding party quickly went on with their eating, talking and laughter so that when the posse arrived they believed that since the bride and groom couldn't be found they would set off on the trail of the three horses that led away from the farm as anyone could see they were fresh tracks, and the posse reasoned that it wouldn't be hard to catch up with a man hampered with a woman.

As the posse disappeared in a cloud of dust, the almost suffocated bride was quickly dragged out of the feather bed. The experience hadn't dampened her spirits in the slightest.

That posse trailed what it thought was the bride, the groom and the best man. When the trail divided and one horseman seemed to turn around and head back towards Kearney, it was logically assumed that the best man was the one who had turned around and the two going on were the bride and groom.

Wrong. The two horsemen were two very experienced riders who could outdistance any posse, which as was the truth, they had been doing for a good many years. Billy and Clell were experts and they were on the finest of horseflesh available, except for *Queen* of course. The rider that turned around was myself, merely returning to get my bride.

After I arrived back at the Browders, Zee kissed all of her sisters, brothers, aunts, uncles and the balance of that group of about fifty, and started out her life as Mrs. Jesse Woodson James.

What Zee did not know as we rode away was that she never would see her parents alive again, that they would die broken-hearted and unforgiving.

She also did not know what awaited us both. All that she did know was that she was finally married to the man of her choice, that we were very much in love, and happy. I knew that no matter what the rest of the world might think, I would always be honorable in my relations with her. This and only this could I promise when I said my vows 'til death do us part.'

We went to Texas and Peace Ranch. It was a beautiful and safe place for honeymooners. After two months we returned to Clay, at which time Zee visited her relatives, including Aunt Tilly in Kansas City, but her parents would not see her. But Zee was very optimistic and felt that future times would heal the breach.

Then we went to Tennessee and located in a new home outside of East Nashville.

Frank Takes a Wife

One of the guests at our wedding was Annie Ralston.

During the festivities after our vows had been taken she took me aside for a few moments, and in no uncertain terms let me know that if Zee and I could be married there was no reason whatsoever why she and Frank could not also be married. She admitted that she and Frank had parted believing that there was no future to being married to one of the 'James Boys', but if Zee could get married, Annie said, she was made of the same stuff as Zee.

She told me she expected to hear from Frank to find out if he was still in love with her, as she was still in love with him.

Upon reaching Peace Ranch, one of the first things I did was tell Frank of Annie's sentiments. This was what Frank was also longing to hear, and the very next day Frank left, for it was time for my brother to take his sweetheart for his wife. Frank knew that the Ralstons were as opposed to him marrying Annie as the Mimms were to our marriage.

When Frank arrived in Kansas City he met secretly with Annie and they decided to elope, not to attempt a wedding. No feather bed for Annie.

They did elope and were married in Omaha, Nebraska in June 1874. Annie was 22 and Frank was 10 years older. The only notice that the Ralstons had after Annie left with trunk and valise was the note Mrs. Ralston received which stated, "Dear Mother, I am married and going West. Annie." It was to be several months before her parents were to know to whom Annie had been married.

Even after the Ralstons had received knowledge of just whom Annie had married they kept it secret until August 11, 1875 when their farmhouse was surrounded and then searched by the Pinkertons. There was no violence on that occasion.

Frank and Annie arrived just one week before we left Peace Ranch. Yes, Peace Ranch was a wonderful place for a honeymoon, that is, if you wanted peace and quite, and if you were a hunted person, that was exactly what you did want.

A Little Competition – But Nothing I Couldn't Handle
The Kansas Pacific Railroad Robbery

Six men hunkered down against the trees. Six fine horses were ground-staked nearby. The day was cold and a thin, icy mist clouded the wooded area just north of Kansas City, Kansas. The woods and surrounding fields were turning brown, already foreshadowing the onslaught of winter, on this December day in 1874.

Frank James and Clell Miller were heel-squatted, rolling and smoking the long black cheroots they favored. I was standing nearby, stroking my beard, and contemplating what lay ahead.

After Zee and I rented a farm and established our first home in East Nashville, Tennessee, I had headed back to Clay County and the farm. I had some unfinished business which had been interrupted by my wedding.

Information had drifted in to Frank and Cole Younger about the Kansas Pacific Railroad which was shipping consignments of gold over its line frequently. The railroad seemed like a natural target to me, but there were complications. Complications I didn't like.

Jim Cummings, who had been with us at the Liberty bank robbery and at Richmond and Clell's brother, Ed Miller, were good mixers. They got into an interesting conversation in a saloon one day with two bar patrons by the name of Fairchild (his real name turned out to be Bill Ryan) and a certain Bud McDaniels. Fairchild and McDaniels had a snootful of bourbon and as it often does, the whiskey had loosened their tongues.

Bragging at the wrong time – and to the wrong person – has brought many a good man down. It was no different with this pair. They began tooting their horns to my men, Cummings and Miller. They were full of talk about a group they belonged to who had plans to rob the Kansas Pacific railroad on its next run.

When Cummings and Miller reported back to me – what they had been told in the saloon – I knew that this "outfit" – whoever they were – would probably rob the train using my own tactics and that the James-Younger outfit would take the fall.

It gave me something to chew on. The first thing I did was to check my own sources. Sure enough, those two saloon boasters had their facts right. Gold was being shipped on that train.

It seemed like a good idea to surprise the other gang – and rob them while they were contemplating robbing the train.

I drew and re-drew every detail of my plan in the soft dirt outside the farm. Then I thoroughly erased it with my boot heel. I've always mistrusted plans drawn on paper – they can be saved as evidence and used against you. My way was better.

Our information called for the other gang to stop the train close to Kansas City. We'd pretty well confirmed this knowledge. I decided to spring my little surprise on them by intercepting the express some eight or nine miles west of a small water station.

At this time, the other gang would probably be on board. So what? If they were on the train, we would just herd them in with the passengers and train crew like the cattle I knew them to be. The names of the guys involved had been told to me and I knew there wasn't one among that bunch who would stand up and face hot lead if it came to a showdown.

Now we were camped out some twelve or fifteen miles south of Leavenworth, and only a few miles' ride from the tank stop on the Kansas-Pacific and some eight or ten miles west of Kansas City. It was pretty country, with which we were all familiar. There was quite a thick growth of timber and a small stream called the Kaw River, which paralleled the railroad, which was good for watering the horses.

We had spent the day deciding where to place our obstruction on the tracks. The express was due to pass this point around 4 p.m. We had picked a good spot but would not put our plan into effect until shortly before the train was due.

When the train stopped, the express car would be taken off and pulled on east, near a half mile where the horses were to be located in a tree-sheltered bend of the stream, a couple of hundred yards back from the trail road. A short distance east from this point was a road leading south, where the outfit could cross the river and make for Missouri and the Ozarks.

All was in readiness.

The six of us consisted of Frank James, Clell Miller, Jim Cummings and Ed Miller – the two bar eavesdroppers – Billy and myself.

About three o'clock we started building the obstruction which consisted of brush, forked limbs, a half-dozen railroad ties and a couple of old rails.

The train was right on time. About four o'clock the rails started vibrating with its impending arrival and a whistle rent the air.

The engineer saw that obstruction on his rail line allright but Clell ran alongside and caught hold of the engine just before it came to a complete halt. Frank and Jim hurried to the rear end of the express car where Frank caught the brakeman just as he was stepping off the car.

Jim Cummings mounted the platform of the express car just as the guard was opening the door to learn why the stop had been made. Jim quickly covered the surprised fellow with his guns.

I entered the first passenger car with both guns visible, followed by Billy, covering my backside. I was expecting it, but it was still a startling sight to see two other men, guns drawn, covering the passengers at the other end of the car. One of them looked up and quickly remarked, "Hi there boss, we've got these people under control. Want to go on to the next car or what are your orders?"

I smiled at this man. Whoever he was, he had a fast mind. He was able to do two things quickly. Pretend to be part of my gang and more importantly to realize and acknowledge who was in charge. Well, I'd been expecting the other group to be on the train, and now here they were. What to do with them?

My mind was churning. I told him, "Ed is at the other end of the passenger section of the train. Bud and Billy will take care of things here.

You and I will go on to the next car."

This stranger had no way of knowing who Ed, Bud and Billy were but it was a good way of letting him know he was surrounded – that is if he had any fancy ideas. It turned out that he didn't – much to his credit.

As he and I entered the coupling area between the two coaches, I said, "You made a quick, and by the way, correct decision back there. Now who the hell are you?"

"My name is Bill Ryan and the other guy is Bud McDaniel", he told me.

Ah! So these were the two blabbermouths who had been spouting off in the saloon. Maybe now they would learn to keep their mouths shut!

"I know Bud," I told him, "but up until now I've only heard about you. I'll tell you what I'm going to do. You and Bud can have the loot from the passengers and I'll take the express car for mine."

Ryan seemed relieved. "That's fair," he answered quickly, before I changed my mind. "Exept we'll need a little help to get out of here."

My reply was sharp and to the point. "When you and Bud get through with the passengers, join us up the track a ways and we'll give you a start."

With that I called to Ed and Billy and we three headed up the track to where the express car had been pushed.

Frank and Clell Miller had uncoupled the express car from the rest of the train and had stopped it a few yards from where the horses were tied.

The messenger readily delivered the keys to Frank and Jim when the demand was made. Everything was running on a perfect timetable. What made it even more perfect was the contents of the boxes – it turned out to be gold dust and gold bars stamped with a private company name. While our take was being loaded in double-end canvas sacks, which would balance the load over the horses, Billy signalled me. Ryan and McDaniel were approaching, having finished robbing the passengers.

As they did I explained to the men the deal I had made with them.

Jim Cummings was annoyed. "That's stupid, Dingus. Why don't we just relieve them of the loot from the passengers and leave them here?"

Jim Cummings was among the few who could get away with calling me "stupid" and he knew it. Nevertheless, it didn't set well in my craw.

I gave him a withering look, a look that had seen plenty of practice. He drew back from my hard, cold stare.

"Because I made a deal, and when Jesse James gives his word, that is all that matters."

A compliant silence greeted this statement. We took Ryan and McDaniel from the scene by letting them ride double with Billy and me. The outfit separated as previously planned, all to meet at the cabin in the

Ozarks in St. Clair County.

It had been a long, weary, dreary, cold – but profitable – day. What more could you ask for?

I Trick the Sheriff

Though having extended the hand of friendship and assistance to our two fellow train bandits, McDaniel and Ryan, Billy and I were vigilant and alert as we headed for Jackson County after the robbery. While the two rode behind us, they were not allowed to have their guns loaded. There was no way anyone with a loaded gun was going to be behind me!

I rode ahead, with McDaniel riding double. Billy rode behind me with Ryan. I figured if the rider behind me attempted to load a gun he would have to do it without Billy seeing him. An impossibility, I figured.

In any event, as we rode, I chattered with first McDaniel and then Ryan about their future. Both expressed a keen interest in joining up with my outfit. I didn't make any commitments to them but, I did outline my simple but strict rules of conduct. Rule No. 1 was that I was the leader and what I said goes – no arguments. Rule No. 2, if anyone was ever arrested he was to keep his mouth shut – no confessions, no admissions, no naming of any men he'd ridden with. Rule No. 3, no drinking while riding with me. Rule No. 4, an equal distribution of the spoils.

When we reached Jackson County, I decided the two might be useful in the future and as we left them there, I told them I'd look them up for future exploits.

After dropping them off, Billy and I rode hard for a cabin in the Ozarks which we owned. We arrived shortly after the others.

At the cabin, an old rock furnace covered with an equally old stove top served well for both heating and cooking. An antique lamp and battered lantern contained enough oil for light. The nights were now getting mighty cold and Jim Cummings and Billy chopped down and carried inside quite a pile of heating wood for the old furnace. There was a good fire going. All of us were seated around it savoring a meal of bacon and coffee. We were enjoying these few luxuries and felt pretty content.

Suddenly and without warning – no one had heard a foot step outside – the old cabin door crashed in and four armed men – a sheriff and three deputies – catapulted into our midst. They had all of us covered instantly after their abrupt entrance.

I rose from my warm seat by the fire, hands in the air, and coolly complimented the sheriff on his quick work. "No need to do any shooting,"

I assured him.

The four deputies were lined up in a semicircle in front of us, making a barricade between us and the door. Their guns were loaded and aimed at our heads. It was a ticklish situation. I knew the handling of it, the getting us out of this scrape, would be up to me.

I told the sheriff that we would turn our guns over to him, butts first. When I said this I could see the surprise in my men's eyes. The deputies also looked suitably astonished. But unbeknownst to the others, I had a plan. That's what leaders were for, weren't they?

In fact, I had rehearsed just such a situation over and over again in my mind. Well, the real thing had to happen some time – and now I was facing it!

I continued the compliments and I could see that sheriff's chest swell up in gratification. A little secret here. Compliment your enemy and he'll drop his guard – no matter how minutely. There was absolutely no reason why the sheriff would be on guard because we all had our hands up – reaching for the air above us. We also all still had our guns.

I was the first to reach slowly and gingerly down to my left holster and cautiously remove my gun, butt end first. The sheriff reached out to take it. As quick as a wink I reversed the gun and sent a ball through the sheriff's wrist, disarming him, and instantly covering the three deputies.

The roar of my '45 had no more than sounded than the rest of my men followed my lead and closed in on the bunch. Clell Miller, with his usual bravado, was for putting a bullet through their heads but I wouldn't permit that. I told Clell and Jim Cummings to disarm the deputies, empty their ammunition, and return the guns to them. Frank and Ed Miller went outside and searched the men's horses, taking what ammunition and outside guns they found.

I then instructed Billy to stir up the fire and put a can of water on to boil. After it did, Clel Miller and I dressed the sheriff's arm, applying some iodine and wrapping it firmly with a bandage. While the wound had put the sheriff out of business, it wasn't so bad as no bone was broken.

The sheriff pledged his undying gratitude, which was sort of a pun, because he well knew that a marksman such as myself could have shot him through the heart. He allowed as much by saying, "You, sir, are a gentleman."

I luxuriated in the fact of being called a "gentleman" by a sheriff, no less! I told him with a wry smile, "Well, that's the first time I've been called a "gentleman" by a law man, but suffice it to say I've never caused life to be lost when it's unnecessary, except maybe once." Then I added, "and that was in the war, of course." I was thinking of Gallatin, and Captain Cox/Sheets.

Frank interrupted us at this point by coming in from the outside and observing that the deputies' horses were exhausted, evidently not having been fed for 24 hours. Nor had the men eaten anything, they said. I think Clell Miller wanted to be thought of as a "gentleman" also because he immediately set to, fixing up as much of a meal for the unarmed deputies as our limited larder could offer. Clell also saw to it that their horses were given a good feed from the ample supply of feed we did have. Frank, having returned to a cozy place by the fire, was rolling one of the black cheroots he favored. *"Now the battle's ended. If friend or foe, let him be gently used."* At my inquiring raised eyebrow, Frank stated, *"Henry VI."*

The eats, and especially the strong black coffee Clell had made, seemed to revive everyone. We all sat around the fire for a time. The conversation was friendly, the jokes bantering. Anyone observing us from a distance would have thought we were all members of a jolly camping party.

How they trailed us they never divulged. Nor did they make mention of the train robbery or that they knew who we were. This may have been discretion on their part, considering their now helpless situation. At any rate, when they departed – without guns or ammunition, the sheriff, plainly a wiser and meeker man, thanked us all for our considerate attention to his wound.

Regardless of the apparent friendship struck up with this posse, we packed our gear and cleared out of that part of the country very early the next morning while stars were still in the sky. We hit the Grand River and followed it down to an old trail leading back into a secluded canyon over in Benton County.

Frank and Clell Miller cruised out to a little mountain supply store and packed in a motley assortment of edibles. I had to laugh at the pile of stuff they unpacked; it looked as though they had just ransacked the store's shelves and taken anything that said "edible" on it. Two of the most peculiar things they bought, as I recall, were two cans of white asparagus and a can or two of "boned rattlesnake meat."

While the railroad detectives and authorities were fussing and fuming over this latest outrage to their "dignity," the outfit was enjoying some memorable feasts in our Ozark mountain camp. Sure, we ate the rattlesnake meat – and it was delicious as always – tasting a bit like white chicken – but we also dined on an endless supply of cottontails and squirrels, wild turkey, and a young two-point buck.

We didn't own one shotgun, but this was an advantage instead of a handicap as far as bagging game was concerned. Invariably, Clell and I would bring our game into camp with the head shot off and the meat well bled. It kept us sharp in our markmanship.

If I had to choose one man from my outfit who approximated my facility and dexterity in markmanship, it would be Clell. Frank was good and so were Jim and Ed. They would quickly show up the average shooter as an amateur. But Clell had the ability to put his lead exactly where he wanted it to go. I did too, of course, but I also practiced every chance I got. So shooting the head off a turkey or a squirrel at fifty yards was a good way of keeping my hand in.

I felt a great deal of satisfaction – from having proved that I could still shoot faster than anyone, including Clell, when I shot the sheriff and also from all the good meals we were putting away. But after ten days of our mountain life we concluded that the most frantic efforts of the railroad authorities had subsided and we split up.

Ed Miller and Jim Cummings left for Cass County where Jim had been staying with kinfolk. Frank and Clell headed for Kansas City to talk to a friend there who might know about the retribution slated for the Kansas-Pacific robbery. Bill and I took a trail leading north to Independence, where we could cross the river and head for Tennessee and Christmas with my beloved Zee.

Frank learned, and later passed on to me, that a few days after the robbery Bud McDaniels was arrested drunk, in Kansas City. He had in his possession $1,000 in cash and some jewelry. He tried to claim that he had earned the money by working in a Colorado mine, but the jewelry was readily identified as having been taken from the passengers in the train.

A detective by the name of O'Hara was detailed to try to get a confession out of McDaniels and to learn the names of his confederates, but McDaniels refused to talk. (I guess that conversation we had as we rode double was worthwhile!). He was promised a full pardon if he would name his accomplices. But even then, he refused to talk.

A few days later, having been confined to a Lawrence (Kansas) jail, Bud McDaniels escaped to the woods. There, he was shot by a deputy. He died without giving away any of his knowledge.

There was no news about our other double-rider, Bill Ryan.

The only other news of any interest that Frank discovered was that both the train robbery on December 8 and a bank robbery at Corinth, Mississippi on December 7, were being attributed to the James-Younger outfit. The fact that it would have been impossible for the outfit to be in both places on succeeding days didn't inhibit the press at all, although one news account covered the impossibility by stating that although the James boys could not have committed both, they undoubtedly planned the Corinth affair.

Also, the Younger brothers were positively identified in both robberies. In truth, they were not present at the train robbery, being at Peace Ranch in Texas at the time.

I forgot to mention Frank's remark in the cabin the morning after the incident with the sheriff. He came up to me with a serious face and told me, "Well, you certainly put another one over on the sheriff of Nottingham."

"Huh?" I puzzled. "Nottingham, where the deuce is Nottingham?"

Frank was not much for levity, but he got a kick out of it when he told me, "It's right here next to Sherwood Forest, Robin."

9

The Crime of the Century : The Outlaw Amnesty Bill : Fear :

Jesse Edwards James : Huntington, West Virginia Bank Robbery :

Money for a Negro School

Allen Pinkerton was raging like a caged hyena. The so-called invincible Pinkertons were losing to a bunch of farm boys and his national reputation was at stake. Whitcher, the Pinkerton emissary, had been killed. The train robberies were continuing.

A high level meeting with the railroad committee was called and a brazen and ugly plan outlined. The plan was to eradicate those tiresome James boys once and for all. A Kansas City Pinkerton branch had been established with this single purpose in mind.

The Kansas City branch of the agency had made contact with a farmhand called Jack Ladd who worked for a farmer named Dan Askew. Askew had been a strong federal sympathizer during the war and it was well known he hated the James family.

It was true that Daniel Askew was a neighbor of ours and that we were well known by sight to his farmhand, Jack Ladd, as was Jack to us. Whenever we encountered Ladd, we always exchanged meaningless pleasantries. It was on January 21 that Frank and I were both at Ma's house, planning on visiting for a spell. I had sent Billy to Tennessee to look after Zee. On that day we ran into Jack Ladd, who stopped us with a cheerful "hello". He asked how long we'd be staying in the neighborhood, and without giving it a second thought Frank answered pleasantly "about a week".

Jack Ladd immediately informed the Pinkertons. Five detectives were hastily dispatched to our area, to wreak revenge for Whitcher's death. It was on January 25 that Jack sent the wire, having seen both of us in the yard that day.

Jack's frequent journeys to and from the the telegraph station were noticed by a friend of ours in Kearney, and he immediately alerted us that this seemingly innocent farmhand had been sending more than one wire from Kearney to Kansas City and Chigaco – in code! The least unusual

On the night of Jan 26th 1875, Pinkerton detectives threw two incendiary devices through the kitchen window of the James' home (left) in an effort to flush out Frank and Jesse. As Doctor and Mrs. Samuel attempted to push the blazing objects into the safety of the fire grate, one exploded with such force that young Archie Samuel, half brother to Frank and Jesse, was killed by a piece of the metal casing, and Mrs. Samuel's right arm was so badly injured, that it subsequently had to be amputated below the elbow.

activity in our area was enough to alert Frank and me. We became suspicious and immediately left home at dusk that night.

Shrouded in the utmost secrecy, a special train was run down from Kansas City to Kearney that night carrying five Pinkerton detectives. At a stop outside of town they were joined by five local men who had told that they knew the location of both the James and Askew farms.

The entire group met at the Askew farm, Ladd, the five Chigaco detectives, the five local area men paid for the night and the night only, and old Daniel Askew himself threw themselves with gusto and zest into their meeting. Askew was surprised to see the five local men as he was convinced he was the only Clay County resident who was against the James boys. The five locals all agreed that it was vital they not be seen by any James cohort, for if anything went wrong, there would sure to be retaliation by James' associates.

The entire group, with the exception of Daniel Askew, left and surrounded the James farm. The Pinkertons' plan was to light up the inside of the farmhouse so that they could shoot Jesse and Frank as soon as they were recognized. This was to be done by throwing a ball of cotton waste soaked with kerosene and turpentine into the kitchen. This fireball would be followed by an actual bombshell that would be guaranteed to kill us both.

After surrounding the house, they noiselessly approached it, and opening a shutter, threw in one of their fireballs.

Aunt Charlotte, our former slave and nanny to Frank and me gave a shriek and the entire family ran into the kitchen. Dr. and Mrs. Samuel, John, Fannie, Susan and Archie Samuels, Aunt Charlotte and her two young sons, Ambrose and Perry, were all distraught.

Zerelda and Dr. Samuel were attempting to roll the fireball with sticks into the fireplace. The entire kitchen was lit up like the 4th of July. It was plain to the detectives anxiously peering in the windows that Jesse and Frank were not among the assembled group.

Nevertheless, they pitched a huge hand grenade into the kitchen.

Dr. Samuel in speaking of it later said:

"The bombshell was thrown into the room while the fireball was still blazing. It was light enough in the room for any person not over thirty yards off to have distinguished our faces. The detectives were not thirty feet distant. Thinking the bombshell to be another fireball, my wife at first tried to push it up onto the hearth. Then it exploded."

Dr. Samuel was thrown against the ceiling. Fourteen year old Archie was severly wounded with a large hole in his left side and Zerelda's right

Archie Peyton Samuel, half brother to Frank and Jesse. Died as a result of wounds received in the bombing of the Samuel's home by Pinkerton detectives on January 26th 1875. Age at time of death, eight years and six months.

forearm was a mass of blood and bone.

Aunt Charlotte's young boy, Ambrose, grabbed a gun and shot outside at the detective. There was a cry as though someone was hit and they left shouting, "We'll be back until we get the whole family!"

The house was on fire. Little Archie was lying still as death on the floor and Zerelda's arm was dangling at her side. Zerelda, ignoring what must have been unbearable pain assisted Dr. Samuel in putting young Archie on the couch and attempted to administer first aid. Aunt Charlotte slipped out to fetch a doctor.

When Dr. Grubs arrived, Archie was still alive, but he died shortly thereafter. No one could do anything for him. Ma's arm had to be amputated. But Ma was heartbroken, not over her arm, but over Archie. Her boy's murder was her greatest source of grief – she seemed to think nothing about her own loss.

At last the morning came, cold and gray and sad. Inside the house was death and agony. Outside, close to the house, dropped during the horrors of the explosion or the panic of the flight, was found a large revolver branded "P.G.G.", these letters being the initials of Pinkertons' Government Guard.

The detectives had all fled, along with their spy and scout, Jack Ladd. His flight was final for neither friend nor foe saw him again.

Archie was buried in the little cemetery at Kearney. Ma never ceased to grieve over the death of her youngest, as long as she lived, and no matter how many other griefs she was called upon to bear. I grieved also, but in my grief, I planned to get even.

The Outlaw Amnesty Bill

The wave of public sentiment was very strong against the tactics employed by Pinkerton in this case; indignant editors throughout the entire country described it as "the crime of the century". Governor Woodson believed that something should be done. If only he had gone ahead with his plans at limiting the activities of private detectives instead of being talked out of it the previous year. So he then came out publicly with the idea of an Amnesty Act.

An Amnesty Bill was put together as a direct outgrowth of the strong feeling throughout the country, and especially in Missouri, that the Jameses and Youngers had been getting a very bad deal. The feeling had become so intensified by the disgraceful attack on the defenseless Samuel home, that six weeks after the outrage, March 17, 1875, the Honorable Jeff Jones of Callaway County introduced an Amnesty Bill in the Missouri

Legislature. Jones represented the Democratic section of the house which was the minority party, but the Bill was supported by Republicans as well and actually received a majority vote from the House Committee on Jurisprudence. The Bill read as follows·

OUTLAW AMNESTY BILL

Whereas, by the 4th section of the 11th Article of the Constitution of Missouri, all persons in the military service of the United States, or who acted under the authority thereof in this State, are relieved from all civil liability and all criminal punishment for acts done by them since the 1st day of January, 1861, and

Whereas, by the 12th section of the said 11th Article of said Constitution, provision is made by which, under certain curcumstances, may be seized, transported to, indicted, tried and punished in distant counties, any Confederate under ban of despotic displeasure, thereby contravening the Constitution of the United States and every principle of enlightened humanity; and

Whereas, such discrimination evinces a want of manly generosity and statesmanship on the part of the party imposing, and of courage and manhood on the party submitting tamely thereto; and

Whereas, Under the outlawry pronounced against Jesse W. James, Frank James, Coleman Younger, Robert Younger and others, who gallantly periled their lives and their all in defense of their principles, they are of necessity made desperate, driven as they are from the field of honest industry, from their friends, from their families, their homes and their country, they can know no law but the law of self-preservation, nor can have no respect for and feel no allegiance to a government which forces them to the very acts it professes to deprecate, and then offers a bounty for their apprehension and arms foreign mercenaries with power to capture and kill them, and

Whereas, Believing these men too brave to be mean, too generous to be revengeful, and too gallant and honorable to betray a friend, or break a promise; and believing further that most, if not all of the offenses with which they are charged have been committed by others, and perhaps by those pretending to hunt them, or by their confederates; that their names are and have been used to divert suspicion from and thereby relieve the actual perpetrators; that the return of these men to their homes and friends would have the effect of greatly lessening crime in our State; by turning public attention to the real criminals, and that common justice, sound policy and true statemanship, alike demand that amnesty should be extended to all alike of both parties for all acts done or charged to have been done during the war;

Be it Resolved, by the House of Representatives the Senate concurring therein;

That the governor of the State be, and he is hereby requested to issue his proclamation notifying the said Jesse W. James, Frank James, Coleman Younger, Robert Younger and James Younger and others; that full and complete amnesty and pardon will be granted them for all acts charged or committed by them during the late Civil War and inviting them respectfully to return to their respective homes in this State, and there quietly to remain, submitting themselves to such proceedings as may be instituted against them by the Courts for all offenses charged to have been committed since the said war, promising and guaranteeing to them and each of them full protection and a fair trial therein, and the full protection shall be given them for the time of their entrance into the State and his (the Governor's) notice thereof under said proclamation and invitation.

The Jameses and Youngers were in favor of the bill and had assured Governor Hardin through intermediaries that if the Bill passed, we would surrender and stand trial. It was felt by the entire outfit that no jury in Missouri would ever convict one of its own, given the witnesses we could produce for alibis for any crime we had been accused of after the war.

I personally had a reason for hoping for a chance to live safely in my native Missouri; Zee had informed me that I was going to be a father. At the time I learned that I was going to be a father, I could not help remember Genesis 9:1, 6, 7 which states: *"And God blessed Noah and his sons and said to them, 'Be fruitful and multiply and fill the earth. Whoever sheds man's blood, By man his blood shall be shed, For in the image of God he made man. And so for you, be fruitful and multiply; Populate the earth abundantly and multiply in it'."* I felt that I was living in accordance with God's will.

Between the time of the bombing and the vote on the Amnesty Bill, almost the entire nation's press condemned the bombing of the James home by the Pinkertons. It was labelled throughout the country in much of the press as "the crime of the century" and compared to the assassination of

President Lincoln and in Missouri the Legislature passed a resolution calling the bombing "the most cowardly and brutal outrage ever committed in the State". The vote was 84 to 1 in the House and 20 to 5 in the Senate.

However, when the Amnesty Bill was voted on March 20, 1875, the Concurrent Resolution (of the House and Senate), had 58 ayes and 39 nays, short of the two-thirds needed. Those voting "nay" appeared to be in favor of amnesty, but the wording eulogizing the James-Youngers by name was just too much for some of the legislators.

Fear

The defeat of the Amnesty Bill on March 20, 1875 was a great disappointment. Apparently it was, also, to the five local men who had joined the Pinkerton regulars in bombing the James/Samuel farm.

These five met with William Pinkerton and the farmhand known as Jack Ladd and made their thoughts known. Their concern was that someone might get to Daniel Askew, who knew all their names, and make him talk. Their reasoning was that once I realized "Jack Ladd" was no longer in Askew's employ, I would "smell a rat" and take steps to right the wrong.

They were 100 percent right. I had held off investigating the bombing because of the promises the Amnesty Bill held out. Once the Bill was defeated, I switched my thinking to revenge. I was bitter about Archie, whom I'd loved very much. Every time I looked at Ma with her right sleeve dangling empty, all I could think about was the Pinkertons.

The Pinkertons made a startling and completely unlawful move. They sent Jack Ladd back to Clay to carry out their instructions. On April 18, 1875 he successfully completed his mission by shooting his former employer, coconspirator and supposed friend, Daniel Askew. This successfully ended any possibility of learning the names of the Clay County local men who were present the night of the bombing. I now had no one to direct my bitterness towards – except the Pinkertons.

After Askew's killing, Frank and I reasoned that we would be held accountable for his death. Frank left for Peace Ranch and urged me to do the same. But there was a difference in our situation at the time. Frank was not an expectant father, and I was. I fervently desired my son (I knew it would be a boy!) to be born in Missouri. Instead of leaving for Texas, I spent a lot of time at my desk issuing letters denying any responsibility for Askew's death to the press. They were duly published as was an impassioned editorial bearing Major Edwards' byline, proclaiming our innocence.

The press had always supported the James boys, after a fashion, and the letters and editorials were convincing. People began to believe that indeed we did not kill Askew. By this time it was the middle of July. Zee had gone to Kansas City to stay with her sister where I hoped she'd be able to stay until my son was born.

Somehow, word got out that Zee was at the home of John and Sally Sullivan and was pregnant. Major John Edwards, my good friend and loyal supporter, decided to check out the news for himself. He had no sooner entered the Sullivan's house when it was surrounded by an angry posse.

"Jesse, we saw you go in and if you don't come out we'll do the same to this house that we did to your farmhouse. We know your wife can't ride and she'll never get away, even if you do!"

This challenge enraged Major John Edwards, as he later wrote about it in the *St. Louis Globe Democrat.*

"It's just old Major Edwards and if any two of you skunks wish to shoot me, O.K. I'm coming out and you can look me over. And if I'm Jesse James, why then you can shoot me!" he yelled back.

After a time, the group besieging the house agreed that he could come out, with the light at his back. If recognized he would not be shot.

With all the courage of a fighting Confederate, which he had been, the good Major walked out of the house. The light was at his back. His hands were upraised and he was unarmed. The posse could see him plainly. There was no question as to the man's identity and the posse agreed that here in the flesh was the same man they'd seen entering the house.

They did not shoot, and somewhat mollified and defeated, they left.

After this incident, Major Edwards and I met secretly. He convinced me that Zee and I would have to leave Missouri in order to have the baby in safety. For once I let my head prevail, instead of my heart. I had been set on having that baby born in Missouri, but as someone once said, you can't have everything.

As Major Edwards and I parted, I grasped his hand and said, "Major, I would like to name my child Jesse Edwards James."

That good man was direct, as always. "I would be greatly honored if you did," he replied.

Jesse Edwards James

I packed up Zee, the household goods, and other essentials for our move into what was called a prairie schooner. This was a canvas-covered wagon similar to but lighter than the Conestoga wagon used by pioneers crossing the North American prairies. It was common for families to use a schooner for a major move. Often they would live in it until their house and land could be secured.

In early August I arrived with Zee and a "farmhand" in the area of East Nashville, Tennessee. On close inspection the lad with me seemed mighty young to be a farmhand, being only 17 years of age. Only a very close observor would discover that this boy wore two guns under his duster and had a carbine in his saddle bag. Even so, if someone had managed to discover the weapons it would not seem out of the ordinary because many men during those times carried and wore guns.

With Archie gone, I felt like Billy was indeed part of the family.

I purchased a small farm in this area, basically for the raising of stock and horses, under the name "Howard". Why "Howard" I really can't explain. It seemed like a good enough name at the time.

We had just barely moved in when Zee gave birth to a healthy baby boy. The doctor attending the birth asked what we were going to name him. We told him we hadn't made a final decision but, for the moment we would call him "Tim".

However, as soon as we were alone, Zee and I named the boy, "Jesse Edwards James". But for many years to come we always called him "Tim", for obvious reasons.

I went to sleep that night with the words from Proverbs 17:6 reverberating through my brain: *"Grandchildren are the crown of old men, and the glory of sons is their father."*

I hoped that these blessings from the Bible would be mine and that I would, indeed, be the "glory" of my sons

The Huntington, West Virginia Bank Robbery
Takes an Unexpected Turn

After Jesse Edwards James' birth – in fact the next day, four men rode into Huntington, West Virginia, from different directions, meeting at the center of town at the bank. Two dismounted and entered. The other two drew their colts and Smith & Wessons and began shooting into the air to clear the streets.

The four men were Frank James, Cole Younger, Tom McDaniels and Jack Keene, who also passed as "Tom Webb" at times. It was Frank and Tom McDaniels who entered the bank, pointed revolvers at the cashier and the one other citizen present, scooping the money from the safe and cash drawer, and depositing it in the ever present grain sack.

Their getaway was not as smooth as their entrance. A posse of twenty men, heavily armed, rode out of Huntington close on the heels of the four.

At several other points along the trail, other posses joined in the chase. Obviously the telegraph office had been put to good use along the route.

The posse got so close that actual pistol fire was exchanged. The desperate bandits abandoned their horses more than once, stealing new and fresher mounts wherever they found available horseflesh. They were heading to the southwest, through the mountains of West Virginia and Eastern Kentucky.

About ten days after the robbery, two young farmers, brothers named Dillon, living in the neighborhood of Pine Hill, Kentucky, read newspaper accounts and figured the bandits were headed straight for their area. They polished their muskets and loaded them with ammunition to be in readiness. "Gee, maybe one of them is Jesse James," they speculated. "The papers say it might be because it sure was the type of bank robbery the James boys favor."

On the third night of their vigil, a moonlit night, the Dillons saw four men stalking toward their farmhouse from the road. They pointed their pistols and fired. The foursome fired back.

Since all were on foot, the Dillons went home and the next morning returned to the scene of the gun battle to see if they could pick up the trail of the fleeing gunmen. Both Dillons felt sure they had hit one of the strangers. Sure enough, at the scene were bloodstains and the trail of blood led several hundred yards down to a cornfield. There they found a man lying on the ground between two rows of corn with a terrible wound in his side.

The wounded man was carried to the Dillon home, laid upon a bed and a doctor summoned. The patient was delirious calling out for "Bud", and then anxiously inquiring, "Where are my friends? I'm dying."

However, when asked the names of his friends he replied, "I've never betrayed a friend yet, and I won't now." And he died – with sealed lips.

While the Dillon brothers and all the available men in the area were out scouring the landscape for the remaining three robbers, a trio of men arrived unannounced at the Dillon home. They asked to see the body. The women at first refused. But the manner of the three gentlemen, all well dressed, and talking respectfully and even reverently, began to break down the women's resolve. Finally, one of the three quoted from Hamlet:

> *"He is dead and gone, lady,*
> *He is dead and gone;*
> *At his head a grass-green turf,*
> *At his heels a stone."*

Listening to the sad rhythm of this quotation, the women succumbed to the gentlemen's charm and allowed them to enter. The three men gazed earnestly at the face of their fallen comrade, now housed in a wooden coffin. The biggest man of the three, Cole Younger, wept openly. The third visitor inquired, "Where's the man who killed him?"

The women nervously replied, "He's nowhere around here. He was a member of a posse that's out looking for the other three. Don't know his name. He ain't from around here."

The big man wiping his tears away with a handkerchief stated, "Well, we do thank you madame, and we bid you and our friend there goodbye."

With that the three left, mounted their horses and cantered away across the cornfield.

Their route continued southwest until they arrived late one night two weeks later at "Mr. Howard's" home and barn near Nashville, Tennessee. No posse had dogged them during this latter part of the trip. The three sat up until the middle of the night with me and Billy. Cole expressed a lot of confusion and doubt about his actions. Although he was the biggest, by far, of any of us, Cole had his sensitive side, and even though he often fought and challenged me on my leadership abilities, he did listen. I assured him he'd done the right thing. "It has always been our vow that if anybody is injured so he impedes the other's safety, he is to be left where he might be found and perhaps saved. I've always said it. If it turns out to be me that's wounded, leave me – as I'll not be responsible for slowing down the outfit so everyone is caught."

"Yes," mumbled the big man, still sniffling into his kerchief, "but you didn't see Tom's face in that coffin." Later, after several cups of Zee's strong coffee, he finally allowed as how I was probably right and leaving Tom was the only thing he could have done.

Frank was still brooding, also. "Tom kept the other rules of the code by not revealing our identification. As the bard put it in Henry V, *"Here was a royal fellowship of death."*

As I looked upon this disheartened trio, I knew I had to make my point even stronger. "It's the only conduct for any of us," I told them firmly. "No matter what happens, we must not reveal the identity of the others. And if someone is mortally wounded, he must be left behind so as not to endanger the others!" Jack Keene seemed to be listening carefully and taking my remarks to heart. And a good thing, too. For Jack was captured by detectives in nearby Fentress County, Tennessee. Unfortunately, he had about $4,500 on his person and was unable to explain just how he had come to have such a large sum. He was taken to Huntington, identified as one of the bank robbers, indicted, tried, convicted and sentenced to serve twelve years in the West Virginia penitentiary. Keene, however, stood by our code. He refused to identify any of the other members of the outfit, even though he was promised a shorter sentence if he did.

The affair of the Huntington, West Virginia bank robbery concluded with the division of the money. Each of the living took one-quarter and the fourth share was set aside for the family of our dead companion, Tom McDaniels. I, of course, did not share as I was not a participant. I was too busy helping Zee out with the care of our one month old son, Jesse Edwards James.

Money for a Negro School

As the mild winter turned to spring, I watched the children going to school and dreamt of watching Jesse Jr. joining them when old enough. I had schooling when I was young and hoped that someday Jesse Jr. would have more schooling than I had, and maybe become a doctor or lawyer or minister as I had always wanted to be.

I also noticed that the colored children had no school and this bothered me. I especially thought of Perry and Ambrose at home and how they didn't have any schooling either.

What was even more important to me was that the colored children should have the same as the white, for hadn't my Lord set it out in Galatians 3:28, *"There is neither Jew nor Greek, there is neither slave nor free man, There is neither male nor female; for you are all one in Christ Jesus."*

One evening I was talking with Zee about schooling and how important it was for children to be able to learn to read and write and learn arithmetic. I mentioned to her that the colored children, both here and in Clay County, did not have a school to attend. I talked about Perry and Ambrose, and how faithful they were to the family, especially how Ambrose, had returned the fire of the Pinkertons on that fateful night when Archie was killed.

Zee knew that I was having a guilty conscience and finally after agreeing that all children, whether white or colored, should have at least some education in school, stated, "Before we left home, I heard of a man named Turner, who was, I'm told, an important Negro educator and is trying to start a school for Negro Children in Clay, but just needs money to get it started."

This was something that interested me and I'm sure it showed in my face as I asked, "Do you think that I could find him?"

It was said with a smile from my beloved Zee, "Yes, I'm sure that you could if you wanted to; and by the way, Billy sure is getting restless, why don't you and Billy go to Clay and find out about this man and maybe talk to him, or whatever. Besides, you should see your mother anyway."

I answered, "Yes, and I should see what's happening at Peace Ranch as well."

Three weeks later on a nice spring day in Missouri, J. Milton Turner was seated on his porch with a friend discussing the very subject of financing a school for Negro children when suddenly two riders appeared, tossed a bag upon the porch and rode away shouting, "Use the gold to start your school."

Unfortunately, J. Milton Turner was very honest and law abiding and turned over the gold to the authorities. The search for the owners of the gold was ineffectual and prolonged. Somehow the money that had appeared so dramatically in early spring just evaporated slowly while in the hands of officials, until by school time, so little was left that it would be several years before enough would be in the hands of Mr. Turner for the start of the school, and especially too late for Perry or Ambrose.

All of Robin Hood's gifts did not end up in the proper hands either.

10

After my attempt to fund the Negro school failed, Billy and I headed on to Texas. Our destination: Peace Ranch.

Our procedure was simple. I rode ahead and Billy monitored my back. Whenever we came in view of others, we attempted to make it appear that Billy was not following me – he seemed to just be a casual rider who was trailing behind. If I turned off onto another trail, Billy would watch my turn and often he would just ride by, nonchalantly making the same turn somewhat later. In this way we appeared to be two separate riders and no one could discern that I actually had a watchdog.

We had stopped in a small Texas town before we got to Peace Ranch and were strolling down the main street when I spotted two men I knew really well. Billy was on foot, not too much farther back from me.

These two men were "Pluck" Murray, an ex-guerrilla and Oscar Thomson, son of Sheriff John Thomson, whose horse I had shot back in Clay County. The Sheriff was the one who moaned to Ma that I had disgraced him in front of all his men. I almost walked on by Pluck and Oscar, but then I thought this might be a good chance to see how young Billy would handle the situation. So I stopped to have a word. I turned to the two, "Hello Pluck, Hello Oscar! Say, I've been wanting to see you for years. Ever since the time I had to shoot your Pa's horse."

Oscar paled a little, but he cleared his throat and got out, "What can I do for you Jesse?"

Pluck was still silent, looking on anxiously. I couldn't tell if either of them was carrying a gun. But I felt calm and safe inside. "Golly, Oscar, nothing at all," I told him, "But I reckon that I can do something for you."

I reached for my wallet. Oscar's paleness had turned a dead white and I realized he thought I was bringing out my six-shooter. After all, he had been with his father that day in Clay. When he saw I was brandishing my wallet, he took a gulp of air and a bit of pink returned to his cheeks.

"I've always been sorry I found it necessary to shoot that fine horse of

your Pa's," I confessed. "Captain Thomson was a brave Confederate soldier. I didn't want to shoot him, so I shot his horse instead. I had to do it, Oscar. I always intended to pay your Pa for the horse, but I never got the chance. Since he died, I've been hoping there would be someway I could square up the debt. How much was the horse worth?"

All the time I was talking I was watching Billy out of the side of my eye. Sure enough, he was loitering a few yards behind me, leaning on the rail in front of the general store, his hand casually caressing his right pocket where I knew he had his pistol. "The kid's all right," I thought to myself, not for the first time.

I had plenty of time to reconnoiter because it appeared the cat had Oscar's tongue. He just stood there, his eyes bugging out, taking a gulp of fresh oxygen whenever he had a mind to. Finally he was able to stammer, "Well, Pa wouldn't have taken money for the horse, but he did say he'd turned down $100 for him."

I peeled off a $100 bill and handed it to him. "We're even," I said. "I wish all my debts were that easy to cross off!"

My thoughts went much deeper. I was thinking specifically of Luke 19:8, 9: *"And Zaccheus stopped and said to the Lord, Behold Lord, half of my possessions I will give to the poor, and if I have defrauded anyone of anything, I will give back four times as much."* And Jesus said to him, *"Today salvation has come to this house because he too, is a son of Abraham."* But what of me, Jesse James? I was responsible for the deaths of several innocent people, from Jolly Wymore during my first bank robbery, to the engineer on the train during that robbery. How could I give back four times as much when it was innocent lives that were lost because of me? Would I be able to even the scale in any way? Would giving my own life do it? I doubted it. But I truly wanted to try to even those scales, even if by just a little bit.

We three gossiped for several minutes about friends and foes in Clay. All the time I was watching in all directions. Except directly behind me. I then walked away without a glance backward.

Two days later when we were nearing the ranch, having avoided the larger towns, we rode into a small town with a river crossing. The town seemed very quiet and peaceful. I felt we were in a safe area and I suggested to Billy that we ride together. But that stalwart young lad disagreed. "No," he said, "It's not right to relax our vigilance. I'll ride behind like I've been doing. You never can tell.

I couldn't help thinking what a valuable little addition we had made to the outfit that day some time back when we scooped up our young orphan and made him part of the James clan.

Billy explained that after we had gone through the town and crossed the river and were on the open road again, he'd ride up to me and journey close to me.

I had always impressed on Billy that the only honorable way to shoot a man was when that someone had called you out, or was facing you. Billy had practiced over and over again what to do if someone drew to my backside. He knew to call out to the man who was pulling a gun to my rear, and then to give him the first shot before firing. I knew that Billy would perform much as I would. That first shot he fired would probably be wild, but the second shot would reach its deadly mark. We had practiced a good deal on just such a situation.

I stopped in the peaceful little Texas town to water my horse, then I started out of town. Billy rode a couple of squares behind me to give the impression that we were not together. As I was leaving the outskirts of town he was about a block behind me.

Suddenly I was facing guns held by two ugly-looking sidewinders, as we called untrustworthy cowpokes in those days. A sidewinder is actually a small rattlesnake of the Southwestern United States and Mexico and to call these two beady-eyed gents by that name was an insult to the snake. At any rate, I was looking down the wrong end of two guns when Billy went into action and his years of training really paid off.

As I saw the galoots, I whirled my horse, I heard four rapid shots and instantly saw two riders slip from their saddles and eat the dust.

It was a hard thing to say when Billy had saved my life, but I felt the boy had to learn the kind of actions I expected of myself – and that I expected of him.

I rode back to Billy and observed, "They didn't have a chance. They were both shot in the back."

Billy didn't say a word, but he got my meaning.

I looked the two over thinking it might be Pluck and Oscar, but I didn't recognize either one of them. I muttered, "Don't recognize them. They must be Texas Pinkertons coming up on me from behind like that."

Billy and I said little to each other for the rest of the ride that day and we endured a silent dinner. I was stuck on the fact that Billy hadn't followed my explicit directions to call out to the two of them before shooting. Tough to criticize a boy (man?) when he's just saved your life. Even tougher to criticize a boy on the verge of manhood.

Needless to say, I couldn't sleep that night. I heard Billy tossing in an equally fitful slumber and suddenly in his sleep I heard him say, "Whatever I did, I did it to protect Jesse from behind in an emergency – and I would do it again. I'd even shoot the man in the moon if it involved Jesse's safety."

After I heard this I felt like a heel. I got up an after a good tussle with my conscience, went over to his bedroll. I stood at the foot of that bedroll and gently nudged it until Billy began to awaken.

I said gently, "Don't worry, Billy." That's all I could get out but I think he smiled in his sleep. I do know that he turned over and fell into a sound sleep because he stopped thrashing around.

"Don't be too hard on the boy," I cautioned myself as I too, finally fell asleep.

Our arrival at the ranch was greeted enthusiastically by quite a large group of the boys. Frank was there, together with Cole, Bob Younger, Clell, Bill Chadwell (whose real name was Bill Stiles), and a newcomer going by the name of Charlie Pitts, whose real moniker was Samuel Wells. Both Frank and Cole vouched for Charlie Pitts and gave him high marks and I liked him immediately. I felt that we had enough men with those on hand at Peace Ranch to undertake a small train robbery. Cole Younger and Bill Chadwell had the information.

Somebody else, I believe it was Frank, brought up the name of Hobbs Kerry, a man Frank had promised to meet in about two weeks about a bank in Canby, Kansas that Frank said he thought would be easy pickin's for us. The entire outfit set to oiling their guns, saddle soaping their saddles, and we left Peace Ranch. As our foreman, Tom Howard, put it, "I'm sure glad to see you go. Two more weeks with all of you here and the entire larder for next winter would be gone."

Always nice to be wanted.

The Missouri Pacific (Rocky Cut) Train Robbery

Frank, Cole and I met with the man they'd been telling me about, Hobbs Kerry, near Sedalia, thereby keeping Frank's word that we would do so. The others waited in camp.

After listening to Kerry's description of the Canby Bank, and his reasons for feeling that it would be an easy undertaking, I decided against that particular robbery *at this time,* I stressed, so as not to hurt Kerry's feelings. Both Frank and Cole heard me out, then reluctantly agreed.

However, they both overruled my objections to allowing Hobbs Kerry to go with the outfit to rob the train. They argued that if he were along I could get to know him, saying they both knew I'd get a good feeling about him. I finally caved in by saying it was all right with me if he went along, but only if he would be put in charge of the horses while the rest of us did the actual robbery.

It was my mistake. If only I had known before what I was to learn later, there would have been no Hobbs Kerry at Rocky Cut.

I always made the decisions as to who would ride with whom when we split up before a robbery. This time was no exception. I decided we would go in two groups. One group would consist of Frank, the Youngers and Clell Miller. No neophytes in that group.

I wanted to know the other group much better than I did. They say there's only two ways of getting to know a person – and that is by working with them or being married to them. I would add a third – riding with them. In my group, in addition to the ever present Billy, were Bill Chadwell, Charlie Pitts and Hobbs Kerry. Lots of unknown quantities in this group!

Before we started out, I had a long talk with Billy so that he would know exactly what tactics we were going to use. I told him I would ride with one of the newcomers, while Billy would always be at my rear, to protect my backside. None of the others in my group were to realize what he was up to. It's true that Billy took a lot of ribbing about always being behind, but he and I knew just how well this system had paid off in the past. We also both knew that there was a price on my head now, and that made a rear-guard action even more possible.

During the ride I had plenty of time to chat with my three co-riders. Both Bill Chadwell and Charlie Pitts talked about Southern Minnesota, which was natural because they both came from there. They both insisted that a real haul could be gotten by robbing the bank in either Mankato or Northfield.

Bill Chadwell seemed to be more informed than Charlie and I found out that he hailed from Southern Minnesota and really did know the lay of the land. I was still dubious, however, until they informed me that both banks were owned and run by old-line federal militia. At that, I began to think that maybe they had something and one or the other of the banks could well be my next objective.

The two separate groups of my outfit joined together just a few miles west of Otterville. Here, I carefully outlined the final plans for the train robbery, drawing a diagram in the dirt with a stick when it was necessary to resort to a picture. I then had a separate talk with the new man, Hobbs Kerry, and went over very carefully where he was to hold the horses and how he was to control them, while the rest of us were doing the actual robbery. I explained to him that even though his role in this robbery was a minor one, he would receive the same cut of the loot as the rest of us. I then carefully reviewed my rules of conduct for each member of the outfit that rode with me and Hobbs Kerry said he was in accord.

If only I had been clairvoyant! But then, not many men are.

Frank and Cole had done their scouting well, and knew to the minute when the Kansas City and St. Louis express would arrive. I cannot remember which one of them observed that it was a very rocky cut in the mountains there at Otterville, but one or the other did and soon everyone was refering to our location as Rocky Cut. While all the men were gathered around, I stressed once again, particularly for the new men, that there was to be no shooting at anyone on the train unless there was a chance of injury or death to one of the outfit. They all nodded solemnly. My plan for robbing the train was so simple that Cole began refering to it proudly as "our plan". Cole was always trying to position himself ahead of me as the "the leader", but I smiled at his silly jockeying for the position this time. I didn't care who wanted to take credit for the "plan" so long as it was executed properly.

Otterville was nothing more than a flag stop on the Missouri-Pacific and nothing more. It boasted a dismal telegraph shack and that was about it. Eight of our outfit of nine dismounted and crowded into the little depot. Here we encountered a German gentleman who talked very broken English but seemed to understand our instructions perfectly. I asked him how many red lanterns he had. The old German gentleman pointed out three. I told him to clean two of them and put in lots of oil and to set one out on the track for any eastbound train from Kansas City.

The flagman objected in his broken English as there was no train due from Kansas City. But after I gave him a sample of my "deadly look" – ice blue eyes boring into his – he resigned himself to the inevitable and did what he was told. We also cut the telegraph wires, just in case anyone got some funny ideas. I told him to clean and fill the third lantern, which he did with alacrity. He stood on the rails and swung the red globe energetically as the train came into view. It came to a dead stop.

At this, we all sprang into action. Clell Miller and Bob Younger began firing their guns randomly at the sky to keep the passengers inside. We moved a couple of red lanterns for enough to the rear of the train so that if a follow-up locomotive were to approach it would have the red signal to stop far enough in advance so no one would get hurt. I was determined to take all the precautions which were possible this time.

Bill Chadwell and Charlie Pitts took over the engine. Frank, Cole and I entered the express car. Billy remained on guard just outside the express car door. Hobbs Kerry was a way off in the woods minding our horses.

The guard gave us no trouble. He immediately produced the key to the safe and we made the usual transfer from safe to grain sack without incident.

I immediately whistled for the horses and Hobbs Kerry duly arrived with them. He had followed that instruction well. I only wished later that he had followed all of my instructions as well.

After we had all mounted, I turned in my saddle so everyone could hear and shouted, "Well, if you see any of Alan Pinkerton's men, tell 'em they'd better come and catch us!"

I never could resist showing up the authorities, tweaking their noses, making sport of them. Call it juvenile if you like, but it made me feel like a million dollars. I knew we had made a significant haul and I felt good.

Within an hour we had divvied up the money and separated. As we did, I made plans for our upcoming trip north to rob either the Mankato or Northfield banks – the ones Bill Chadwell and Charlie Pitts had been touting. As I thought about the future I knew I would make one firm decision. I would replace Hobbs Kerry with Jim Younger the next time we rode.

The man hadn't done anything to make me mistrust him but I was just going on instinct. Harking to that still little voice within that if you listen carefully, can save you a lot of trouble.

Turns out I was right. A few weeks later Hobbs Kerry was arrested in connection with the Rocky Cut train robbery and disregarding my hard and fast rules never to name names, he sang like a canary. He gave the authorities the names of all the men who had ridden with him that day, except Billy.

Looking back, the man had given me a peculiar feeling the first time I met him. In the future, I vowed to listen more carefully to my instincts, and to go along less with whatever Frank and Cole had to say. They were well-intentioned always, but sometimes misguided. If the James-Younger outfit were to prosper and stay out of jail, it would be up to me.

A Friend in Need

After the Rocky Cut robbery at Otterville, Billy and I went into hiding at our camp in the Ozarks. The plan was for the rest of the outfit to show up in about three weeks.

We did a lot of hunting. We bagged wild turkey over in the big timber and along the river, several miles east of camp. We also shot rabbit and squirrel. With just the two of us to feed, it didn't take much hunting to overstock our larder.

After dinner, Billy and I got into some serious conversations and did a lot of reading from the Bible. My well-thumbed and pencil-marked Bible, originally my father's, got quite a workout and I gave earnest thought to what I read. I talked a lot about the Bible's teachings to Billy. Billy was a sharp lad, getting sharper every day as he grew into manhood. He hadn't had much formal schooling, but he could read and write and had an acute mind. In addition to our Bible discussions, we exchanged our philosophies on life, Billy's ideas just beginning to be formed – mine having been shaped and solidified many years ago.

One night we got to reading in the New Testament – Matthew 25:34-40 which states:

"Then the King will say to those on his right, 'come, you are blessed of my father, inherit the Kingdom prepared for you from the foundations of the world. For I was hungry and you gave me something to eat; I was thirsty and you gave me drink; I was a stranger and you invited me in; naked, and you clothed me; I was sick and you visited me; I was in prison, and you came to me.
"Then the righteous will answer him saying, 'Lord, when did we see you hungry and feed you, or thirsty and give you drink: And when did we see you a stranger and invite you in, naked, and clothe you? And when did we see you sick, or in prison and come to you?'
"And the King will answer and say to them, 'Truly I say to you, to the extent that you did it to one of these brothers of Mine, even the least of them, you did it to me'."

As we were reading these paragraphs and pondering on them, an old friend, Charley Mead, floated into my mind. I told Billy that Charley resided near Moberly, Missouri, over in Randolph County. The last time I heard his health had been very poor. I hadn't seen or heard from him in well over a year and I wondered how he was getting along.

Charley had once performed an act of kindness for me which incidentally saved my life. I told Billy about it and added that I was ashamed that I hadn't written to him to see how he was getting along. Billy got real interested in Charley's welfare and the upshot was we both decided to ride over to Moberly to see how he was. Billy thought a personal visit was better than writing a letter any old day.

We began to prepare for an early-morning start. Billy was all excited about the trip. Whether he was just bored with our enforced isolation in the Ozarks camp or whether Charley's story had captured his imagination I did not know. In fact, he was so anxious for the trip that he rolled out a little after midnight, thinking it was morning and he was dressed before he discovered the time. We had a good laugh about that when, as was sure to happen he overslept the next morning and I had to pull him out for breakfast.

We ate, saddled the horses, and were about to leave when Billy suggested we take along some of our ample larder. He quickly dressed some fox squirrels and a couple of young bush rabbits, wrapped them and said he was taking them along for Charley.

I appreciated his forethought. As it turned out, no present could have had more meaning than that food.

With no other horses to slow us down, *Queen* and *Rhoda* left a hundred miles behind in less than ten hours. We really made good time.

Charley lived a few miles west of Moberly and we reached there about ten in the morning. I knocked at the door and Mrs. Mead answered, a little boy and girl about five and six years of age, clinging to her skirts. What a stricken home we found! Marks of destitution and want were apparent on the mother's sorrowful face as well as the pinched faces of the little ones.

Her husband, Mrs. Mead told us in a defeated voice, had died some three months previously, after a long illness. The family had been left without a cent. Not only were the Mead family penniless, they were in debt. They had mortgaged their little house and farm for $300 in order to raise cash to pay for Charley's medicine and doctor.

Charley's forty acres seemed barely able to support a cow and garden, but, by golly, this forlorn little group, I felt, deserved the chance to at least try. The pitiful condition of the Mead family was shock enough, but as Mrs. Mead explained her situation to me, and the dreadful months of Charley's sickness which she had endured, she upset me even more by breaking down and telling me that not a soul, neighbor, Christian or otherwise, had called to ask if aid was needed. This cold-hearted and selfish behavior on the part of the community which presumed to be both civilized and Christian, made me furious. I knew that quick action of some kind was needed, and I vowed to undertake it.

As I listened to the unhappy news, Billy suddenly remembered the squirrels and rabbits and he hurried out and brought in the package. Mrs. Mead's dull glaze of defeat quickly turned to joy in anticipation of the promised feast. By their very actions the famished little tots finished the story of privation which their mother could not because of the tears on her eyes.

As Mrs. Mead began to cook, I knew that my next business was Moberly. I got the name of the bank holding the mortgage from her and told her to go ahead and eat. We would return in an hour. I also told her not to cook for us. We weren't hungry, as we had eaten a huge breakfast.

We reached the bank before noon and I asked for and received a statement of interest paid to date, and the amount of the mortgage. I paid it off and received the note and lien stamped "Paid in full". It felt peculiar to be doing honest business with a bank. And there was a moment or two when I felt like pulling my gun when the young, bumbling clerk took his time getting out the papers. But that wouldn't have done the Mead family any good, so I restrained myself.

Our next stop was the dry goods store. With the help of a rather attractive female clerk I selected complete outfits for the two kids. After this, we headed for the grocery and provisions shop where we loaded up, the only restriction being how much the horses could carry.

The livery stable was nearby and after seeing that our horses were fed, we stopped in a restaurant and ate our noon meal. We sat at a table which afforded me an excellent view of the front door and Billy had an equally perfect view of the back door from his seat across from me. We felt perfectly safe, and somewhat elated at all we had been able to accomplish. Also, there is no better feeling than doing something for someone else.

When everything we had ordered was put down in front of us, Billy got off a lovely rejoiner. "Well, I sure doubt you can eat all of that there food after the big breakfast you put away!"

I had to laugh. We'd had nothing for breakfast. He had a big, satisfied grin on his face and I remembered what I had told Charley's wife. "Aw," I muttered, "I was talking about yesterday's breakfast."

Billy's fast reply was, "Oh, I guess I just heard *part* of your conversation. Sorry about that." With that, we both got a fit of giggles, the way you will when something strikes you funny. The folks in that restaurant must have thought we were a couple of goof balls.

As we were eating, feeling on top of the world, I thought of something I'd overlooked. That was paying the taxes! After a visit to the unsmiling tax man, we completed packing up the horses with all the provisions and clothes we'd bought. We looked like a couple of itinerant peddlers when we rode out of town.

The poor woman's tears of anguish and grief turned to tears of joy as I handed her all the papers as Billy busied himself with bringing in the goods and groceries. All she could do was cry, she was so overcome with relief.

It got to Billy, and he started dabbing his eyes. As for me, I figured it was hay fever that was making my eyes smart and water so.

I told Mrs. Mead that I had not done anything that Charley wouldn't have done for me if our situations were reversed. Then, while she wasn't looking, I slipped a folded package containing some notes under the bundles on the table. Billy pretended not to notice, but he had seen and he had a satisfied smile on his face.

A Friend in Need

Like the mother, the little boy and girl couldn't find words to speak, but as we grabbed our hats and started to go, they threw their arms around us and gave us loving kisses. I thought, "I wonder if when I die from that bullet in the back, my friends will do the same for Zee and little Jesse?" But then I was lucky in being surrounded by kinfolk and when that time comes, I won't grieve because I just know my family *will* be taken care of.

As we rode towards camp I was never happier, I began keeping time with my horse's hoofbeats by humming my favorite "Dixie" to myself. I said out loud to Billy, "What in the world would have happened to them if we hadn't happened over there today?" Billy pointed out that I had had a little guidance from the Old Testament. I had been reading that passage about feeding and clothing the poor just before the thought of Charley popped into my mind.

I then recalled the entire passage I'd been studying and I smiled to myself. There was no question that Providence had given me a nudge, and no question that the Lord works in mysterious ways, His wonders to perform.

A Deed of Honour

As we two self-satisfied Santa Clauses left Moberly, I thought of General Shelby. "You know, Billy, we still have two weeks before we meet up with the rest of the boys. How about us going over to Lafayette County and payin' General Shelby a visit?"

Billy was all for it. He was really enjoying being alone with me, travelling with me, and being my solitary sidekick. The ride was a long one, but once again the horses we were mounted on, being the best, just melted the miles away. During the journey, as always, whenever another rider appeared or we approached even the smallest of towns, Billy would fall back and follow me from a distance. He stayed far enough back to give the impression that we two were not together. Yet, he stayed close enough to be sure that no approach or move was made toward my backside.

When we arrived at General Shelby's we found that he was away for two days. But we were urged to stay, rest our horses, and see the general upon his return. To this, I agreed.

The next day Billy and I were out in the pasture happily hunting quail when we saw a group of horsemen ride up to the gate. We both had the same thought – somehow word had gotten out that I was at General Shelby's home – and this was a posse out to catch Jesse James.

We took off in a fast run for the stables to get our horses. But before we reached them, the horsemen turned and rode away. They had General Shelby's servant, a young Negro boy, hands tied behind him, mounted with them.

I knew this boy's history very well. During the Civil War he had drifted into the general's camp to get something to eat. He had ended up being adopted by General Shelby, and since that time had been like a son to him. Yes, he was black, but no one ever mentioned that, at least not in front of the general.

Seeing the posse hadn't come for me, Billy and I headed quickly to the house to ask Mrs. Shelby what was going on.

She was understandably distraught but managed to tell me that the boy had gone into town with a load of firewood to sell. He had been set upon by a group of white ruffians the last time he made the trip, so this time he took an army pistol with him, taken from the general's room. When the ruffians attacked him, he pulled out his pistol and shot one of them in the leg.

The Negro lad well knew that the whilte folk would get after him for this. He immediately unhitched his mules, mounted one of them, and started on a run for home. But he was too late. He was within a mile of the house when the posse of white men on horseback came into sight. Although he urged the mule to its utmost speed, he had just reached the gate when the posse caught up with him. We had seen the rest.

I immediately decided I would rescue the lad. Mrs. Shelby urged me not to attempt it, but I told her that as I was a guest of the general, and since he was not at home to take command, that it was my duty to protect the adopted boy in his absence.

Billy and I saddled up and rode after the mob. We saw them just ahead of us halted at a bridge. They were dismounting. Billy immediately dropped back to assume his usual position – protection from the rear.

I rode at the mob at a full gallop, seeing that they were attempting to tie a rope over the branch of a nearby tree. There were twelve men in the group, all armed, but they didn't deter me. "What are you going to do with that boy?" I shouted.

"Lynch," cried the man in charge.

"Well, what's he done?" I asked.

"He shot a white boy. The niggers are getting too bold, what with all this freedom. We're going to make an example of this one."

"No, you are not," I stated firmly. "This is General Shelby's boy and I am the general's friend. If that boy has harmed a white boy, he must have a fair trial for it!"

Just as one of the twelve started reaching for his gun, another in the group recognized me, and yelled, "That's Jesse James!" The man starting for his gun let his hand drop as though it had been burned, and the entire mob seemed to shrink within themselves. There was a noticeable change in attitude after my identity was known. "What should we do then?" asked the leader.

"The best thing for you to do is to take this boy to Lexington and turn him over to the sheriff and put him in jail. Let him get the same sort of fair trial that a white boy would. That will satisfy General Shelby. It will satisfy me. And it ought to satisfy you!"

There was a little stir among the men, then the leader nodded thoughtfully, and agreed to my suggestion. Billy and I rode with them towards the outskirts of Lexington to make sure they did as I'd told them. Then, with a somewhat lightened heart, we rode away – towards a meeting with my outfit for the trip North.

Later, we learned to our satisfaction, that the Negro boy had been tried by an all-white jury, was able to prove he had plenty of provocation for his shooting, and was acquitted. Needless to say, I had earned the eternal gratitude of General and Mrs. Shelby.

On the trail Billy piped up with, "Jesse, if you're really Robin Hood, then who am I?"

I chuckled. "Well, if you could sing we'd call you Will Scarlet."

Billy turned red as a ripe beet. He well knew he would never earn the nickname of Will Scarlet because his singing voice sounded more like a wild turkey caught in a trap than a nightingale.

"Never mind," I clapped him merrily on the back, "We'll find an appropriate nickname for you one of these days. Like everything else, it just takes time."

II

Preparing for Northfield : The Northfield Raid : The Retreat : We Meet
Some Real Folks : Double Trouble

We held our final meeting in Jackson County before leaving Missouri for Minnesota. It did not go smoothly. In fact, the various irritations, contentions and "chips on the shoulder" expressed during this meeting presaged an even worse experience to come.

Cole Younger had long been smouldering under some of my rules and regulations, which all the men knew by heart by now: no drinking while riding on a "raid" no matter how long before the raid the drinking took place, a careful choice and determination of the exact job to be pulled, the exact location, time, and all other aspects of the robbery to be determined by one man only – with little input from the others – and that man was me.

I could understand Cole's defensiveness. After all, he was being told what to do and when to do it by a much younger man than himself. But even though I understood his viewpoint, he was a constant burr under my saddle. The only reason that deterred Cole from asserting his total leadership, and changing the name of the outfit to the Younger-James gang, was the fact of the Huntington, West Virginia bank robbery. I had not been there. And it was the only bank robbery which turned sour.

At this meeting, Cole stroked his beard and stated in a loud voice that it was pure ridiculous to ride all the way to Minnesota on a horse when trains were available. In a patronizing tone of voice he pointed out that good horseflesh could easily be purchased in Minnesota.

I allowed him to ventilate his lungs but told him that I would insist on riding my own horse. So would Billy. Frank, who was quite capable of siding with Cole at times, piped up that he would ride, too. He'd obtained a dun colored horse in Kansas City just the week before, on which he was pretty high. He said it was one of the finest horses he'd ever ridden. When I asked Frank if he had actually purchased the horse or if he'd stolen it, he gave me a queer look and quoted from I Henry IV, Act 1, Scene 2. *"Who, I rob? I a thief? Not I, by my faith."* Sometimes getting a straight answer out of Frank was an exasperating and tough job. He spent hours reading and

memorizing Shakespeare with a passionate compulsion and he knew when he made appropriate quotes from his hero that he impressed everyone with his scholarship. Truth was, he had scholarship in only one area – and that was Shakespeare. Nevertheless we all listened to him with appropriate reverence and at times, even awe, when he went into his act.

The dun horse, Frank told us, was known around Kansas City for its speed and endurance. Frank was sure he had a horse which could compete with and stay up with Queen and Rhoda which Billy and I would ride. Despite Cole's whining insistence that taking the train was the wisest course to follow, Frank would ride.

This small dispute was settled when I pointed out that Cole could get to the assignment any way he wanted, as long as when the final "boots and saddles" was called, he was ready to ride.

So the three Younger brothers, together with Charlie Pitts and Clell Miller donned business suits and went by train. They would purchase good horses in Minnesota after leaving the train. As it turned out, it was Clell Miller's first opportunity to wear a business suit, and unfortunately his last.

Now all we had to settle was *which bank to rob!*

I kinda had my sights set on the First National Bank of Northfield. It had a strong Northern Abolitionist history. Two of its heaviest investors were General "Silver Spoons" Butler, Military Governor of New Orleans after its fall to the Federal forces in April, 1862, and his son-in-law, J. T. Ames, notorious carpetbagger governor of Mississippi. Northfield, itself, was founded by John W. North, Abolitionist lecturer and the head of the delegation to the Republican convention that nominated Abraham Lincoln. It was a town of some 2,000 to 2,500 inhabitants, situated in Rice County, on the line of the Milwaukee and St. Paul Railway (hence Cole's insistence on rail travel). Cannon River runs through the town, spanned by a fine iron bridge. In addition to stores, schools and mills, it contained our target – the First National of Northfield! The bank's northern connections were like an elixir to me!

I set our meeting for September 6, 1876, in the brush near Waterville, Minnesota. Here, we'd lay our final plans for the robbery to take place on September 7, 1876.

During the entire trip north on horseback, Bill Chadwell, who knew the area we were entering intimately, and I rode together. As we did I checked and rechecked in my mind the escape routes from Northfield. In Bill's considered and carefully calculated opinion, the best route was on horseback almost directly west from the town until the Minnesota River was crossed twice. After that he urged a gradual southwest course to Sioux Falls, South Dakota. I mulled these ideas over very thoughtfully, and finally agreed to these plans.

My reasoning was this. The robbery was sure to be thought of as the work of the James-Younger gang. The travel path any posses would expect us to take would be southeast towards Missouri. So far so good. But there was more to come.

A second possible route would be to ride southeast. This was a shorter escape trail which would lead back to Missouri much quicker. But it had its drawbacks. It was much slower. Directly west was our best bet, according to Chadwell, and I agreed. He pointed out that this course was fast riding country. We could cover as much as 80 miles per day, even in bad weather.

When the two parts of the outfit met in the brush on September 6, 1876, the Younger contingent said they had secured mounts at Le Sueur from a cousin of Bill Chadwell. That out of the way, we discussed our escape routes carefully, deciding that my group which had ridden north by horseback would take the westerly route, while the train group would take the shorter, southeasterly route, straight back to Missouri. Cole seemed quite pleased at this decision.

We went over the plans for the robbery more than once. Bill Chadwell and Clell Miller, with Bob Younger's back-up if necessary, were to destroy the telegraph. Other positions and assignments were handed out, soberly considered, accepted and agreed to.

And so we slept.

The Northfield Raid

There were three approaches into Northfield so, as was our time-honored custom, we split into three groups. Group one was composed of Bob Younger, Charlie Pitts and Bill Chadwell. These three, with the addition of Frank, were to be the four inside men that day. The second group was made up of Frank, Cole and Clell Miller. Group three was myself, Jim Younger, and Billy.

I looked on with a sense of satisfaction as group one rode directly to the bank, dismounted, and waited for group two to join them. The four who were scheduled to enter the bank did so. Everything was proceeding according to plan.

What I did not know, and which would have led me to call off the raid if I had, was that Bob Younger, Charlie Pitts and Bill Chadwell had been drinking liquor steadily from the time they arose until 2:00 p.m., the time of our attack. They had broken one of the outfits cardinal rules. As a result, they would suffer the consequences.

In any event, the three, together with Frank, entered the bank. Cole Younger sauntered towards the front door while Clell went towards the side door. Jim Younger and I were mounted in a sentry position, each about one block away from the bank, in opposite directions. Billy was nonchalantly leaning against the hitching post in front of the bank, holding the horses, but with an alert right hand touching, but not showing, his gun. Just in case.

Then everything seemed to go wrong at once!

The very first thing was that a man named J. S. Allen, a hardware merchant, was trailing my four into the bank. Clell Miller siezed him by the throat as he crossed the threshold. For some inexplicable reason, Clell tightened his grasp on Allen's neck and ordered him to leave, threatening him by saying, "and if you speak a word to anyone, I'll kill you." Threats are one thing, but it would have been wiser for Clell to have just shoved Allen *into* the bank, where he could have been covered by the now unholstered '45s, instead of shoving him *out* of the bank. Mistake No. 1. The mistakes were to accelerate after this.

Mr. Allen took immediately to Clell's "suggestion" but as he exited, he dashed around the corner and began to yell, "Get your guns boys. Those fellows are robbing the bank." So much for threats. As this alarm was given, Clell and Cole ran out, remounted, and joined Jim Younger and myself. We began riding up and down the street in front of the bank firing wildly, hitting store signs, raising up the dust of the main street and a hootin' and a hollerin' for everybody to get inside their houses. However, surprisingly enough, these citizens were not about to take orders from strangers. From several different directions came rapid and frequent return gunfire.

Inside the bank things were no better. When my four men had originally entered they'd encountered no customers and only three employees, each at their proper work station. The teller, A. E. Buner and the assistant bookkeeper, F. J. Wilcox, were where their bosses intended them to be, but the head bookkeeper, Joseph Lee Heywood, was positioned at the cashier's desk.

Charlie Pitts grabbed this man, Heywood, rushed with him to the front of the vault and commanded, "O.K., cashier, open that safe!"

Something about Charlie's over-agitated state disturbed Frank and he stepped in. "I'll handle this," he told Charlie. Frank beamed hardened eyes on the cashier. "Sir, I understand your concern for your bank, but I must tell you that unless you open that safe *at once* you'll be shot dead."

Heywood replied mournfully, "I can't open it. The time lock is on and won't open until 3 o'clock when the head cashier gets back."

The muscles around Frank's jaw tightened. "You're lying," he told the hapless bank clerk. But Heywood stood his ground.

All the loose currency Charlie and Frank could find went into the grain sack. But it was a pitiful amount and certainly not worth all the time and trouble it took and the risks we'd taken.

These thoughts were quickly dispelled, however, when Charlie and Frank heard us cry from outside the bank, "Come out boys! They're killing our men!" As they turned to make a fast exit, Mr. Heywood decided he'd try to be a hero. He grabbed a gun from behind the cashier's desk and his trigger

Colt pistol used in the Northfield Raid by Cole Younger.

finger was just about to move when some instinct made Frank turn and look at him. Frank aimed and quickly shot Heywood through the head.

The grim statistics outside the bank added up to the loss of one of our horses, which had been shot dead, and Clell Miller, who had been shot in the cheek and clavicle with with such force that the bullets knocked him off his horse and he lay dead, flat on his back, in the street.

Chaos ruled outside. We had expected the Northfield residents to cower beneath our onslaught, but instead the citizens were fighting back with desk pistols, derringers and shotguns. The steam whistle at the river mill was screaming over and over again and girls were yanking steeple ropes so that the church bells were ringing, sounding the alarm. Laborers were throwing down their rakes and hoes in the fields to rush to the street, manually pushing wagons in front of the bank and at the road exits to try to impede our escape.

As Cole and Jim Younger and Bill Chadwell leaped into their saddles, all thought of further gain from the bank eclipsed by their need to escape, a well-aimed bullet caught Bill Chadwell, and he keeled over instantly dead.

Bob Younger's bay horse was the one that had been killed, so Bob ducked behind some crates and boxes piled up near the general store for cover. It did him no good. Gunshot found Bob Younger's right arm and the ball crashed into his elbow. Jim Younger, astride his horse, took a bullet in his shoulder, Cole Younger got it in the thigh and Frank James was shot in the leg. A bullet pierced Billy's side. (That bullet would remain inside Billy for 58 years and when he died, he was still carrying it with him.)

There were now seven bandits alive, but only six horses. Cole Younger pulled his brother Bob up behind him and we raced out of town.

The cost to the outfit in dead and dying was too high. There was only one man of the entire gang unharmed, and that was myself. Was I smarter, faster or luckier than the rest? All of that, and yet none of that, too. This day would be a day we'd long remember – with gloom and sorrow and regret.

The Retreat

As we seven outlaws on our six horses rode out of Northfield, dripping blood behind us to make a trail anyone could follow, wincing and grimacing in pain, we had some more bad luck. Obviously, my men who had been assigned to destroy the telegraph were in no condition to complete that job, two being dead and one with his right arm out of commission. Bob Younger's right elbow was completely destroyed; his entire right arm lay limp at his side. He struggled to hold onto Cole with his left arm, reeling from his affliction.

Even so, we made a good start down the Dundas Road, but it was obvious to us all that the horse carrying both Cole and Bob was having a hard time keeping up. Something had to be done about this situation or they'd both be in trouble. Just before we reached the town of Dundas we relieved a farmer of one of his team of horses. This helped.

At the next farmhouse, we stopped and I explained to the farmer that we were deputies in pursuit of horse thieves. We wanted to borrow a saddle. The other blood-covered men stayed behind some trees as I approached the farmer, together with Bob. "This young man didn't have time to get his saddle when he joined up with us," I lied cheerfully, "And he's been thrown off. He got his arm hurt." The farmer readily gave us the "loan" of a saddle. When it came right down to it I could still "fast talk" and get what I wanted. Good to know I still had something going for me, after the debacle at Northfield.

Bob mounted shakily on his newly gotten saddle and was able to keep pace with the rest of us for the next several miles by sheer guts. But the events of that black day were not going to ease up. It was about 4 p.m. and we had reached the outskirts of Millersburg when Bob Younger's borrowed farm horse stumbled and fell. Bob Younger broke his left arm.

Now we were back down to seven riders and six horses again and Bob was totally out of commission with two useless arms, and suffering from severe trauma and pain. The only way he could ride was in front of one of the others, who would have to ride with Bob's added weight, plus the inconvenience of holding Bob with one hand and the reins of the horse with the other. Mighty awkward and a situation just calling for trouble. The only horseman we felt could do that was Billy. He was the lightest and Queen, his horse, could handle the extra weight. Needless to say, our pace was considerably slowed.

The next town up ahead was Shieldsville. We'd have to get through it some way. What we didn't know was that the county seat, Faribault, had been notified of the robbery by telegraph and had sent a posse out. They were sitting there in Shieldsville just waiting for us to show up. As soon as we entered the edge of the town of Shieldsville, the posse was alert and gave chase.

Our situation could not have been grimmer. I had six severly wounded men to contend with most of them moaning and flinching in pain as blood poured from their wounds, coating their beards, making their shirts look like they all wore red, and mixed with the dirt and dust on the horses' flanks and dripping into the road. Obviously, a decision had to be made – and fast. The posse was gaining on us. The next hour or so could easily see the demise of the entire James-Younger outfit. Three had already been wiped out. Were we all slated to die that day?

It became apparent to me that the only thing to do was to go into the thick brush. This would not be a new experience for any of us. We had ridden between trees and through underbrush so thick we sometimes had to lean over our horses heads with a machete and cut a pathway, many, many times under Quantrill, Anderson and Todd in both Missouri and Eastern Kansas. I motioned for my men to follow me and we blended into the woods.

The Minnesota posse stopped at the edge of the timber.

Darkness soon began to fall, and with it the rains came. I don't remember ever passing a more miserable night. The outfit took their blankets off the horses, spread them over bushes in an effort to make some kind of tent and tried to get some much-needed rest. But the shelter was ineffectual and rain fell through gaps in the blankets, splattering together with the blood, to make a mournful rhythm. It was like some scene right out of *Dante's Inferno.*

Cruel decisions would have to be made. I was not only the leader, but the only one in any condition to do so.

I stood over my little beleagured group as they huddled miserably under their makeshift tents. As they all watched me anxiously with pain-filled and weary eyes, I cleared my dry throat to speak.

It was a difficult thing to say, but I had to say it. I finally stated, "Men, it's always been the rule that if one of us cannot travel, then he is to be left behind. Bob must be left here. We'll split up into two groups with the six good horses we have and ride out of Minnesota."

Cole Younger rose out of the wet darkness like an avenging angel.

"Like hell we will! I'll not abandon a brother of mine! If Bob dies, we'll die with him."

I held to my decision. "It was Bob, Charlie and Bill that broke the rules by drinking all morning. That's why we're in this predicament. I say we leave Bob at the first farmhouse we come to, then take the two routes Bill said would be the fastest and least dangerous out of this state."

Cole roared like a wounded mountain lion. "Jesse, I'm warning you, I've still got my gun!" His face was a mask of determination and hostility as his right hand went to his holster. "God damn it, you heard me. I will not leave my brother. You can go to hell as far as I'm concerned, but Jim and I will not leave Bob behind. Right, Jim?"

Jim's voice floated out from the gloom, "I'm with you, Cole. Brothers cannot be separated."

The mood was too serious for quotations. Frank said staightforwardly, "Yes, brothers must stay together. Jesse and I ride, and I guess Billy goes with us. How about you Charlie?"

Charlie Pitts took one look at my forbidding and pitiless face. He knew I wouldn't forget – or easily forgive – that Charlie had been one of the imbibers. My anger, though slow to break, could be merciless against anyone who had ever broken one of my rules. "I'll stay with the Youngers," Charlie said, hanging his head a little. That took care of that. Now all we had to decide was what routes to take.

In an attempt at reconciliation with Cole I explained to him that the fastest route was through Waterville and down by Mankato, then directly west. Cole nodded his head solemnly, as I spoke, and I could see that in addition to his anxiety about his brother he was suffering grievously from his wounded thigh. He had tied a strip from his linen duster as a tourniquet about the wound and at least it had stopped bleeding. But it must hurt like hell. He agreed that this was the best route, and that's the one he, his brothers, and Charlie Pitts would take.

Bill, Frank and I would head directly west, intending to veer slightly northwest until we would leave Minnesota near Sioux Falls, South Dakota.

At the first suggestion of the sky's lightening, the two parts of our outfit split. The rain was still pelting down on our sorry-looking congregation. As Cole and Jim Younger nodded curt goodbyes they both wore a look that seemed to say, "Partner, if any of us make it, it will be a miracle. And if any of us do, the ones that don't will never blab on the others."

As we three riders left the brush, gloom was so thick it was like a fourth horseman named *pessimism* rode with us. Nevertheless, we persevered, taking a directly west road towards the Minnesota River, my photographic memory serving me well as I recalled every little detail that Bill Chadwell had outlined. I knew that the route we took was not the fastest way to Missouri. But even with the rain dampening our spines as well as our spirits I also knew that if we could stay with it we would be able to cross the Minnesota River twice before nightfall. That would put 100 miles between us and the town of Northfield and the other four badly wounded members of the outfit back in the brush. I knew *Queen* and *Rhoda* were capable of this undertaking, and if Frank's dun horse proved as good as they'd said, even in this weather, it just might be done.

The dun horse was capable. By nightfall, as predicted, we had twice crossed the Minnesota. All three horses were spent. But they had done it! Not once during that long, wearying, fraught-filled day had there been a problem of any kind. Maybe – just maybe – our luck was changing, I dared to hope.

The next day was almost a replica of the previous one. By the end of the third day, Sioux Falls was a reality. It was here that Frank and Billy were to have their wounds attended to. The story, readily accepted without question, was that they had been shot by horse thieves. This kind of activity was so prevalent hereabouts, and our horseflesh was obviously the finest, that no one gave my story a second thought.

While my little group had reached its hardfought-for destination and the wounds had been attended to, an entirely different saga was unfolding for the Younger band.

The Youngers, of necessity, travelled very slowly due to Bob Younger's condition and the fact that they were four men mounted on three horses. The group floundered in swamplands with almost a thousand manhunters looking for them.

What they did not know was that a picket line – a human chain of deputies, law men and posse members – was being set up in the old Army way, so that places on the rivers which could be forded, streams, and all roads were encompassed by this picket line – men strung out in a line ready to shoot at anything which came their way. When they came to a ford of the Little Cannon river, it was guarded by three men who fired upon the fugitives. They retreated into the timber. They waited. And they waited some more. Finally Cole, falling back on his guerrilla days, scouted the river and determined that the three had left.

The four weary travellers crossed the ford. They had broken through the picket line! They soon discovered the burden of attempting to have four men ride three horses. They were also discovering, to their intense chagrin, that the horses they had purchased at Le Sueur were not of the same calibre as Missouri horses, which were bred for stamina. At a lonely farmhouse they had a bit of luck. They were able to trade two of their horses for fresh mounts. Not because the farmer wanted to, but because two pistols held by two grim looking men have a fast way of breaking a man's resolve.

It was no use obtaining a horse for Bob. He could not ride alone. They spent a dismal night in the rain near German Lake. They had not eaten in several days as they couldn't take the time or use the ammunition on hunting. They chewed grass and hunted for wild mushrooms as the nights grew increasingly cold. Cole, Jim and Charlie's wounds had dried up some, helped by linen-duster tourniquets, but the blood had mingled with the filth and dust and grime in their clothes so that their apparel was glued to their skin. Bob looked so awful that the thought passed over Charlie's mind several times that it would be better to shoot him.

The next four days were long and hard. They were in desperate need of food, sleep, medical attention, and dry clothes. They were in desperate need of everything. Then, out of the blue, they stumbled upon an abandoned farmhouse. Here, they stayed gratefully for two nights and one day. Cole and Jim and Charlie all believed it was close to Makato. Bob was beyond offering an opinion of any kind. Finally, Cole decided to venture into Makato. His thought was that the train might stop there and just possibly this beaten down little band might be able to ride to Missouri the way they had come – by train.

Cole started out, alone. He soon found that the road was highly travelled. It was filled with men on horseback as well as posses. They were looking for outlaws on horseback who had robbed a bank at Northfield. It didn't take Cole long to figure out that his plan would never work. He retreated to the farmhouse. Since the posses were looking for "men on horseback" he reasoned, the group would go on – but with a difference. They would leave the horses behind and go forward on foot. Onward they plodded towards Medelia. A lad of 17 spotted them as they passed his barn

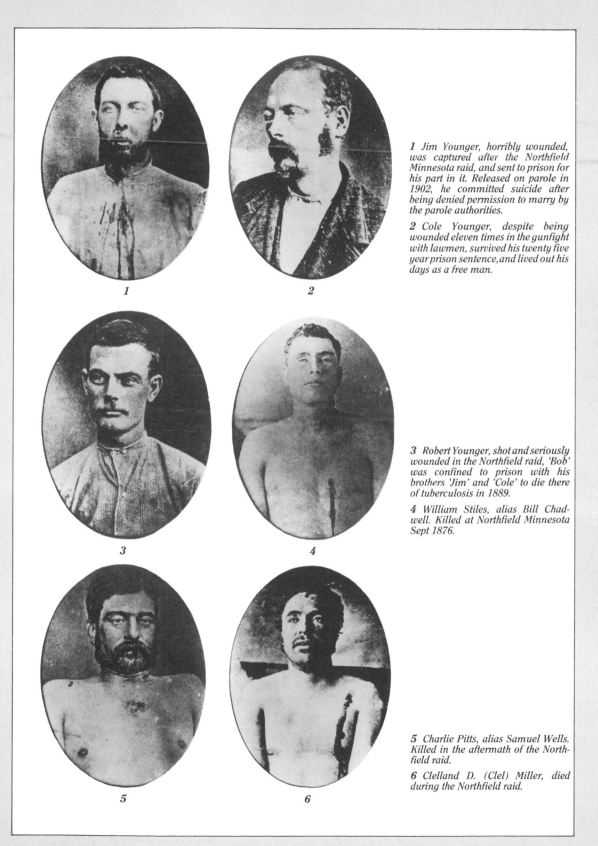

1 Jim Younger, horribly wounded, was captured after the Northfield Minnesota raid, and sent to prison for his part in it. Released on parole in 1902, he committed suicide after being denied permission to marry by the parole authorities.

2 Cole Younger, despite being wounded eleven times in the gunfight with lawmen, survived his twenty five year prison sentence, and lived out his days as a free man.

3 Robert Younger, shot and seriously wounded in the Northfield raid, 'Bob' was confined to prison with his brothers 'Jim' and 'Cole' to die there of tuberculosis in 1889.

4 William Stiles, alias Bill Chadwell. Killed at Northfield Minnesota Sept 1876.

5 Charlie Pitts, alias Samuel Wells. Killed in the aftermath of the Northfield raid.

6 Clelland D. (Clel) Miller, died during the Northfield raid.

while he was milking. They had unfortunately stopped at the main farm-house asking to buy some food explaining they had been fishing and eaten all their grub.

Young Oscar had an alert mind and he didn't believe the story the way his Pa did. He talked his father into letting him go to Medelia to report the strangers to Colonel Vought. A posse of seven men responded immediately and rode to the boy's farm. Others joined them there. The word spread rapidly and as many men as could headed their horses in the direction of Oscar's farm. Everyone wanted to be in on the final capture and kill off the famed James-Younger outfit.

It didn't take the men long to locate the footsore fugitives in a mucky morass known as Hanska Slough. After the thunder and smoke of the guns died down, there were only three men alive – barely. Charlie Pitts was instantly dead with a Minie ball which crashed through his chest at the collar. Bob Younger suffered a bullet through the right lung, but amazingly survived. Jim Younger had five wounds including one that crushed his upper jaw so that he shed teeth like confetti and could never chew food again. Cole was stricken with eleven gunshot wounds and a blackened eye whose bruise spread until it covered the entire right side of his face.

The Youngers' surrender was to mark the beginning of a long stay for them in Minnesota. Bob would die in prison. Jim Younger would commit suicide. Cole would serve 25 years behind the high walls of Stillwater prison.

Of course at the time Frank and Billy and I had no idea what terrible events were happening to the Younger party. We spent four days at Sioux Falls posing as cattle buyers with Billy as our trainee. Mercifully, Frank's wound was healing and Billy was suffering soreness from his, but little pain. We ate well.

The newspapers were full of the raid and the ensuing chase. We did know that the weather was terrible from the newpaper reports, but we all somehow felt that the Youngers had made it through. How wrong we were! I didn't give Charlie Pitts much thought because I knew he would soon dis-appear from our lives by choice, if not his, then mine. I was bitter about the men disregarding my orders and drinking and I felt that by doing so they had ruined our chances of a successful raid. In fact, I was bitter about the whole experience. Although I'd liked Bill Chadwell well enough, he had broken the rules and suffered the consequences. I had no feeling of remorse about his death.

The matter of Clell Miller was entirely different. I had become excep-tionally fond of and close to Clell. Although not a guerrilla, himself, he had always carefully and scrupulously followed the rules. When arrested, he had kept his mouth shut when it would have been to his advantage to talk. He had never touched liquor when a raid was planned. Like Billy, I had begun to look upon him as a younger brother. And now Clell was gone. Due to no fault of his own, I thought mournfully, but to others' stupidity and flagrant disregard for instructions. Or for even good sense. Any fool knows you cannot drink and shoot straight at the same time.

Our trip from Sioux Falls to Sioux City, Iowa was leisurely. We no longer rode in a headlong panic. First, because there was no pursuit whatsoever. Secondly, both Frank and Billy were still troubled by their wounds. The last newspaper report we'd read had stated that all the outlaws who robbed the Northfield bank were still in Minnesota. Their imminent capture was predicted.

When we arrived in Sioux City, Iowa, we immediately bought a paper to learn that the Youngers had been captured and that Charlie Pitts was dead.

Sad to say, but Pitts' death was somewhat of a relief. It relieved me of the responsibility of deciding what to do with him after his failure in Northfield and secondly I would no longer have to worry about him confessing to the authorities.

Despite our conflicts, I knew the Youngers would never reveal who their companions had been. Although suspicion would fall on us, there would be no proof. The Youngers might be accused of it but, again, there would be no verification as long as we were not captured. We left for Council Bluffs, Iowa, in pretty good shape physically but dispirited by the news.

The next morning I woke with a scream, frightening the living daylights out of Frank and Billy. They stared at me in horror. I was actually visibly shaking. Once the tremors and chills subsided I told them that for the first time in many, many months I'd had my frightening dream again. This time it was more vivid than ever before. In the dream, I was standing without my guns and waiting for the shot from behind. The shot came. I was dead.

"Billy," I said, "You'll stay with me and watch my backside?"

Billy's answer was simple and sincere. "Jesse, I'll be with you as long as you want me."

In Council Bluffs we read about the Youngers' capture. They had refused to name their accomplices, as I'd known they would. The reports also stated that all the men who had taken part in the raid on Northfield were in custody, except two. And those two, the papers said, were still in Minnesota and would be caught soon.

It wasn't hard to understand why the authorities had made a wrong count. First, the entire raid took less than 10 minutes, and during the ride from Northfield where we might have been observed a keen eye would have seen only six horses. So with three in custody and three dead that left only two more to catch.

As we left Council Bluffs I patted *Rhoda* and looked approvingly at *Queen* and the dun and I never felt better about my decision to take tried-and-true Missouri horseflesh all the way to Northfield. But my dream still troubled me, as Billy rode behind me to protect my rear. The thought persisted that if I was going to be shot, standing, without my gun belt, what good would his riding behind me do?

Also, what good did it do me to *know* I was going to be shot if there was nothing I could do to prevent it? Puzzling and troubling thoughts. I knew that I would never allow myself to be captured. I could not stand prison and I'd always thought that I would like to go out of this life as I had lived, firing my guns and with my boots on. Would matters become so desperate that I would allow myself to be shot in the back, somewhere down the line? What would be the circumstances? What was to become of Billy? Of Zee? Young Jesse?

As I often did when troubled I turned to the Bible. This time I was using my small New Testament and my hands turned to Timothy, Chapter 1, verses 12 through 16, which hit me hard:

> *"And I thank Christ Jesus our Lord who hath enabled me, for that he counted me faithful, putting me into the ministry;*
>
> *"Who was before a blasphemer, and a persecutor, and injurious, but obtained mercy, because I did it ignorantly in unbelief.*
>
> *"And the grace of our Lord was exceedingly abundant with faith and love which is in Christ Jesus.*
>
> *"This is a faithful saying, and worthy of all acceptation, that Christ Jesus came into the world to save sinners; of which I am chief.*
>
> *"Howbeit for this cause I obtained mercy, that in me first Jesus Christ might show forth all long suffering, for a pattern to them which should hereafter believe in him to life everlasting."*

Although I had been removed from the roster of the church; my faith had never wavered. A comforting thought came to me. If Paul, a murderer, could be accepted by our Lord as his apostle, could I not also be accepted into the real church, the one in heaven?

We Meet Some Real Folks

After two days at Council Bluffs, we pulled out early and the next afternoon we were devoutly thankful to be in our home state. I could have gotten down off of my horse and kissed the good, rich, brown earth of Missouri. Towards evening we came upon a small but very neat farm house located about midway between the state line and St. Jo. A large water tank fashioned out of sycamore standing out in the barnyard caught my eye. It seemed to offer a good opportunity of giving the horses a cooling drink.

As we rode between the high weight lever swing gates, the owner came from the barn carrying a feed pail and extended us a friendly greeting. He was a large boned man of about 40, with black hair and two vertical frown lines between his brows which were immediately dissipated by a picket fence which dominated his face. "Good Missouri farm food are responsible for those," I thought to myself, while leaning off my mount to extend a grateful hand to him.

As we dismounted and uncinched the horses to water, I noticed that he owned one of the old time tread power outfits. It stood next to the tank and was connected with the old wood pump. It was smaller than the regular horse tread, but nevertheless and exact duplicate with the same cleated treads and enclosed side around the inclined platform. I knew an animal had to be used to walk the tread to pump the water and as this contraption was too small for a horse to tread, I wondered what kind of an animal the owner used.

I didn't have to wonder long. The farmer, whose name was Mr. Evans, opened a small gate in the front garden and in shot a big, shaggy shepherd dog, laughing us a storm.

The dog beamed so much joy and delight at us that I likened him to the head of a welcoming committee whose duty it was to greet the governor of the state. Dogs laugh? Of course they do. Just like people. And this dog so obviously rejoiced in his task that we all stood around grinning at him, like a gaggle of schoolboys. Up he jumped on the old tread and soon had it humming so fast a good stream of water ran into the tank and the horses thankfully drank. Mr. Evans told me that he had to keep his gate closed at all times. Otherwise if his dog wasn't watched he would go in and pump water until it overflowed the barnyard. I never saw a creature happier at its work! In fact it was the best show I'd seen in a long while.

Mr. Evans told us that he was formerly from the South and it soon became apparent that he hadn't left any of his Southern hospitality at home when he settled in Missouri. By then it was late afternoon and we readily accepted his invitation to dinner.

The Evans family consisted of the father and mother and their two boys and two girls. Contentment seemed to pervade all of them. Their general aura of happiness plus the genuine welcome they extended to us, made us feel instantly at home, almost as though we were once again among "kinfolk".

After a wonderful dinner that evening we were entertained by the children. They sang songs of the old South, and hymns whose lyrics translated into a hope for a higher better life.

When Frank told Mr. Evans that it was our aim to find accommodations somewhere for the night, as it looked a little like rain, an offer to stay with them was readily tendered.

Having our own bedrolls we unfolded them in the hay barn and when the delightful evening's entertainment had concluded, happily bid the family good night and retired to our bunks.

Weary as we three were, it was a long time before we slept. The next morning I asked Billy if his wound had kept him awake. He said no, that it was the contrast between the ugly happenings at Northfield and the peace and happiness of the Evans farm. Billy was pretty good at expressing his thoughts, but he was inarticulate when it came to telling me what was going on in his soul at that time. A part of him longed for the traditional values of a settled and conventional home, he told me falteringly. And yet another part of him throbbed and hummed when it came to executing a raid. Two different paths. Which should he follow?

I promised Billy that morning that in the future he would be able to enjoy the tranquillity he sensed in the Evans household with me and Zee in the near future. I realized that even if I were drawn again into acts of outlawry, Billy would have to be spared. I couldn't risk Billy becoming jaded and bitter, as I had.

It had rained during the night and was still drizzling this Sunday morning. Mr. Evans insisted we should remain until it cleared up a bit and we happily agreed. Their next and not unexpected suggestion from Mr. Evans was that we should accompany them to church that morning.

Too late to rescind our acceptance, I detected a look of distress on Billy's face as he tried to catch my eye and shook his head emphatically to negate the proposal. It was then that I remembered his hated stepfather, from whom he'd fled, had been a preacher. Billy evidently had pretty negative feelings about attending church.

But the damage had been done and we were committed. The Evans family had been so generous and kind that we would look like ingrates to refuse their invitation when it seemed a small way to show our appreciation.

Billy had to endure more. A large tin tub was set up in the kitchen and filled with hot water. "You first," Mrs. Evans said to Billy.

"Not me, Jesse first." Billy said, creeping behind me as though to hide. "I'm going to help Mr. Evans in the barn."

"Not so fast," I grabbed him by the arm as he was taking off in any direction but the kitchen. "Let's get some of that road grime off of you, young sir. It'll be good!"

Acting like a baby (which in a sense, he was), Billy was finally persuaded to shed his clothes and immerse himself in the dreaded tub.

"Don't forget behind your ears!" Mrs. Evans called out cheerfully, laughing at his typical boy's actions to get out of taking a bath.

"Want me to scrub your back?" Mr. Evans joined in.

"No, I can manage myself," Billy piped up, soaping himself as rapidly as he could so he could get out.

A towel wrapped around his middle, Billy fled to the barn to dress. He had scrubbed his face almost raw, so the the pink skin glowed and his blond hair stood out in fragrant, newly-washed tufts. In his knapsack he had an extra pair of clean pants which he donned. He carefully arranged his trousers outside his boot stops, a major sartorial change on his part. Preening self-consciously like a store model on display, he sheepishly invited our opinions on how he looked. Frank, who had smartened up his own appearance as best he could, plunged in. "You look like the very devil, squirt," he told him. His confidence somewhat undermined by Frank's candor, Billy proceeded to pull off his boots and replace his trousers inside, the way he generally wore them.

The little country church was located at a crossroads about a mile from the Evans house. We all rode there and tied up our horses in the rear. We hitched them close, ready for an immediate exit if it became necessary. We followed the Evans family inside. I spied a vacant seat near the entrance where I could see everything and everyone and kept my linen duster on which covered my two six shooters.

Frank and Billy were also armed and their dusters covered their weapons, as well. Frank and Billy, looking nice in his clean trousers and shined boots, were led directly up to the "Amen corner". After making a careful observation of the assembled churchgoers I concluded that we would not be challenged by anyone in the group and I settled back to enjoy the service. I was also enjoying Billy's discomfort. He glared daggers at me and Frank every time we gifted him with a pleasant smile.

There was no doubt about it. Billy detested church and preachers. They reminded him of his hateful stepfather. At this point he looked as though he'd rather be facing enemy rifles in Northfield than where he was.

It took this country church preacher about two hours to properly whip the congregation into a guilty and depressed state. By the time he was through, he had the whole human family – but most particularly those seated within his church – hogtied and bound and consigned to the brimstone pits. At times, as the preacher reached new heights of zeal, hammering the pulpit for emphasis, I looked searchingly at Billy, half expecting him to whip out a '45 from under his duster and shoot the poor, misguided man.

Finally, more out of exhaustion than inclination, the preacher came to a sing-song climax and quit and the little congregation was able to escape and get some fresh air. Mr. Evans and Frank started out the door but Billy made a beeline for the preacher. Frank started after him, sensing trouble, but was unable to reach him before the young squirt demanded to know from the old circuit rider, "Where the hell he expected to be while the rest of us were burning in the brimstone."

Before the befuddled and slow-thinking preacher could reply, Frank had Billy by the arm and led him quickly outside. Frank was no ardent churchgoer himself, but he was smart enough to realize it wasn't a good idea to call attention to ourselves at this time.

Billy's rebellious outburst seemed to relieve his pent up emotions and he rode back to the Evans farm in much better spirits than on the way over. I couldn't help but be amused by the entire matter. I also couldn't help thinking that here was a preacher who was the wrong kind. Instead of inculcating his flock with fear and hatred of our Lord and God he should act as my father had done by preaching the love of God to his people, thereby gathering the forgotten sheep to him.

We stayed at the Evans farm Sunday night, enjoying another evening of entertainment. But early Monday morning we packed our rolls and cinched up the horses to undertake the remainder of that long and memorable ride. In the course of talking with Evans I learned that he, himself, had suffered depredations and losses from Jayhawker raiders. But according to his Bible he had deduced that to *"turn the other cheek"* was what the Lord wanted him to do, and this he had endeavored to fulfill. I replied that the Bible also says *"an eye for an eye"* and we had an interesting discussion regarding the Scriptures.

I discovered that Evans had read a great deal from the Bible, as of course I had too. Frank entered our conversation by quoting from his favorite bard, and I told Evans that many of the Jayhawkers' outrages had been avenged.

I had a funny feeling that at this point Evans knew who we were, but being a true Southern gentleman he never said a word. Also in keeping with Southern customs, he refused to take any pay for our meals or our accommodations insisting that he had already been amply repaid by the pleasure of our company. The only thing I could do to show my appreciation was to slip a brief note under a plate thanking them for their kindnesses. It contained a twenty dollar gold piece and my note explained it was for the girls and boys, in appreciation of their entertainment.

A quotation swam into my mind. I couldn't remember its author. *"Friendship is the shadow of the evening, which strengthens with the setting sun of life."* It neatly summed up the warm feelings I had for the Evans family and the time spent in their hospitable home. Frank, Billy and I would also cherish memories of this short respite in our tumultuous lives for a long time to come.

We still had something like over a hundred miles to ride before we could reach our Ozarks camp. There was no use crowding the horses to attempt this in a day, so we did it in two days readily finding a good camping spot that night. It seemed like a special dispensation from providence that we were permitted to ride in safety to our quiet and secluded retreat. Six out of the original nine that had crossed over the Minnesota border a month before would probably never set foot on Missouri soil again. Three had gone to their lonely graves, three were incarcerated in a Minnesota prison, perhaps to eventually be hung by a trial jury. Who knew?

After the sunny moments the Evans family had brought into our lives were over, an air of gloomy dejection once more pervaded the camp. The high spirits which had marked other homecomings after successful adventures were absent now. It was a long time before the picture of Clell Miller reeling and falling in his tracks would fade from my daily thoughts. It will never fade from my memory. We rolled into our beds that night with a feeling of relief that this long heartbreaking ride into the face of tragedy would soon be over.

Double Trouble

We stayed at the Ozark camp a few days and then decided there was only one place to go – Peace Ranch. I thought briefly of joining Zee in Tennessee or going back to Ma's farm, but both decisions had their drawbacks. I didn't want to bring any hint of trouble or turmoil to Tennessee and my family. The farm at Clay was too carefully watched and monitored to be safe. Yes, Peace Ranch was the answer.

When the three of us arrived we found little had changed except that our foreman and manager, Tom Howard, was struggling with a Texas fever. It had infected almost every herd in Texas. Peace Ranch had not escaped its virulent onslaught. Tom Howard reported he'd been able to isolate and destroy the infected steers, both bulls and cows, but the problem of what to do with the rest of the herd remained. Finally, Tom and I decided to try to sell the herd in Texas.

The marketing end of the cattle business had always been taken care of by Tom and he soon made an excellent deal to sell the remaining herd to a buyer on the Arkansas River. Unfortunately, during the roundup of the cattle, Tom's horse stepped in a gopher or prairie dog hole and fell, pinning Tom beneath him. Tom was killed by the accident, joining his father and his two brothers who had died on Southern battlefields.

Frank's mood had been gloomy since we'd left the Evans farmhouse and upon hearing of Howard's death moodily observed, "Trouble always come double. Look out now, fellers, for something else."

This did little to brighten our spirits.

Now the big question was once the roundup had been completed, who would make the delivery to the buyer? I had no choice but to assume Tom's name and make the deal. I spent the next few days and nights copying Tom Howard's signature, and reviewing everything we had known of the man. The delivery of the cattle was duly made and the transaction went off without a hitch. The buyers had not known Tom personally, so they readily accepted my impersonation. I had acted as a cattle buyer many times in the past so I knew the lingo. When the time came to execute the contract, I signed Tom Howard's name without a hitch. Since everyone was referring to me by that name I actually began to think of myself as "Mr. Howard". After all, it had been the pseudonym I'd chosen to use in Tennessee, so it seemed quite natural. I decided then and there to continue to use it.

With the sale of the cattle, Peace Ranch ceased for all practical purposes. Now we had no cattle – no foreman – and no Youngers. The ranch had belonged to everyone in the outfit, not just to Frank and me, and now with the Youngers gone it seemed as though its very heart had been cut out and ceased to beat.

12

A Plan to Rescue the Youngers : Return to Tennessee . Noted
Guerrillas : Life in Tennessee

Cole, Bob and Jim Younger had escaped the hangman's noose. Cole, in particular, put on a good show before the authorities, citing scripture, airing his deep and abiding love for mankind and the Baptist church, cunningly shedding a tear or two at the appropriate time. At the Younger brothers' trial each confessed his crimes, sorrowed in their guilty remorse, and pleaded for leniency. As a result, the judge sentenced them to the state penitentiary at Stillwater, Minnesota, there to remain for life.

Naturally, this was a situation I couldn't accept. It was up to me to get them out.

During our final months at Peace Ranch we entered into many long and earnest discussions of how to accomplish this. One plan after another was dissected, its weaknesses discovered and debated upon, and finally discarded.

The plan we finally worked out would require at least twelve men and fifteen horses. Just who among the boys sprung this plan, I don't remember. But I do recall that I heartily agreed with it. The main point to be kept uppermost in mind at all moments was that we not only wanted to rescue the Younger brothers, we wanted to defy the whole much-hated state of Minnesota. If it was possible to combine a plan of disgracing the entire state together with rescuing the boys, this would be the plan I desired.

No one had ever been rescued from a penitentiary. So what? No one had ever robbed a bank before I did, and nobody had ever robbed a train. As someone more learned than I once remarked, "there's a first time for everything."

Our first requirement was for an individual familiar with the telegrapher. Stanley Little, assuming the role of a county sheriff, filled this bill admirably. With Stanley playing his role to the hilt, the rest of us would ride in twos and threes to a short distance from Stillwater. Here, we would meet, together with a good team and a closed carriage.

The plan demanded that at or near 7 o'clock Stanley would send a telegram to the warden at Stillwater prison advising him that as a county sheriff he was bringing in three prisoners. His story would be that he's missed his

last train connection. He would deliver the prisoners by carriage. He didn't care to hold them overnight. He and his party would probably reach the prison by 9 o'clock.

The carriage would presumably contain the three prisoners, together with three guards. Two others, riding on the rear of the carriage, would drop off and cover the gate guards as the carriage entered the prison.

Upon entering the prison office, Stanley, in his role of county sheriff, with his three guards would immediately cover those within, lead a prison officer to the cells of the Youngers, and release them. Those men in the prison office would be trussed up, gagged, and left to bide their time. It might be that we'd swap our clothes for those worn by the prison guards. This might help to effectuate our escape. If not, we felt we could still escape easily by using our guns. The boys outside the prison gates would be holding our horses in readiness. Once we had mounted with the Youngers it would be every man for himself in the race for Missouri.

The possibility that one or two men might be caught before the state line was reached existed, of course, so every man would have to be ready to take that chance for the Youngers. When we went over this point Billy cheerfully remarked, "They can't do any more than hang us!" Some pessimist that boy was turning out to be!

Whether hidden flaws existed in this plan we never knew since it never materialized. However, at this time the plan looked good from every angle. There was no question in my mind we probably could have carried it out, thus adding another sensational chapter to the memorable history of the Northfield raid.

The principal thing that deterred us was the continued physical deterioration of the Younger boys. One or all three of the boys were constantly confined to the hospital for their wounds. When we heard this discouraging news from family visitors and friends we realized that not one of the Youngers would have the physical stamina to withstand the rough and tumble ride for freedom which would be necessary.

We waited for a long time, hoping to get word of the boys' recovery. After a year or so, other problems confronted us, and still word that the Youngers were in good health had not come. The problem which faced me at this point was the mustering of the necessary number of men to execute the raid. During this time, I only approved of eight men to undertake this rescue. In addition to Frank, Billy and myself, they were Jim Cummings, Stanley Little, Jim Reed, Jim Anderson and Bill Ryan. I knew the success of the plan depended upon choosing men of the same viewpoint – men who were completely unafraid, men who were willing to die in the attempt if necessary, men who would not drink, and most importantly of all, men who would not ride with the bloodlust to kill, but would ride with one intention only – to rescue.

I'm not just making excuses. I met with over 20 men in an attempt to find the numbers I needed. Without disclosing the details of the plan I discussed the rescue in general terms. I found all 20 men lacking in one quality or the other. In particular, Ed Miller worried me. Although he put up a brave front there was just something furtive about Ed which gravely concerned me. It was a feeling that Ed blamed me for his brother Clell's death and some day would do something to avenge that feeling. At times I found myself wondering if Ed Miller would be the one to shoot me in the back, that's how intense was Ed's silent message of resentment and accusation.

I had a really tough time trying to put together the right combination of men. When I had seven good men who were all enthused and would have gone down the wire with me, obeying all the rules, the Younger boys were in the hospital. By the time there was a chance of pulling off the plan with the brothers out of the hospital and back in their regular cells, the good ones had drifted away.

Thoughts of Cole, Jim and Bob were rarely out of my mind. True, Cole and I had disagreed vehemently that night in the brush, but that didn't change my feelings for any of the Youngers. No truer or more steadfast men ever lived. (With the exception of Bob, I allowed myself, whose weakness was drink.)

My thoughts returned time and time again to that fateful night. Just maybe, my little demon conscience said, if Frank and I had stuck with the Younger boys, we would have all made it. (Or maybe all been killed?) I was the leader. Did I turn tail? I didn't think I had. I had followed the rules of the guerrillas all the way, and of course the guerrilla rules were my outfit's rules. We had split up, like always. It was Cole who had refused to follow the rules. On the other hand, said my conscience, if Frank had been wounded would I have been willing to leave Frank at the first farmhouse so as to allow the rest of us to escape? I probably would have acted much like Cole if Frank had been the injured member of the party. Or would I? And so the war in my head raged on.

These conflicts tore me up. I suffered intense restless nights and nightmares wrestling with my conscience, seeing things one way for a minute, and an entirely different way in the next. I came out of it with one firm resolve. If the entire outfit collapsed we would have no resources to send to the boys in Stillwater prison. We were still sending them as much cash as we could put our hands on for life in prison, as outside, always had a price.

The depression that had me in its lethal grip during this period of my life was so strong that I contemplated suicide. Several things stopped me. Thoughts of Zee and young Jesse and my heritage were the major deterrents. I wasn't about to admit to the world that a person of the Woodson-James heritage would take his life. I thought of Ma's mysterious story of the two bastards and the hint that Frank and I were descended from a king. Would this be suitable royal conduct? I thought not.

When these black moods passed, as they eventually did, I had brief moments of exuberation where I would see into the future with the "Howard family" somehow emerging as a family to be remembered and honored. The only person I ever talked about these feelings with was Frank. Although he offered what sympathy he could I could detect within him a hard core of doubt. If he had been the terribly wounded person at Northfield, he seemed to imply, I would have left him. Following your rules, Jesse, he seemed to say, are more important to you than saving a brother.

One night at the ranch he looked me firmly in the eye and spoke his mind. "I know how this is troubling you, Dingus. But if you had been the badly injured person I would have followed the rules, also, and left *you* at the next farmhouse and made my getaway. Both of us have lived by our own rules and standards too long to make any other decision. Maybe that's why I haven't been able to embrace our faith as I should. The two just don't seem to coincide."

I knew he spoke the truth. Even though I might have been the one left behind at the farmhouse, I would have loved and respected my older brother whether I lived or died. I told him so.

Unwittingly, Frank had put his finger on the truth. We were both children of our time and circumstances. We couldn't escape our environment.

Frank would have made a great teacher. It was too bad the Civil War interrupted those plans. I now had a good fix on why he had settled on Shakespeare as being the bearer of his personal truths, rather than on the Bible. He was my brother in all ways – not only by birth.

Return to Tennessee

Just about all meaningful activities had come to a halt at Peace Ranch with Tom Howard's death and the sale of the cattle. We decided to close it down and each of us would scatter to our chosen destination.

Frank, Billy and I decided to stop in to see Ma in Clay County, taking the risk that it was heavily watched. We never went too long without a visit to the old girl and we both agreed now was the time. While there, we came to the conclusion that Tennessee was the place to go to make over our lives, if this were possible. It was at Ma's farm that Frank decided to start using the name of Woodson.

When I looked surprised at his decision he said, "Well, Jesse, Maybe *I'll* be the one to fulfill the legend of our forefathers and become the famous descendant if I use the name Woodson."

I grinned sardonically. "Frank, if we haven't already fulfilled that prophecy as 'The James Boys' I don't think it ever will be fulfilled."

"Our lives aren't over yet, Jesse. And I know that being called Mr. Woodson will be a lot easier than being known as Frank James."

Ahead of "Mr. Woodson" lay three peaceful years as a farmer. He became a registered voter, a raiser of prize hogs, the owner of a high-prancing racehorse which he would ride (with great pride) in the county fair, and most importantly of all – a faithful and loving husband and father.

I returned to what was called the "bottom" section of Tennessee and began a new life under the guise of Mr. Tom Howard. We told those who evinced curiosity that I had retired from the life of a cattle buyer (which was at least somewhat close to the truth) and was settling down to become a farmer. I purchased a little farm and tried to sever my connections – and my thoughts which was more difficult – from the past. Billy, known as our hired hand, began to work the farm and enjoy quiet evenings along with Zee and little Jesse (known as "Tim").

Disturbing nightmares peopled with the Youngers and Clell Miller began to fade. But the fear of detection was ever present.

The Pinkerton detective agency was still doing its best to track down the James boys. They had gained a reputation and were enjoying being known as the most feared agency in the country. After Allan Pinkerton's coup with Abraham Lincoln they had succeeded in breaking up the Reno gang – all of which added to the lustre of their (to me) feared name. The agency sent its most respected and feared detective, Yankee Bligh, to Minnesota to interrogate the Youngers after they were captured. But the Youngers were silent. The agency could find no trace of the James boys.

The agency could rightfully boast that they excelled at killing children and tossing bombs into houses to blow off the arms of defenseless women. They were unable to boast that they had captured the James boys. This caused them a certain frustration.

Owing to the fact that Frank and I, as well as the Youngers, had always been scrupulously careful not to let any photographs of ourselves fall into hands other than the family, most of the Pinkerton agents had no idea what we looked like. Naturally, this created a certain obstacle for them.

By now there were several good-sized rewards offered for our capture and rumors of our whereabouts were rife. From time to time we would hear reports that the James boys were dead. Another newspaper report swore Frank James was dying of consumption over in the Indian Territory, as a result of his war wounds, and another stated authoritatively that Jesse James was dying of wounds received at Northfield.

Tom Howard, the farmer, and a certain Mr. Woodson who also farmed and raised prize hogs, paid no attention. As Mark Twain once remarked, "The reports of my death were exaggerated."

Noted Guerrillas

As I settled down into my new life in Tennessee, I began to relax a little. At least I'd been able to fulfill my promise to Billy to lead him to a more peaceful existence approximating that of the Evans family. That pleased me. However much I tried to forget the past, the nightmares persisted. Often I would awake in the middle of the night, bathed in sweat and trembling, and unable to get back to sleep again. They were always the same, with slight variations. I was shot in the back. I knew the person who did the shooting. How or why, was never made clear. And who this person might be was equally clouded. But it seemed to me as though the prediction was coming nearer and nearer every day.

During this time a book was delivered to me bearing Major John Edwards' return address. As I removed the wrapper I saw that the title was "Noted Guerrillas" by Major John N. Edwards. Major Edwards was a dear and loyal friend, so much so that I'd given young Jesse Edwards his middle name. To say that I devoured the book is an understatement. I read every line many, many times.

Obviously I was more interested in the portions which mentioned me.

"To most of the guerrillas the end of the war brought an end to their armed resistance. Some were killed because of the association with Quantrill during the war, some were forced to hide, and some were prosecuted and driven into defiance because they were human and determined to protect their rights, their families and their homes. Jesse James belonged to this latter class. He strived hard to put the past behind him. He sacrificed much to take his place again in society, but though he tried hard and patiently, he was not permitted to do so."

The above paragraph had me dumbstruck. It was the absolute truth,

I swear upon my father, the Reverend Robert James' name and Bible.

That one man could so thoroughly understand my situation was very heartening. I read on eagerly as the Major described my attempt at surrendering:

"Jesse James, emaciated, tottering as he walked, fighting what seemed to everyone a hopeless battle of the 'skeleton boy against skeleton death' – joined his mother in Nebraska and returned with her to their home near Kearney, in Clay County. His wound would not heal, and more ominous still, every now and then there was a hemorrhage. In the spring of 1866 he was just barely able to mount a horse and ride a little. And he did ride, but he rode armed, watchful, vigilant, haunted. He might be killed, waylaid, ambushed, assassinated; but he would be killed with his eyes open and his pistols near him."

The paragraph I had just read brought back to me those difficult and painful days at the homes of the Mimms, where my beloved Zee first cared for me, and where our love began. Some good had come out of that tragic past, but I wondered what it had done for Zee – she was the wife of a hunted outlaw, a woman who couldn't use her rightful name, and she was unable to call her son by his.

I remembered Zee's sweetness, her many kindnesses and the care and attention she had given me. I also remembered the bad days of having to drain the pus from the wound every few hours, and lying back on my banked pillows feeling as though I was going to die any second. Or even worse, that I wouldn't die, and that the pain would go on forever.

I continued to read:

"What else could Jesse James have done? In those evil days bad men in bands were doing bad things continually in the name of the law, order and Vigilante Committees. He had been a desperate guerrilla; he had fought under a black flag; he had made a name for terrible prowess along the border; he had survived a dreadful wound; it was known that he would fight at any hour or in any way; he could not be frightened out from his native country; he would be neither intimidated nor robbed, and hence the wanton war raged upon Jesse and Frank James, and hence the reason why today they are outlaws as they are and persecuted in county, or state, or territory – they have more friends than the officers who hunt them, and more defenders than the

armed men who seek to secure their bodies, dead or alive."

These words enforced my own beliefs that the course I had taken was the only one open to me. If not for the life of banditry, I would have ended up as did many of my comrades – dead. Every one of them, to a man, who had ridden with and made a name for himself with Quantrill had been hunted down and killed – for a crime no more monstrous than having served on the Southern side.

I was feeling a little smug at having escaped their fate. But had I really? And for how long? I wondered who it was who would make a name for himself by shooting me in the back. Was there a man somewhere who professed to be my friend who would one day spell my demise?

I continued to read, with fascination:

"Since 1865, it has been pretty much one eternal ambush for these two men – one unbroken and eternal hunt twelve years long. They have been followed, trailed, surrounded, shot at, wounded, ambushed, surprised, watched, betrayed, proscribed outlaws, driven from State to State, made the objective points of infallible detectives, and they have triumphed. By some intelligent people they are regarded as myths; by others as in league with the devil. They are neither, but they are uncommon men. Neither touches whiskey. Neither travels twice the same road. Neither tells the direction from which he came nor the direction in which he means to go. They are rarely together, but yet they are never far apart. There is a design in this – the calm, cool, deadly design of men who are not afraid to die. They travel this way because if any so-called friend – tempted by the large rewards offered for the life of either – would seek to take it and succeed, the other, safe from the snare and free to do his worst, is pledged to avenge the brother slain through treachery, and avenge him surely. That he will do it none doubts who know the men. In addition, the Jameses trust very few people – two probably out of every ten thousand. They come and go as silently as leaves fall. They never boast. They have many names and many disguises. They speak low, are polite. They never kill except in self-defense. They have nothing in common with a murderer. They hate the highwayman, and the coward. They are outlaws, but they are not criminals, no matter what prejudiced public opinion may declare, or malignant partisan dislike make noisy with reiteration. The war made them desperate guerrillas, and the harpies of the war – the robbers who came in the wake of it and the cutthroats who came to the

surface as the honorable combatants settled back again into civilized life proscribed them and drove them into resistance. They were men who could not be bullied – who were too intrepid to be tyrannized over – who would fight a regiment just as quickly as they would fight a single individual – who owned a property and meant to keep it – who were born in Clay County and did not mean to be driven out of Clay County – and who had surrendered in good faith, but who because of it did not intend any the less to have their rights and receive the treatment the balance of the southern soldiers received. This is the summing up of the whole history of these two men since the war. They were hunted and they were human. They replied to proscription by defiance, ambushment by ambushment, musket shot by pistol shot, night attack by counter attack, charge by countercharge, and so will they do, desperately and with splendid heroism, until the end."

As I finished this portion of the book I rejoiced that even if Frank and I were to die, there would be left behind a written record of our lives which accurately explained our situation and motivation.

If anything happened to Frank, of course, and I was still alive I would kill the perpetrator. Just as I vowed to kill Captain Bill Anderson's murderer, I would vow to eliminate Frank's. Oh, don't tell me the gossip! I know it by heart. I am well aware that people are saying that I killed a man named Captain Sheets at Gallatin, instead of Captain Cox. But I'm not stupid. Many men adopted different names during this period and I am 100% convinced that Sheets and Cox were the same person. Anyway, all these people who are so knowledgeable about the event weren't there. I was. And the man known as Sheets/Cox virtually admitted his true identity to me before I shot him. I don't regret it. Any man who served under that valiant and courageous captain would have done the same. I saved them the trouble. I did it.

Next, I began to scan the book eagerly looking for the names of my other guerrilla friends, whose roster was fast becoming extinct. I looked for the names of all the guys who rode with me at Liberty, and I especially hunted for the names of Jim and Cole Younger, those stalwart companions now reduced to making twine at Stillwater Penitentiary. This is what I found:

"There were among the guerrillas few better pistol shots than Cole Younger. He spoke rarely and was away a great deal in the woods. What was he doing, his comrades began to inquire, one of

another. He had a mission to perform – he was pistol practicing. Soon he was perfect and then it was noticed that he laughed often and talked a great deal. There had come to him now that intrepid gaiety which plays with death. He changed devotion to his family into devotion to his country and he fought and killed with the conscience of a hero.

After the war closed Cole returned to Missouri, determined to forget the past, and fixed in his purpose to reunite the scattered members of his once prosperous and happy family, and prepare and make a comfortable home for his stricken and suffering mother. Despite everything that had been said and written of this man, he was during all the terrible border war a generous and merciful man. Others killed, and killed at that in any form or guise or fashion, he in open and honorable battle.

In battle he never had those go where he would not follow, aye, where he would not gladly lead. On his body, today there are scars of thirty-six wounds. He was a guerrilla and a giant among the band of guerrillas but he was one who killed in the open and honorable battle. As great as had been his provocation he never murdered; as brutal as had been the treatment of every one near and dear to him, he refused always to take vengeance on those who were innocent of the wrongs, and who had taken no part in the deeds which drove him, a boy, into the ranks for a cause, a creed, an idea, or for glory. He was a hero, and he was merciful.

The war closed, and in the last stages of consumption, Mrs. Younger dragged her poor emaciated body back to Jackson County to die. She had no home, every house she owned or inhabited was burnt. Every store of forage and all her stock was stolen. She had no place to lay her head that could be called her own. All that remained to the Youngers was their father's land. Her boys came home and tried as best they could to forget the past and look solely to the future.

Cole Younger cut logs and built a comfortable log house for his mother. He made rails and fenced in his land. In lieu of horses or mules, he plowed with oxen. He stayed steadfastly at home. A vigilance committee composed of sulking murderers and red-handed Kansas robbers went one night to surprise the two brothers and end the hunt with a massacre. Forewarned, James and Coleman fled.

The mob attacked the house, broke in the doors and windows and rushed upon the dying woman with drawn revolvers, demanding to know, upon her life, where James and Cole were. Furious at not finding them, after having searched for them everywhere and stolen whatever about the scantily furnished house tempted their beggarly greed they laid their hands upon John, the youngest brother, carried him to the barn, put a rope about his neck, threw one end over a joist, and told him to say his prayers; for he had but a little time to live unless he declared instantly where his brothers were. He defied them to do their worst. Three times they strung him up and three times he refused to breathe a word that would reveal the whereabouts of James or Coleman. The fourth time he was left for dead. Respiration had perceptibly ceased. The rope had cut through the skin of the neck and had buried itself in the flesh. His poor mother cut him down. It was half an hour and more before he recovered. Not yet done with him, the mob wounded him with sticks, beat him across the shoulders with the butts of their muskets, tormented him as only devils could, and finally released him half dead, to return to his agonized and brokenhearted mother. Soon afterwards Mrs. Younger died.

Cole Younger never entirely recovered from the shock of this night's work, lingering along hopelessly yet patiently for several months until his mother died.

The death of his mother did not end the persecution. He was repeatedly waylaid and fired at. His stock was killed through more devilry or driven off to swell the fains of insatiable wolves. His life was in hourly jeopardy; as was the life of his brother, James. They were chased away from their premises by armed men. Once Cole was badly wounded by the bullet of an assassin. Once half-dressed, he had to flee for his life. If he made a crop, he was not permitted to gather it, and when something of success might have come to him after the expenditure of so much toil, energy, long suffering and forbearance, he was not let alone in peace long enough to utilize his returns and make out of his resources their legitimate gains.

Of course there could be but an ending to all this. Cole and Jim Younger left home and Jackson County. They buckled on their pistols and rode away to Texas, resolved from that time on to protect themselves, to fight when they were attacked, and to make it so hot for the assassins and detectives who were eternally on their trail that by and by the contract taken to murder them would be a contract not particularly conducive to steady investments. They were hounded to it. The peaceful pursuits of life were denied to them. The law which should have protected them was overridden. Instead there was no law.

The courts were instruments of plunder. The civil officers were cut-throats. Instead of a legal process, there was a vigilance committee. Men were hung because of a very natural desire to keep hold of their own property. The border counties were overrun with bands of predatory plunderers. Some Confederate soldiers dared not return home and many guerrillas fled the county."

As the tears welled up in my eyes, the many thoughts that went through my mind and deepest thoughts and into my heart were not only that this was truly the story of Jim and Cole, but deeper yet my misgivings of that night in the brush outside of Northfield. My God, was what I did the wrong thing to do? I could understand the deep feelings of brotherhood and loyalty Cole must have felt. I saw now, for the first time, that there was no way he could have left Bob behind. Bob had not been a guerrilla, and Bob was not familiar with the old guerrilla creed which I had adopted for the outfit, that if a man was wounded and holding back the rest of the group from escape because he could not ride, he was to be left behind while the others rode away. Bob and Cole were united by something stronger than a guerrilla bond – they were united by blood.

If only Frank and I had stayed with the Youngers! But would it have made a difference? If so, would we have all made it safely back to Missouri? I sincerely doubted it. Although my head had always been more inventive and clearer than the others in the outfit, I doubted that I could have led those severely wounded men, hampered by a totally incapacitated man, to safety.

True enough, if the decision had to be made to leave Frank behind, I would have agreed and ridden on – but probably because Frank, as an ex-guerrilla, would have been part of that bond and would have agreed to the stipulation. So much for Frank, who knew the rules. But what about my beloved Archie (I never considered him as a half-brother). What if Archie had lain there, mortally wounded? Would I have left Archie? Would I have insisted on a guerrilla rule that Archie knew nothing about? Of course I wouldn't!!

Hot, salty tears began to sting my eyes and soon I was sobbing, unleashing emotions that had been welling up in me for months. Oh my God!! Cole had been right!!

Would I have had the guts to have done what Cole did! I'll never know.

I was bowed under by guilt thinking of Archie's death and the loss of Ma's right arm. Both were all my doing, I thought dolefully. Both were my responsibility. Neither Frank nor I had been at home that night to protect them.

With these disquieting thoughts wracking me emotionally, I read on:

"Neither the Youngers nor the Jameses have been permitted to rest long at any one time since the surrender of the Confederate armies. Some dastardly deeds have been done against them, in the name of the law. Take for example, Pinkerton's midnight raid upon the house of Mrs. Zerelda Samuel, the mother of the James boys."

What followed was an accurate accounting of what had taken place that dreadful night. I particularly responded to the passage which read:

"Pinkerton's paid assassins did this because his paid assassins knew better how to kill women and children than armed men in open combat."

Major Edwards seemed to be reading my mind. That's exactly the way I felt about the cowardly Pinkerton agents. I finished the book and then idly turned to the flyleaf to discover that there was a personal autograph, "To my good friend Tom Howard – Major John N. Edwards." I was sure that about 75 miles away a similar autographed book had been delivered "To my good friend Ben Woodson."

Major Edwards' book "Noted Guerrillas" won a great deal of public opinion to the side of the James Boys, people who believed that the war was all in the past, and that with the passing of time, no good was to be gained by the continuation of the old feuds. However, as the Outlaw Amnesty Bill had conclusively shown, there was just no line of action that could reclaim us at this late date.

As I often reflected, I was sure glad I'd given my son "Edwards" for his middle name. Some day young Jesse will understand why. And I hope he will be as proud as I was to have such an understanding, trusted and loyal friend as the Major.

Life in Tennessee

While we lived in Tennessee under our assumed names, both Frank and I were always on guard, always fearful, always on the alert. What amused us both were the dime novels of the day in which the James boys were reported to be in Carmen, Matamoras, Chihuahua, and along the Rio Grande. What we really got a kick out of was that when we were in Texas, nobody knew, and now that we weren't there, the books were being written that we were. Ah, such is life.

For over two years our rural paradise endured, BUT it was an unsafe paradise, which we both were aware of. Elaborate precautions were taken and observed. Every stranger that came to either of our farms was immediately a suspect. The detective forces of half a dozen states were always on our trail, always working on clues. There were large sums of money and great advancement and fantastic notoriety awaiting the detective who could land either one of us by capture or death.

Even in the matter of family life we both were extremely careful. Always we were referred to by our alias. Frank was always called Ben and I was Tom. My son could in no way be referred to by the name I wanted him to learn, but instead was always referred to as Tim. Zee was known as Josie and Anna became Fannie.

Although our two families lived many miles apart, the close bond that Major Edwards had revealed in his book was true. We kept in close touch at all times. By happy coincidence, February 1878 was the month when both Zee and Anna bore children.

Zee had twins, whom we named Gould and Montgomery for the two doctors that attended Zee. Unfortunately, the twins were frail and died at one week of age. They were buried with two simple headstones giving their first name, date of birth and death – on the farm then being rented by me.

At the same time, a son was born to Frank and Annie, who was named for his grandfather and father – Robert Franklin James, but who was immediately put into a girl's baby dress. Unfortunately, Annie's breasts went dry. Sue (as the baby was called) was fed on mother's milk provided by "Josie Howard" who had lost her twin boys. Quite neighborly of the Howards (only 75 miles away) to do that for the Woodsons. However, none of the neighbors knew of this except one, a storekeeper, named Isaac T. Rhea.

It was at Isaac T. Rhea's grain and flour business one evening that a Mr. Woodson, also known to Mr. Rhea, arrived in the store. Mr. Rhea, who was talking with Mr. Tom Howard, saw Mr. Woodson come in and called him over to the desk and stated, "I reckon you two men are not acquainted. Mr. Woodson, this is Mr. Howard."

I shook hands with the newly met Mr. Woodson and we first talked of the weather, but Mr. Woodson mentioned that his wife was having a time with their new-born daughter due to the fact she had no milk. I told Mr. Woodson that this was indeed quite a coincidence, as my wife had milk since our twins had died. Mr. Woodson seemed extremely polite as he offered his condolences, and Mr. Woodson seemed to be such a nice person that I suggested that we should consider Mrs. Howard taking the little girl to breast feed if it could be arranged with the Woodsons.

We left together to see if this could be arranged. I'm sure that Frank felt as smug as I did, that this arrangement had just been made in front of the very respected Mr. Rhea. If anyone questioned why two families, 75 miles apart, would do such a thing, we had a good story – just coincidence, and the help of fate, and Mr. Rhea of course. In fact, as we left, it was Mr. Rhea who thought, as he was to tell me later, "what a fine couple of men they are, and their families must be also to do that kind of thing, for a stranger."

I really got to know Mr. Rhea quite well and after many more meetings with him, our friendship grew and he loaned me $265.00 at one of those times when I really needed it.

Both Frank and my interest in horses did not stop with merely riding for our work. We loved horse races. It was Frank who came to me about the Lexington, Kentucky races which were to start the first part of May, 1878. Frank did not have the Kentucky bred horses that I did. Queen and Rhoda were seven and five years old respectively, and according to Frank and Billy, right at their peak. They were the fastest horses Frank had ever seen. Frank wanted to enter the two horses.

Frank explained that he wanted to enter both of them in what was known as a two-mile race open to all and, in reality, a free for all. The entry fee was $500.00. I immediately felt this was a deterrent, even though the first money was $10,000.00 and second money $2,500.00. Upon the urging of Frank and Billy, I decided such a challenge was just what we needed at that time.

Billy and I rode Queen and Rhoda to Lexington, taking our time and conditioning the horses for the race as we travelled almost the entire width of Kentucky. When we arrived the entry fee had already been paid by the "co-owner" of the horses, a Mr. Woodson. The racing touts paid little attention to the two families from Tennessee as this size purse brought out many strangers to racing and the best horses in the South and several from the North. So we were ready, after finding us a pair of jockeys. My, those jockeys are small!

A little bay was leading when they passed the wire on the first mile; when they reached the half mile post on the second lap, Queen went around the bay as if he was standing still and Rhoda followed. The horses belongng to Woodson/Howard took both first and second money! When the band struck up "Old Kentucky Home," I swear, Queen tossed her head in response. After all, she was a daughter of the Blue Grass State!

Later in the summer came the State Fair at Nashville. I decided that I would enter Queen as it should be easy money and I could sure use it. Billy and I rode over a couple of days in advance and found a professional jockey and Queen was entered, but she finished fourth and out of the money.

When this happened I knew that the race had been fixed! Obviously, the professional jockey was part of the fix. I was so mad that I was ready to blow the whole thing open. Fortunately, Billy calmed me down enough to make me realize that if I did this, with all the detectives around, I was sure to blow the fact that I was not just Tom Howard, farmer from the Big Bottom Country.

I told Billy that at least I was going to take care of the damned jockey. Again, Billy prevailed, explaining that that was all that we needed was to blow our incognito status. After all, at most fairs a lote of detectives attend to spot known gamblers and other outlaws. I barked back at Billy that I knew that. I wasn't as dumb as I looked!

Billy smiled back and said, "Well, we both know Queen is great, but I wonder if she could win with a big guy on her, like you."

I weighed 170 pounds and that was giving away a lot of poundage to the other horses with those little professional jockeys. But damn it, I knew I could ride as well as any man alive and I determined to prove that Queen was great.

I entered her the next day under a different name with me as the jockey. Boy, did I get some sarcastic comments, sly smiles and large guffaws. Also, I was so mad that I put $200.00 on Queen to win and with the high odds against her, I figured I'd really clean up. Of course, I had Billy place the actual bet.

That race was a one horse race. Because of my weight we were behind right after the start, but that horse of mine was fantastic. We won the race by over a length. Those that had made the guffaws, sly smiles and sarcastic comments had to really eat crow. However, I had to be magnanimous and not push too hard. I think the most satisfying thing was riding the race in front of a crowd undoubtedly filled with Pinkerton agents.

By the way, when I say that I needed money, I'm serious. You know I tried to live the life of a good Christian. I did not smoke, drink, nor did I ever take the name of the Lord in vain. But I had changed my mind on one activity that I enjoyed. I couldn't find anything in the Bible against playing poker.

I liked to play, but I just wasn't very good. My big problem was that I seemed to tip my hand. Believe me, not being able to bluff in draw poker is a real detriment. I would lose the big hands because my face was too easy to read.

I found out that in the gambling circles I was known as a pretty easy mark, but I also heard that the warning was out, not to try to cheat with me in the game. It is true, I believe that if anybody tried to cheat, I would have caught him and my temper is such that if that happened, I would have immediately taken care of it in my way, and Billy wouldn't have been there or even if he was, wouldn't have been able to calm me down fast enough.

The way I figure it, I just about broke even with my winnings in horse racing and my losings in poker.

As the winter came on 1878, in addition to the playing poker, there was, as there always is in the farmland, a little extra time for the farmer like Mr. Howard to spend at the nearby store, whether it be the foodstore, the grain store, or the clothing store. Of course, in many instances, it's the same store which we referred to as just the Country Store.

I spent a lot of time at Isaac Rhea's store. I felt comfortable there, and as safe as I could be in any store anywhere. The manager of the store was a Mr. Kroger and I liked him as he had been a Southern soldier for four years. I liked to bring up the James boys in talking with Kroger and others just to attempt to get their reactions toward us. It was sort of like a bellweather to get an inkling of how the winds were blowing in regard to the feelings about the James boys.

When I brought up the James boys' names with Kroger, he replied, "I don't uphold the Jameses at all in their outlawry."

When he said this I came back with, "Well, don't you think those man have been driven into outlawry because they belonged to Quantrill's guerrillas in the war?"

I sure didn't get any sympathy or moral support from Kroger who replied, "Well, I fought in the war myself on the Southern side for four years, and I wasn't always treated the best after the war during the reconstruction, but that didn't drive me to robbing banks and trains."

Along with always on the alert, I kept a close eye on everything. Every letter I received was gone over both before and after it was opened. I felt that each letter might in some way be a trick or ruse to discover my true identity. This was one of my phobias.

One day I received a letter from Isaac T. Rhea and upon opening it I found that there were pencil marks inside the flap. It was obvious to me that it had been opened. Although the letter was not important, it being merely a notification of my present bill due to the Rhea Company and a statement as the nearest offices that were open and the times they would be open, it indicated to me that the postmaster had opened the letter for some verification that Mr. Tom Howard was in reality Jesse James.

I determined that the next stop was to go to see the postmaster and determine the entire situation. If what I suspected was true, it would mean that I would have to leave my home pronto, and it just might mean that Postmaster Jackson might not leave, ever, that is, except in a pine box.

What happened was that on the way to the postmaster, I just happened to run across my friend Mr. Kroger and I sensed that he noticed my agitation. I didn't tell him why I thought my mail was being opened, but that I suspected it was, and after showing him the letter I said I was going over to "kill" that postmaster for opening my letters.

Fortunately for both Postmaster Jackson and myself, Mr. Kroger remembered that Mr. Isaac Rhea often opened some of his outgoing mail, just to check on mail from his establishment. Well, I believed Mr. Kroger and I calmed down and I did not confront Postmaster Jackson and nothing occurred.

I watched my mail even more carefully thereafter and I have to admit, I never found another letter that gave any sign of having been opened, and again I was saved from my temper, and of course allowed to live the life of Mr. Tom Howard, farmer of the Big Bottom area of Tennessee.

Through the balance of the winter and all through the Spring, our completely peaceful life continued. On July 17, 1879, Zee gave birth again. It was a girl whom we immediately named Mary. We felt that if Mary was a good enough name for the Virgin Mother, it was the name we wanted for our daughter. She was a healthy baby and Zee became a happy and fulfilled mother. Mary's birth made up for the death of the twins. Now we had a real family, a son and a daughter.

However, this idyllic life that us Howards were living was doomed. Just three weeks after Mary's birth, I was recognized by a traveller going through from Clay County. This man was not one whom I trusted and realized that there was a tremendous price on my head, at least tremendous for almost all farmers of the day. I was shaken. Although he promised not to divulge my identity or whereabouts, I just couldn't trust him. The false casual way he asked about Frank made me very suspicious. Of course, I told him that Frank had been in Texas for the last three years and I hadn't even heard from him for over two years.

Immediately after the man left I packed up Zee, young Jesse and the baby with as much of our belongings as possible and with Billy and the horses rode off towards Nashville and the one place where there would be help, a Mr. Woodson.

I made one detour. I went into Nashville and found Mr. Isaac Rhea and his main office and paid him $265.00 I owed him.

13

And so we headed for the Woodson home, two horse team wagons loaded with our worldly goods, the fine horses tied up behind. I had made a decision. I was going to return to my old ways and I hoped to convince Frank to do the same. I was basically broke. Despite the exaggerated claims of my wealth made by the newspapers and dime novels, the reality was that I had lost a bundle on the cattle at Peace Ranch and that a robbery would often net us no more than $3,000.00 or $4,000.00. When that money was split between 10 men, it didn't amount to much. It was time I refurbished my larder.

There was a big difference between Frank's life and mine at this time. Frank was happy and unworried. His name, Ben Woodson, was listed in the City Registry and his job of hauling supplies was unspectacular but steady. Frank had made the transition from a renegade and outlaw to an upright citizen.

From his point of view, my decision to return to outlawry seemed bizarre. I explained to him that I had been recognized and although time had passed peacefully, really nothing had changed. There was still a price on both of our heads. I told him, and truly believed, that it wouldn't be long before Frank was recognized also. I added that I had told our mutual acquaintance who had recognized me that Frank was in Texas and that I hadn't seen him in two years. But how long would it be before someone discovered that story was just not true?

Frank was obstinate. He didn't want to return to robbing banks and trains. Our discussion went on back and forth for over five days and we hashed and rehashed all the pros and cons many times. Both of us were at the breaking point when Frank finally conceded by quoting from his favorite author, *"Thou art mine own flesh and blood."*

I'm afraid I snapped back at him, "Just what does that mean Buck?"

Frank narrowed his eyes impatiently. "What it means is that blood is thicker than water; and if you gather a good outfit and obtain information of a bank or train that has a sizeable kitty, I'll be at your right side when

the time comes."

Once Frank's decision had been made, Billy and I saddled up and headed for Kentucky, leaving Zee and the rest of the family at the Woodsons. We intended to make contact with friends and relatives in Kentucky to re-form the outfit. We also wanted to seek out Stan Little, who had always been our inside man on train information. Although he wasn't actually present during the robbery, Stan always got his cut if the train robbery was successful – a powerful incentive for providing us with accurate information.

Safely in Kentucky, we hooked up with our cousins, the Hites. Both Woodson ("Wood"), and Charley Hite were delighted that I'd come to them for help. From the Hite household, I got out word that I was interested in forming a new outfit, and I made contact with Stan Little.

My plan was to rob the train at Glendale. I began interviewing potential members of the new gang. Of course I talked with and considered both of the Hites. In addition, I interviewed Jim Cummins, who had ridden with me before, Ed Miller, the brother of Clell who was killed at Northfield, and Bill Ryan, Dick Liddil and Tucker Basshan, all of Jackson County.

After doing all I could in Kentucky, I returned to Nashville and had a final conference with Frank. We agreed that five men would actually participate in the train robbery. Besides Frank and myself there would be Billy, Jim Cummins and Ed Miller. Dick Liddil and Bill Ryan were to be considered full-fledged members of the "new" outfit but were not to be direct participants in the Glendale train robbery. Cousin Wood Hite was assigned the job of bearing the message to both Jim Cummins and Ed Miller as to where we five would meet for "boots and saddles."

Although I had enjoyed the three years of peace and quiet and rural domesticity since Northfield, as I began planning the Glendale robbery I felt a familiar tingle of excitement and anticipation which had been missing from my life. I carefully explained to those not participating in this particular robbery that there would be others to follow, but in this case Frank and I felt it prudent to use just the five men who were familiar with this type of action. The other men would be held in abeyance for the jobs which I felt sure were to follow.

What I did not know at the time and would only find out much later was that Wood, Charley, Dick, Bill and Tucker Bassham were very disgruntled at not being included in the first ride of the new outfit. Without my knowledge, they quietly made plans of their own.

On October 8, 1879 at about 6.00 p.m., at the small settlement of Glendale, County of Jackson, Missouri, the five of us rode in. We saw three men lolling in front of the town's only store. One was the proprietor, whom I later learned was a Mr. Anderson, and the other two were farmers.

We drew our revolvers and rode up on the men, ordering them to the depot at the train station a block and a half away. As we walked into the depot, the train master and telegrapher looked up and greeted Mr. Anderson. Mr. Anderson, who was ahead of all us, replied politely "Good evening, Mr. McIntyre." Mr. McIntyre was just about to make some pleasant small talk with his friend Mr. Anderson when his eyes flickered to the five revolvers which were pointed directly at him.

One Colt, in particular, was aimed right at McIntyre's head. Mine. I had him telegraph a message to Chicago, and as soon as it was received, we destroyed the telegraph instrument and wires. I had learned my lesson in Northfield. This time there would be no communication with the outside world until the train arrived at its next station. By that time we would have been long gone and dispersed into the countryside, as usual.

Next, I ordered the station agent to change the green light to red in order to signal the approaching train, due in at six forty-five. Again, I didn't want any gunplay, nor did I want to injure or kill anyone on the train as had happened when we derailed the locomotive during my first train robbery.

As the train approached, it stopped promptly on the signal. The conductor approached the station to receive the expected orders or passengers. Jim Cummins promptly levelled his revolver at the surprised man while Frank and Ed Miller took the engineer and fireman captive. It was about time to go to the baggage and passenger cars.

As we started down the aisle, I suddenly saw a sight that my eyes and head had a hard time believing. At the other end of the car were five other bandits, handkerchiefs over their noses and mouths concealing the lower half of their faces, guns drawn and ready. Once I was past this shock, I got an additional surprise when one of these newcomers said jauntily, "Hi cousin. We thought you might need some help!" No doubt about it. It was Wood Hite's voice. I then recognized all five of them and made a quick decision. I didn't want any trouble. After all, these men were all ones I'd interviewed and chosen to be part of the new outfit. Wood and Charley Hite were, of course, my cousins. So they had disobeyed my orders. I would deal with that later. For the moment, all I wanted was a successful conclusion to the matter at hand.

"All right, boys, let's all cooperate," I sang out. "Bill Ryan comes with me to the baggage car. Wood, Charley and Dick make lots of noise so the passengers stay on the train. Tucker, you hold those horses so none gets away – or I'll have your skin!" All five immediately sprang to attention and to do my bidding. I couldn't foresee any trouble, at least during this robbery. So far so good.

The express door was closed and locked. Bill Ryan found some coal hammers and we broke in. Once inside, the express manager, who I later learned was named William Grimes, capitulated to our demands completely and handed over all the money, including that which was in the safe. I felt pleased. Everything was going according to my plan. No resistance meant no bloodshed for which I was eternally thankful. My old outfit had been cautioned not to kill except in self defense, but I couldn't know how the members of the new outfit would react if they were challenged. I suspected that Bill Ryan would shoot without a qualm and save his regrets for after the fact.

My spirits improved greatly when I figured the amount we were getting to be about $40,000.00. But, of course, now the split would be between 11 men rather than just six, but all in all, even that didn't upset me. Things were going well and I'd had the opportunity to see all of the men in action and study their methods which would be invaluable knowledge in the future.

With the express car denuded and with a large amount of money a certainty I ordered the men to alight without molesting the passengers. I was anxious to send the train on its way. Also, I was not about to take the chance of allowing these new men amongst the passengers. Who knew what brutalities they might impose on the helpless men and women? If we alit now, we would have plenty of time to make our getaway, because with the telegraph inoperable, news of the robbery would not reach the outside world until the train arrived at the next station.

As the train got up steam to depart, I couldn't resist a bit of braggadocio and twitting of the authorities, whom I knew were sure to hear of it. I sauntered up to the engineer and said, "Things have been happening so fast I forgot to get your name. Mine's Jesse James." The only thing the hapless engineer could manage in reply was a sullen silence.

We rode only a short distance away before we stopped to divide the loot, with Frank presiding. It was divided into 11 portions. After this, the usual split up of the outfit took place, all going their own ways, except for three who stayed together and headed for Tennessee. This was a much different ride for the three of us than that undertaken across Minnesota just a little over three years ago. This ride was fast but nothing like the frantic haste of our Minnesota exit. After all, we were in our home territory of Missouri and knew the route well.

And there was another difference. Even when we rode through towns we rode together. Frank finally said, "Jesse, with Billy riding with us, instead of behind, does that mean that you've gotten over your dreams of somebody shooting you from behind?"

I took my time answering as we clopped along. Finally, I managed to say, "No, Frank, I still have them. But after Northfield I'd rather be shot in the back and end my life that way than to be captured and taken to prison." We rode alone in silence for a bit, then I added, "You know, Frank, some day I'm going to be shot in the back for sure, they'll never let us give up and have a fair trial, but I'd rather die that way with my boots on than to be hung or serve a life imprisonment sentence like Jim, Cole and Bob."

Frank was in a thoughtful mood. "Well, Jesse, I've had three great years since Northfield living as a normal family man in Tennessee. But you're probably right – for me and you – it's too late. But doggone it, it's not too late for Billy."

Billy reacted with alarm. "I wouldn't leave you two as long as you want me. You're the only people I've ever known to give two hoots about me at all!"

Frank had expressed something I'd been thinking about for some time. I'd been holding off, from selfishness perhaps, but now I could do so no longer. I looked Billy sternly in the eye when I said, "And that's why Billy, this was your last ride with us. When we get back to Frank's you're going to take Rhoda and your full share of your rides, which I've never touched, and go and make your own life – forget outlawry – you'll make a fine husband and father, but you can only do it if you go straight. Nobody knows you, or even mentions you in the newspapers so far. But soon, especially after this ride with the new men you'll not have the chance to get out without being known. Frankly, I'm worried about this outfit. It's not like the old one and I'm not so sure if one of them gets caught that they wouldn't confess just to make it easier on 'em. I'm sure they'd immediately name their accomplices. As much as Frank and I love you, just like a younger brother, this was it. We can't get out of this business but you can and will."

After we returned to Frank's home, amidst a great many tears from Zee and young Jesse, Billy left riding astride Rhoda carrying full saddle bags. He was in the stable saddling Rhoda on his last day when I went up to him and put out my hand.

"Goodbye, Bill," I said.

He gave me a stricken look. "Bill?"

"Yeah, I think so, don't you?"

A small smile of satisfaction played around his lips. "Sure, Jesse, if you say so. It's time."

"There's always the mails, you know, son," I attempted to assuage his sorrow.

"'Course," he told me, tightening Rhoda's cinch, "I'll be in touch. And of course Christmas still comes once a year."

"Just remember, you're the best shot and the best rider in the country – excepting for one."

"'Ceptin' for one?" Billy grinned, "Aw, who might that *one* be?"

I pulled him towards me and gave him a hearty bear hug.

"You know dang well who that one is, and don't you forget it."

Billy mounted Rhoda. "I won't ever forget, Jesse. And I'll be in touch!"

"So long, Bill," I cried out and little Jesse echoed me with "Goodbye Uncle Billy," and Billy rode off.

That was the last we saw of Billy Judson, the name he had used while riding with us – from the very beginning. Only Frank and I knew his real name, but it will not be recorded here. We had news of Billy, of course, and we were all delighted to know that under his real name, "Bill" became a farmer, then a lawyer, then a rancher, and finally a successful newspaper editor.

His eventual death was caused by complications due to a bullet breaking loose from his lowest rib where it had been since it entered his body in Northfield, Minnesota. Frank and Jesse Jr., were aware of all these doings in our Billy's life – and eventual death – but of course I was not.

After the young man rode off, I felt a great void in my life. I could not shake a peculiar feeling of loneliness even when I was in the bosom of my family and living with Frank and his family. Finally, I realized that what I had done was to substitute Billy for my younger brother, Archie. As long as Billy had been around I was able to put Archie out of my mind. That was no longer possible. The guilt and depression I felt over Archie's death now returned twofold. My dreams of being shot in the back semed to come every troubled night and there were also dreams of accusations by all the innocent people who had died because of me – starting with Jolly Wymore and ending with Archie.

I would delay sleep as long as possible by sitting up in bed and reading my Bible. The reading of Psalm 51 helped, but nothing truly relieved my pain and feeling of desolation and guilt. It seemed as though the two sides of me were at war more and more. But the day would eventually come and the dreams would disappear.

Mammoth Cave, Kentucky Stage Coach Robbery

The nights were horrible. Jolly Wymore, holding his hand over a gaping, bloody hole in his side accused me. The engineer from the first train robbery, his head caved in on one side and covered with blood, raged at me for ending his life, and a shadowy figure whose face I couldn't see but whom

I somehow knew, shot me in the back. It was a relief to see the first pale fingers of dawn creep over the horizon.

Despite my ghastly nightmares, the days were passable. My acute fear that my acquaintance from Clay County would talk about seeing me in the Big Bottom Land farm now seemed groundless.

The only person who had actual knowledge about a connection between a certain Mr. Howard and a Mr. Woodson was the storekeeper, Isaac Rhea, and I had a strong feeling that this man would not give away any information whatsoever. I had liked him and he had liked me and I thought that a man who would pay his $265.00 bill in full when he could have skipped out on it and never been traced would count for something with Rhea.

Annie and Zee were enjoying each other's company. And young Jesse ("Tim") was thriving, playing with his young cousin and the baby. Frank and I had never been closer. Not only were we living together, but we were farming together. In addition, Frank enjoyed a small but steady income from his hauling business. Even more, we two met with the road commissioner and agreed to haul gravel in our spare time. We soon learned that because we didn't haul gravel on a regular basis, we could put any date we cared to on the receipts and the commissioner would sign them without reading the dates.

If needed in the future, this could provide an excellent alibi for us!

Bill Ryan became a frequent visitor and actually moved in and lived there from time to time.

One day Bill Ryan and I took a short ride into Kentucky. It was September, 1880. Near Mammoth Cave we chanced upon a stagecoach. Inside were six men and a woman. Sam McCoy, the stagecoach driver, stopped promptly as soon as two masked men stepped out upon the road and demanded that he do so.

"Step out of the stage," I ordered the passengers, brandishing my gun. "Put your valuables and money in this grain sack."

A short, roly-poly man with a red face and a fringe of white hair objected. Sweeping off his hat and mopping his red and perspiring face with his handkerchief, he introduced himself as "Judge Rowntree of Lebanon, Kentucky." "I'll be mighty grateful," he said, "If you'll show due respect for my lovely daughter, Lizzie." The man was obviously scared to death and even more fearful of what might happen to his daughter, who he might construe as "lovely," but I warranted was anything but. Young, she was, but tall and thin and gawky with dark brown hair swept back into a bun under a rather fetching bonnet, large dark eyes, but a thin, pointed face with little or no chin.

"Sir," I told the judge, "Have you ever heard of Robin Hood behaving in anything but a gentlemanly way?"

"Er, ah, Robin Hood?" he stammered.

I chuckled. "Yes, and Friar Tuck here, is even more of a gentleman than I. So if you'll hurry up and put your valuables in the grain sack, no one will get hurt, least of all this beautiful flower of Kentucky womanhood."

"Much obliged," said the perspiring judge, hastily removing a gold chain and watch and dumping it in the sack. He then went to stand beside his daughter, putting a protective arm around her waist. That's about as high up as he could reach because she towered a good foot or two above him.

In examining the loot later, I found the judge was telling the truth about his position in life for his watch was engraved to him from the Governor of Kentucky. His daughter's diamond ring also had her pet name "Lizzie," carved inside.

With the business at hand completed, Ryan removed a pint bottle and drank to the passengers and the highwaymen's health alike, calling for all of their "continued good health and good fortune."

The passengers re-entered their coach and Ryan and I rode swiftly away. As soon as we got beyond earshot my temper exploded. I told Ryan loudly and angrily that the rule for riding with Jesse James was "no liquor."

I really laid down the law, explaining to Ryan that no liquor was ever to be used before or after a robbery, but that I didn't care what he did when he was on his own. Later, events proved me wrong. I should have told Bill that he would have to abstain from liquor entirely in the future – not only before or after a raid. But I didn't.

Bill apologized and assured me that he would follow the rules. There would be no liquor. I cooled down, satisfied with his promise and we separated, each taking different pathways home. I arrived back at Frank's a full two days before Bill Ryan showed up. He did not explain, nor did I ask, where he had been. That was his business – not mine.

The Government Paymaster Robbery

Frank and I were in the kitchen, two mugs of Annie's good coffee sitting before us on the pine deal table.

"The robbery went fine," I told him, "Except for the end when Ryan pulled out a pint bottle of liquor and began to drink."

Frank took a swig of coffee and wiped his mouth with the back of his hand.

"Get rid of him," he said tersely.

"Well, I don't think we have to go that far, but somehow that man worries me."

"He worries me, too. I don't really trust him. If he was ever captured, I'm sure he'd blab and tell the authorities who we are and where we are."

I reached for a piece of cornbread which Zee had made the night before, slathered it with butter, and took a bite before I answered.

"Think so? I'm not so sure. Don't forget he's from Jackson County and that means 'kinfolk.' Anyway, we're sorta caught in the middle. If we cut him off now, there's nothing to stop him from running to the authorities and collecting the rewards. No. I think we better give Bill Ryan another chance. He *did* promise!"

"Mebbe so Jesse. But don't forget I warned you. Ryan might just be the one who pulls the trigger and shoots you in the back. Be careful when you're with him!"

Just then the baby, Robert, let out a yowl and Annie came into the kitchen to warm up some milk for the little boy, who was now off Zee's breast. That ended our conversation.

But from that day forward I was careful around Bill. When he arrived back at Frank's house he brought with him a plan for a robbery. He had found out that the government paymaster at Muscle Shoals, Alabama received a fat payroll each week sent by government messenger from Florence, Alabama. It was Bill's thought that we hit this payroll.

I set it up so that Frank, Bill Ryan and I would meet at the bend in the road just one mile from Muscle Shoals. When the messenger arrived it would be Ryan and I who relieved the messenger of the payroll. Frank's job was to guard the rear of the messenger to make sure that he was not followed and that no trouble brewed in that direction. What I was really doing was trying to prevent a trap being sprung if, in fact, Bill Ryan was in truth setting one. With Frank guarding the rear, there would be no chance. He would scout the entire area in a rear guard action.

Needless to say, I didn't discuss this part of the plan with Bill.

In March, 1881, the government messenger was duly relieved of $5,000.00 in gold. Frank and I had set up an alibi in advance. We had a signed receipt that showed we were hauling on the night of the robbery and a dated receipt signed by the commissioner of roads.

On the night of the robbery Bill Ryan was sober, did not have any liquor on him, and did a fine job. There was no sign of a trap being set. As usual, we split immediately after the robbery. While still in Alabama, I met Frank at a pre-arranged site and we rode back together. I told Frank I was very pleased with Bill Ryan and I honestly believed that he had at last seen the error of his ways. In fact, I was a bit puffed up with myself and admitted to Frank that "perhaps I was responsible for having saved a person from the sins of alcohol."

Frank gave me a sidewise glance and demurred. "Hmmmmmm," he said, "I'm not as sure as you are, Dingus. But, yeah, he's been acting okay since the stagecoach robbery."

Sometimes I'm not the best judge of a man's character. Just 15 days after the paymaster robbery, Bill Ryan, using the alias of "Tom Hill" rode up to a saloon at White's Creek, a suburb of Nashville, got himself totally tanked up and made such a complete nuisance of himself that he was arrested. In a loud and boisterous voice he told everyone that doubted him that "Of course I'm Tom Hill, the famous outlaw!"

He sure fitted the bill. In addition to the two revolvers they found on him, he was carrying $1,300.00 in gold. This latter fact, together with his drunken claim of being a famous outlaw, convinced the Nashville police although they were unable to come up with any outlaw named "Tom Hill." They did telegraph his description to the police chiefs of the country and the answer was that his description sure fit that of Bill Ryan of Jackson County. Bill Ryan was soon on his way to the hoosegow of his native state.

When he learned of "Tom Hill's" arrest, we immediately put two and two together and made four, especially when the newspaper account stated that "Tom Hill" had $1,300.00 on him in gold. (Bill Ryan's share of the government paymaster robbery was over $1,600.00 which gave us a pretty good idea of how much he's spent on whiskey before he was caught). Obviously, our safety was now jeopardized. While we were not positive Ryan would talk, we couldn't take the chance.

It had been four years that Frank and I had lived in and near Nashville. All our children had been born here. Frank had won a prize for his Poland China hogs here. I had joined the church here. But now this tranquil idyll was coming to an end. We must leave. As we came to this conclusion, I also became aware of two things – one, it was back to the old ways for me, and two, the time was drawing ever near when my dream would be fulfilled.

We packed up the wagons.

Frank and I were cooling off from our labors with a glass of lemonade.

"Frank, my dream will soon be reality. You're going to have to look after Ma, and Zee and the kids."

Frank nodded. His reply was direct and simple as he sorted through that wonderful storehouse of quotes he'd memorized from his beloved bard. *"Haste me to know't, that I, with wings as swift as medication or the thoughts of love, may sweep to my revenge."*

I knew Frank would do just that, but revenge was not uppermost in my mind.

"For we shall surely die and are like water spilled on the ground which cannot be gathered up again. Yet God does not take away life, but plans ways so that the banished one may not be cast out from him." I was quoting from 2 Samuel 14:14.

After I let the Scripture register with Frank, I told him that I was ready to face death and my maker for my sins. What was more important than avenging my death would be for Frank to go on and live and somehow, someway, keep the two families as well as Ma and the farm together.

Finally, I obtained his solemn promise that he would in no way act to avenge my death, but only after I agreed that the promise was mutual. That if he were the one to be either killed or captured, I would not avenge his death or attempt to rescue him.

Early the next morning, the wagons loaded down with our worldly goods, and the families settled inside, we parted, each to go in different directions.

As we separated the only words I could think to utter were "Goodbye Buck." Frank's simple reply was "Goodbye, Dingus."

14

Remorse : Kinfolk and Detectives : The Winston Train Robbery :
The Blue Cut Train Robbery : The New Outfit Falls Apart

"All right son, you've got something very heavy on your heart. What is it?" Ma was looking very solemn, unlike the happy face she'd been wearing since I came home two days ago.

I never could keep my true feelings from Ma and today was no exception. Looking into her eyes I knew that I had to tell her everything about my innermost fears and anxieties. She would be content with nothing less.

I started off by telling her about my continuing dreams of being shot in the back, probably by a friend. She had known I'd had this dream once or twice in the past, but she hadn't known how serious the dreams had become and how persistent.

Then I told her about my dreams of guilt and how all the people who had died because of me accused me in my sleep. I began choking up as I confessed that I'd never wanted people killed – it had just turned out that way. Next, I asked her if she remembered how we'd talked and prayed after Liberty and how I had written the note to Jolly Wymore's parents.

Ma was listening intently as I poured out my troubled heart, finally telling her that until recently I had always believed that I had killed Captain Cox at Gallatin, but now I wasn't even sure of this.

"Oh Ma, what am I going to do?" I wailed.

Ma went into the kitchen and brought me a glass of beef tea, the kind she used to fix me when I was so sick with my lung wound.

"Jesse, I think you better tell me everything," she said gravely.

I took a sip of the tea. "Ma, if it weren't for me, your son Archie would be alive and you'd have your right arm!" I blubbered like a two-year-old.

Ma stroked my hair gently. "Jesse, that was not your fault. No one blames you for what the Pinkertons did!"

"All well and good, but if it hadn't been for me, if I'd have had the gumption to stick it out and become a good citizen, none of it would have happened!"

"Bosh and nonsense, Jesse. The Federals would have pursued you and

killed you after the war no matter what you did. Now stop this blame-calling and caterwauling and drink your tea."

"How do we know, Ma?" I was inconsolable. "How do we know?"

By this time I was crying and the tears were rolling down my cheeks just the way they used to when I was a baby. All the guilt, the remorse, the tension of living like a hunted animal, all the pent-up anxiety come rolling out of me."

"Neither Dr. Samuel or I have ever blamed you or Frank for Archie's death – in any way. My right arm may not be here, but I have never thought nor did I believe in my heart that you were responsible in any way."

My head was buried in my arms, my beef tea forgotten. I sobbed out the story of the Youngers. I told her about Northfield and how Cole Younger had fought me because I wanted to leave Bob Younger behind. "I would never forgive myself for that one," I told her, and how I often dreamed that the situation was reversed and the Youngers were leaving me, Frank and Archie behind in the same situation. But even more important, if I had not contacted Jim and Cole Younger to take part in the raid in Liberty, they might well have endured and never turned to outlawry.

I could not know that Jim Younger would eventually commit suicide. Although paroled, as a condition of his parole, he was not able to leave the State of Minnesota and was forbidden to marry. These two conditions would be enough to tip the scales for old Jim, beaten down and discouraged as he was by that time by his years in jail. He would take the only way "out" he could think of, by taking his own life. Bob Younger would die in prison, and Cole would serve his sentence and die a free man.

When I talked about the Youngers, Ma began to cry herself.

"I think the only way to wipe the slate clean so I can see my real Pa in heaven is to allow myself to be shot in the back. This will show the good Lord that I am repentent."

With this, Ma began to wail. I had heard people keen and wail before, but I had never neard anything like the deep mournful sounds my Ma was making. It was scary to see that big, sturdy lady break down, but break down she did. She could not talk, but kept on sobbing her heart out.

Finally we both regained our composure a mite and thinking to say something positive, I blurted out,

"Well, at least I have the consolation of knowing that Jolly Wymore's parents know that I was not callous and hard and that I did care and do care about what happened to their son."

With this Ma began to weep and wail louder than ever.

"Oh Jesse," she sobbed. "I lied to you. I never could deliver that letter.

I was afraid that it would be construed as a confession from you and Frank."

When I heard this I went berserk. I yelled at my mother.

"My God, Ma. That's the one thing I've held tight to all these years! The one thing I felt good about was that I acknowledged my guilt to his parents! You can't have done a thing like that!"

Ma raised tear-stained, red and guilty eyes to me. I could see by looking at her that she was telling the truth. She got up, went to her desk and opened a drawer, removed the note and handed it to me without saying another word. I could see that this was the note I had written 15 years before.

I have always been a person of action, not reflection. "At least I can deliver it now," I stated and rose and started for the door.

Ma yelled, "But you don't know where his parents are now."

"No, not for sure, but if it's the last thing I ever do in this lifetime, I'll find them!"

I did find them and I delivered the note to Mrs. Wymore, now a widow. I told her, "Here is a note that should have been delivered a long time ago." I did not tell her who I was, but there is no doubt in my mind that she knew I was one of the James boys.

Suddenly the realization hit me. "But we're not 'boys' anymore. I'm 33 years old, married, and the father of two children."

Kinfolk and Detectives

After leaving Missouri, I went straight for the home of Donie Pence. I felt that here was "kinfolk" as Donie was a very old friend, a guerrilla and brother of Bud Pence, who had ridden with me at Liberty. I never thought for one instant that I would not be received as "kinfolk." The fact that Donie was still Sheriff of Nelson County would certainly not interfere with "kinfolk." I was correct. Donie accepted me as before as part of the family and merely referred to and introduced me as his "cousin," Mr. Howard, to friends and neighbors.

It was really a paradox. Who of the many detectives who were looking for me throughout many states would have thought to look for me at the sheriff's home? None, I hoped, and was correct. While at Donie's, I did what a visiting cousin was supposed to do. I worked around the farm, went to church and even attended the fair.

While at the County Fair, I saw George Hunter, a renowned detective. I watched George with a very close eye and then realized that he did not recognize me. Detective Hunter was talking to another man whom I did not recognize. I later asked Donie (Sheriff Pence), and he told me the name of the person to whom Hunter was talking.

After I had left Donie's home, I wrote a letter to Hunter and explained to him that I had an unfair advantage over him because I knew what he looked like, but that he did not know what I looked like. To prove what I was saying, I told him about the incident at the fair, including the date, time, and the person's name to whom he was talking. I couldn't resist doing this. It made me feel good to know that this type of letter had to drive anybody to distraction, especially a detective.

While I was at Donie Pence's, I kept in contact with all of the members of the new outfit; Jim Cummins, Ed Miller, Dick Liddil, Wood Hite and Charley Hite. Bill Ryan had gone off to prison and so had Tucker Basham. Tucker Basham had confessed and told the authorities the names of the members of the outfit that had robbed the Glendale train, except Billy's. This was the second break from the tradition, but then good men were hard to find, and I was not at all surprised about that dumb-bunny Tucker.

Bill Ryan, at least for the time being, was not admitting anything or telling of our relationship, although I wasn't sure that this would last very long, but when we had left Tennessee and hopefully had covered our tracks so well so that anything said by Bill Ryan would not be of much help, except possibly to give the names by which Frank and I had been going. Strange as it may seem neither, Frank or I changed our names again, but stayed with the names of Woodson and Howard. I was very aware that Tucker Basham had used the name of Jesse James when confessing and naming his co-conspirators and had not mentioned our aliases if he had known them.

Before leaving Kentucky for Maryland and the family, I visited Louisville. As fate would have it, I saw the very famous D. T. (Yankee) Bligh, the Pinkerton who had spent a great deal of his detective life trailing and hunting for the James-Younger gang (as he referred to us). In fact, he had been hunting for me since 1868, but had never met me nor did he have the foggiest notion of what I looked like.

Bligh's success with other bad men had been remarkable due to the fact that he believed in finding out the habits of the bandit, his hangouts, his friends, etc. The only problem with the James boys was that we had very few habits or hangouts that he was aware of. Fortunately, he knew nothing of our love of race horses and tracks, nor of my penchant for gambling.

He did know one thing about me though, that I did not smoke or drink. I had read an article by him where he so stated this about me, including the fact that "Jesse James will in no way allow liquor to touch his lips." Well, I decided that was going too far and thought about a plan that would utterly confuse good old Yankee Bligh.

I commenced the conversation with him on that muggy June afternoon by stating how muggy it was and if he cared to join me in a drink. Bligh accepted and joined Mr. Howard in having a drink at the railroad station at 14th and Main. I explained to him that I was a salesman for a tombstone company. After a while Bligh stated that he was a detective employed by Pinkerton, and that although he had arrived at some success and notoriety, his ambition in life was to see Jesse James before he died.

After the two of us finished our drink, we parted with me telling him to keep up the good work, as the more bandits he killed, the more tombstones were needed.

After I arrived in Baltimore, I sent Bligh a postcard which reminded him of the drink with the tombstone salesman and the postcard went on to say, "You have now seen Jesse James, go ahead and die," and I signed it Jesse James.

While I enjoyed this joke tremendously, I'm sure that it had a deeper meaning for me. As I thought about it later as something stupid that I had done, because now he, at least, knew what I looked like. It wasn't that I ever expected to see him again, but then he was a very intelligent man, and maybe, just maybe, he could remember me enough to draw a picture of me which might be of considerable help to all of those many people hunting for me. Was it because I secretly or maybe not so secretly, was looking for that shot in the back to even up the slate before I met my maker?

By the time Detective Bligh received the postcard, our family was no longer in Maryland. The family of four in the usual two-horse-drawn schooner was travelling west to Kansas City, Missouri. At this time I had periods in my mind of never being found out or recognized alternating with periods of which I was looking to be recognized and get that person behind me so he could collect the rewards by shooting me in the back. Deep inside I still felt that Missouri was still "Jesse James territory" and that "kinfolk" would protect me.

We went for our first residence to that of Zee's sister and her husband, Charles McBride. Being in Kansas City made it easier to operate for my next planned robbery, and more importantly, Frank was in the area and with Frank vacillating between his desire to leave the outfit and his kinship for me, I wanted him at least for one more robbery with the new outfit.

The Winston Train Robbery

I was ready to test the new outfit. At Glendale, it had been a hodge-podge situation. The new outfit boys had been there, but not planned to be so; and although they appeared to do well, it was still a little early for the jury to return a verdict. I still needed Frank, who was increasingly talking of leaving for good, whether it was back to Tennessee, Texas or California. Frank could not make up his mind, but said it wouldn't be long before he left. I had the feeling that, or at least the hope that if Frank went on a robbery with the new outfit, he could evaluate the newcomers and see if they would do for the future and a resumption of the old ways.

I had heard from Stan Little (whatever connections he had among the railroad personnel, he would never say and I'm sure he had his payoffs too) that on July 15th on the Chicago, Rock Island and Pacific there would be a good haul to be had. What was also a part of the information was that the conductor of the train would be William Westfall, the man in charge of the train that carried the detectives to the Samuel farm on the night of the fatal bombing.

When I told Frank of the plan to rob the train and my plan for so doing, he seemed very reluctant, but when I mentioned that Westfall was to be the conductor, his attitude changed 180 degrees and said, "Well, I'd like to face that man just once, face to face." So the plan was completed and the actual robbery was to take place near Winston, Missouri.

This time the approach was entirely different than I had used before, but stemmed from the plan that had been attempted by the previous group that we had beaten to the punch back in Kansas. I, with Wood Hite and Dick Liddel boarded at Cameron and Frank with Jim Cummins boarded at Winston. As soon as we were a short distance from Winston, we were to spring into action. Dick Liddel and I were to get to the engineer and stop the train. Frank, along with Ed Miller, was to get to the express car to secure the valuables there and Jim Cummins and Wood Hite were to keep the passengers in line and at the same time collect the passengers' valuables in the grain sack.

Just as the plan sprang into action, Conductor Westfall walked down the aisle. As he did he was confronted by a tall man with a dark black beard. Frank had his wish, he was facing Westfall. Frank asked, "Are you the Westfall in charge of the train that took the Pinkertons to get Jesse and Frank James in '75?"

Westfall, of course, had no inkling to whom he was talking and automatically answered "yes," which, as it turned out to be, was the last word he uttered on earth. Frank pulled his colt and shot Westfall twice saying, "One is for Ma and the other is for Archie."

Unfortunately, a man who I later learned was named Frank McMillan attempted to make a move towards Frank, and Jim Cummins promptly shot and killed Mr. McMillan.

Except for this small digression, the robbery was executed exactly as planned. After completion, we jumped off the train and disappeared into the darkness. The escape part of the plan worked to perfection. Clarence (he liked to be called Charley), held six horses in readiness in addition to his own and the robbery took place and the train was stopped only two miles off target. After the train was stopped, Charley brought the horses to the train.

Before the split of the loot was done and, of course, before we took our different routes, I told Jim Cummins that there was absolutely no reason for him to have shot the passenger. The passenger hadn't even pulled a gun. Jim was livid and snapped back that Frank had shot a man who didn't even have a gun. We had a somewhat heated argument and I never was able to convince Jim Cummins that there was a big difference. Frank shot Westfall because of the dastardly raid on our home when we weren't there, killing our little brother Archie and blowing off our mother's arm, but that the passenger was merely an innocent bystander.

When we parted I had some real deep misgivings about ever having to ride again with Jim Cummins and I felt sure he had the same feelings. After all, he owed no loyalty to either of us for wrongs done to our family and here we were killing someone; when he reacted when a man made a move towards one of us, he was chastised. You know, he had a point, but I didn't know how to go and make an apology. I guess one of the things I had never learned was how to apologize.

It's strange but in my dreams thereafter, I never once had William Westfall's death come to light in any of the dreams, whereas Frank McMillan became a part of my dreams, although unnamed, almost immediately. The mind compensates for bad deeds in its way when the mind wants to and blocks out those events where there really is no remorse, and I had no remorse over the killing of William Westfall.

After the train robbery near Winston, Governor Crittendon posted a new reward for me in the amount of $5,000.00. I felt that it would be unsafe to leave the family at McBride's as the detectives might go there either to look for me, or just to get information from the McBride's; and if they did that wouldn't be good for myself, my family, and even more importantly, the McBrides.

I told my young son that we were moving to another city although we were in reality moving to a different part of Kansas City. We moved to the Dagett House, which was really a hotel. It wasn't more than a week later when Tim (who I called by that name as I could not call him by his real name, nor could could I ever let him know his true identity, but at least

Governor Thomas T. Crittenden.

I didn't dress him in girl's dresses like Frank had to with Robert Franklin) saw McBride pass on horseback and shouted to him "Hi Uncle Charley, how did you get to this town?" When I heard about this I immediately paid the bill and took the family from the hotel.

After two short moves after the Dagett House, I moved where I could keep tabs on things. We moved to a house on Woodland, where right across the vacant lot at the rear was the house of the marshal himself. I got to know Mr. Murphy quickly as this fitted in with my plan of knowing what was going on. Marshal Murphy was, like all other law enforcement people, very anxious to capture (or kill) Jesse James or any of those left in the 'gang' as he referred to the outfit.

It seemed that almost every night a posse would gather at Murphy's house and start out for the country around Independence and the 'cracker neck' district in search of members of the James 'gang.' I would walk over when the posse was getting ready to start out and talk to them about their plans, and to wish them good luck on their trip. I sure had a hankerin' to go with them, but I knew that if I did, someone in my old stompin' grounds might recognize me. Of course, if someone did, maybe he would shoot me in the back, and then everything would be over. But still I couldn't bring myself to go.

It was from this house on Woodland that I planned and executed the train robbery referred to afterwards by some as the Blue Cut train robbery and others as the Rocky Cut train robbery. I, and I alone, determined that the date of the robbery was to be September 7th. This was very important to me in that it would be the fifth anniversary of our disaster at Northfield. I wanted to prove to Frank that this new outfit I had formed was just as good as the one that rode into Northfield.

The only newcomer in the outfit was to be a man by the name of Charley Ford, who was to ride in place of Jim Cummins. Charley was from Ray County, which is right next to Clay, and I considered Charley reliable and I guess "kinfolk" the same as I did the others. Except for Frank, Jim Cummins was the last of the old outfit to go, but I had made the decision and was not about to reconsider. Although we discussed the personnel from time to time, Frank always abided by my final decision. I'll admit that Frank didn't cotton to Charley Ford, but Charley seemed so eager to join that I okayed it. Maybe it was ego too, because of the way he looked up to me. As he put it, "What an honor to ride with Jesse James!"

The Blue Cut Train Robbery

On September 7, 1881, exactly five years after Northfield had destroyed our old outfit of James-Younger, our new outfit robbed a train at Blue Cut, Missouri. This train robbery was just a few miles from Glendale, the successful train robbery of October 1879. We chose the same railroad, the Chicago and Alton.

The real reason we robbed the same railroad was that we had information from Stan Little. Stan had learned that there was to be $100,000.00 in the express car of the Chicago and Alton on September 7th as it went through Jackson County. Stan, however, was unable to find out which of the two trains on that day would carry the shipment, all he could find out was that the shipment would move on the 7th. This tied in beautifully with my desire to stage a train robbery on that date, and if we were able to obtain $100,000.00, I felt that this would satisfy Frank and satisfying Frank was very important to my plans.

This time we used the plan that had been so successful before by stopping the train by putting debris on the tracks. I felt that it was too soon to attempt to repeat the operation of the Winston robbery. So back to the stopping of the train by putting a blockade on the track. We put stones and logs between stations. This is all the time that would be needed, in Jackson County. Before the train reached the next station we would have split the loot, divided, and gone into the sunset before any pursuit could be formed.

As the train ground to a halt so as not to strike the stones and logs it was a now familiar attack. I went with Wood Hite to the engineer and took command of the train. It was Frank and Ed Miller who went to the express car, where they found the messenger and locked and bolted the door to the express car. When I learned of this I ordered Engineer Foote (I had already learned his name), to provide the pick from the engine, which he did without any hesitancy. The pick was used to open first the door itself and later the safe inside.

When Frank and Ed Miller entered the express car Messenger H. A. Fox did not try to resist at that time. However, Ed Miller was so mad at the delay that he just up and hit Fox over the head with his pistol butt. The problem was that this was the wrong train and instead of $100,000.00, there was only $1,200.00 in the safe.

At the time that I demanded the pick from Engineer Foote, he at first was uncooperative, but when I put my revolver to his head and threatened to kill him and added that this was the revolver that had killed Westfall, he became a quick believer and thereafter cooperated fully, which allowed me to then concentrate on the other proceedings. After the express car was looted we all four joined Dick Liddel and Clarence Hite who had taken over the passenger portions of the train.

All valuables soon joined the cash from the express car in the grain sack. While we were taking the valuables from the passengers, I let it be known several times that as Jesse James, this robbery was to avenge the Chicago and Alton's participation in the new reward offer. I hoped that this allegation would satisfy the railroad men that I really didn't expect the train to have the $100,000.00. Protecting Stan Little was extremely important, and if the authorities thought this robbery was staged because of the railroad joining in the new reward, I would have accomplished my purpose of protecting Stan Little.

After the robbery was completed, I went back to the engine and shook hands with Mr. Foote saying, "You're a brave man and I like you. Here is $2.00 for you to drink to the health of Jesse James tomorrow evening." I also asked him if we could now assist in removing the stones and logs from the track. For some reason he declined, although I believe just to get us on the move.

As we began to scramble up the bank, unbenownst to me, the brakeman pulled a gun that had remained hidden and took aim at me, but before a shot rang out from the side of the engine from which we were departing, a revolver rang out from the area where Charley Ford was keeping the horses. Neither one of the shots hit anything.

As we all mounted our horses which Charley Ford had been keeping so well, I looked over and stated, "Thanks Charley I'm eternally grateful that you were watching my backside." Charley's answer bothered me right then, but even more importantly later on, when he said, "As long as I'm around Jesse, your backside is safe." How did he know?

We quickly divided the loot, or what loot there was. Maybe it wasn't the most opportune time, but I chastized Ed Miller for hitting the messenger over the head with the butt of his gun when the messenger was not resisting us, and that was against my rules.

It was Ed who blew his top at me, and come back with "To hell with your 'rules' Jesse, what good did they do at Northfield?" Before I could answer, Ed Miller blurted out "And what good here for this paltry sum of money, the great Jesse James and we're lucky if we have $300.00 apiece!"

With this I said back, as I too was angry and I guess I lost my temper, "And you sure as heck aren't your brother Clell either!"

The New Outfit Falls Apart

Less than two weeks after the Blue Cut robbery, the trial of Bill Ryan began. I honestly believed at the start of the trial that Bill would be acquitted. The trial was in Jackson County where it would be impossible to convict anyone who had ridden with Jesse James. I knew of many of my "kinfolk" of long standing who themselves went to the trial fully armed and actually slept outside the courthouse. During the trial Tucker Basham appeared and identified Bill Ryan as a member of the Glendale Train robbery and of course (I thought for the good of Bill Ryan), that I (and Frank of course), were members of the gang that robbed the train. Even though the facts were on the side of the prosecution, I still felt that there would be an acquittal.

How wrong I was, Bill Ryan was convicted. This was a shock! What it meant was that Jesse James' country and kinfolk was not what it had been for the James boys. Of course, we were not boys anymore, either. Times change, and they certainly had for us.

During this time, Frank had taken a trip to Tennessee and found to his satisfaction that he was still Mr. Woodson. When Frank returned to Missouri we had a long conversation. Frank said that he was quitting, that under no circumstances would he ever ride again. He further stated that he was wrong the night he and I told Billy that neither of us would quit. He was going to quit and that was that. I did everything I could to convince him that he was wrong but to no avail.

We again discussed my dreams and my belief that I must make amends for the people I was responsible for killing and that I would do so by being shot in the back with my Lord knowing that I was being shot in the back to atone for my sins.

It was Frank who said, "Well, Dingus, if you allow that Charley Ford around long enough he'll be the one." When I disagreed because he'd had the chance during the Blue Cut train robbery, Frank pointed out that not only were the rest of the outfit present who would have shot Charley on the spot, but more importantly that I was wearing my guns.

Frank then said, "If it's going to be Charley Ford, be sure that you take off your guns, he's too yellow to shoot you, even in the back when you're wearing a gun."

It was a sad parting, but I knew that Frank would never ride again. Frank would never rob anybody because he had said he wouldn't. I hoped that he would always be "Mr. Ben Woodson" and I further hoped that he would find peace in his way. I told him all of this and when he left all he could say was, "Thanks little brother. Well, we sure fulfilled the prophecy of the two bastards. We are famous, even if it isn't for the best things." I looked at Frank and the only thing I could say was, "Buck, you're right, but I would give anything to have had it different."

Frank's last comment to me was as usual from his beloved bard, as he stated from Romeo and Juliet, *"Parting is such sweet sorrow, but I shall greet you on the morrow."*

My last comment to him was, *"I just pray that it will be in heaven, not in hell."* I knew then that I would never see Frank in this world.

With Frank gone for good, I fell into a deep depression. It seemed that I was living on borrowed time, but I was determined that this borrowed time was to be spent with my family and in safe surroundings, if possible. This could not be done in Kansas City, it was just too close to home and the chances of being recognized were too great.

Yes, I still had that hope of living, the conflicts were still there. One time I would want to live, such as Frank was trying to do, the next minute I knew that I must die to wash away my sins. Inside me was hell. Maybe I was suffering the tortures of hell so that I could wash them away.

Oh God, please help me. I prayed, but there were no revelations, only the dreams at night, always the same theme. The people who were dead or left – the widows, the orphans, all because of Jesse James.

After the trial of Bill Ryan I moved to St. Jo, Missouri. Why St. Jo? I had been driven from Clay County and the area of Kansas City, but I did want to be in Missouri. When we came from other raids, especially Northfield, I had felt good when we crossed the border and arrived in Missouri. When we had gotten to St. Jo after Northfield, I had that feeling that we were 'home' even though I did not know anyone in St. Jo.

Things were beginning to deteriorate even more with the new outfit. Dick Liddel was arrested in January 1882. It was about this time that I learned that Wood Hite had been killed. When Dick was arrested, I was unable to get any information from anyone about who killed Wood Hite. Two months later Dick Liddel confessed to the killing and again Frank and I were named as the leaders of the train robberies from 1870 to 1881.

If this wasn't enough, Clarence Hite was arrested at his home in Kentucky, returned to Missouri and confessed, corroborating Dick Liddel's statements. There was such a difference between this "new outfit" from the old. Cole Younger was still in Stillwater Prison, and even though he was offered a pardon if he would identify the other members at Northfield, he refused.

These developments made me feel even worse. Here were my real "kinfolk," the Youngers keeping their vows and these new riders with me confessing and naming names – Jesse and Frank James – to robberies they knew nothing about. My dreams were now even clearer, the answer was to cleanse myself by being shot in the back. Oh how I actually wanted that to happen most of the time, and yet there was that turmoil as I would look at Zee and Mary, and most of all at young Jesse, even when I had to call him "Tim."

The next report I read was that Ed Miller was found dead, and the articles all said one thing, Jesse James is believed to have been the executioner. Good God, I hadn't even seen Ed for six months. But what other atrocities could be heaped upon me? With Ed's death this made five of the "new outfit" gone, and with Frank in effect gone from the outfit, this meant that the only man I had ever ridden with that was alive and willing to ride again with me was Charley Ford.

With what Frank had said maybe there was the savior of my soul. If this was to be I would give him every chance. Somehow this made me feel satisfied and I had a turn for the better from my depression. I felt the die was cast, when and where would be shown to me by our Lord at the proper time. I was, for a while, at peace within.

15

The Peaceful Time : St. Jo : The End : Epilog

We settled in St. Joseph, Missouri, in November 1881. The family was Tom and Kate Howard, our son Tim and daughter Sue. Residing with us was our cousin Charlie Johnson.

The days that followed were actually the happiest of my life. My son was now a good-sized lad of six, and father and son were together constantly. I had lots of good times with him, we had fun together, played pranks on each other. It was like Frank and I playing those many years before, except there were no stories to hear of the bloody border raids, no fear, that was behind me.

Whenever the weather was fair we two rode from the city. On one occasion I had "Tim" sit on the top of a rail fence and I showed him how I used to ride with Quantrill, with the bridle in my teeth, an unloaded revolver in each hand snapping the triggers rapidly. I charged at young Jesse. Jesse Jr., thought it was great fun, and I told him all about Quantrill, Anderson and Todd.

When the weather was bad, I read to my son from the Bible, and many times from the dime novels about Jesse James, from the exploits in Texas and Mexico. My, how they all seemed so exciting and chivalrous, and exactly like Robin Hood!

In one of the novels I was reading aloud it came out that Jesse had ridden with Quantrill. Young Jesse interrupted and said, "Daddy, you rode with Quantrill, as you showed me a while ago, did you know the famous Jesse James?"

I was caught by surprise, but before I could answer, Zee, who had been sitting quietly sewing, said, "I think your father met him one time, didn't you dear?" Of course I recovered myself and told my son the only lie I had ever told one of my family. I agreed with Zee, I sure didn't want my son to know who he was at this time, it would be time enough when I was no longer around.

There was another time when my son and I had quite an experience. The home of a preacher living in the suburbs of St. Joseph had burned down and the story was in the newspapers. We rode over to see if there was

House in St. Joseph Missouri where Jesse was assassinated by Robert Ford.

House in which Jesse James died after it had been moved to a new site.

anything we could do to help. There was always the warm feeling that I had for preachers and just maybe I could help in some way, without giving myself away.

As I was observing the ruins with young Jesse, the preacher and his wife came up to us. I turned and, lo and behold, I recognized them both! They had been the preacher and his wife at a church that I had visited in Liberty. They immediately recognized me.

We talked for some period of time and I finally asked if there was anything I could do. When the preacher replied no, he put the emphasis on the name as he said, "No, you have done many things in the past to help others, and I really don't need your help this time, *Mr. Howard.*"

My thoughts were very simple, here was a couple obviously, destitute with their home and belongings gone, and although they could have earned that $20,000 reward that was now on my head, I knew that these fine folks would never utter a word to anyone of my identity. Preachers, if they are real, do not give information for money and that would have been their only motive. Deep inside I felt that this was a sign from my Lord that he was forgiving me and the only thing left was the final act.

So convinced was I that when I left our "home on the hill" as we called it, that I always carried both revolvers fully loaded, three cartridge belts loaded and some cartridges in my pocket. Also, whenever I left for a short trip, I carried a small valise full of cartridges and the Winchester strapped on the inside of a large umbrella. The reason I did this was that I wanted my destiny to be that of fulfilling what I now knew, that of being shot in the back by a friend which would atone for all my sins. I wasn't going to allow another ending to my life.

There was another incident that occurred. One day while my son and I were sitting by the window, I saw the chief of police of St. Joseph and four men coming up the hill toward the house. I went immediately to the barn and saddled a horse. Then I went back to the house, put on my revolvers and cartridge belts, brought my Winchester rifle out of the closet and took dead aim at the chief of police.

The chief put one hand on the gate, but then turned and with the other four men walked away. I later learned that he was just showing some strangers from the city the view from the "house on the hill" was the best view of the city. Obviously, it was the best view – that's why I chose the house to live in.

The chief never knew how close he came to being killed. When he walked away I felt a sigh of relief because now there was one woman and several children, his family, who would not be made a widow and orphans because of Jesse James. Yet, I knew that I would have shot and undoubtedly killed him if necessary, because I knew that I would never be captured. I was destined to die in a certain way or my soul was lost forever.

Charley Ford mentioned that our funds were getting low and that if I was not going to stage another robbery that maybe he should clear out. I did not want this to happen for I felt that somehow he must stay to fulfill my destiny in this world, so I could go on to the next.

I said that I was going to rob a bank as I needed money and showed him a letter about a farm in Nebraska. I took Charley with me to look over banks in the area, and even into Iowa. Finally, we decided on one to rob. I explained to him it could be done with just three men. Charley had a brother whom he said could fit the bill. I had known that Charley had a brother and the immediate thought came to me, maybe when there are two of them together they'll have enough nerve to do the deed. I told Charley to return to Ray County and get his brother.

Charley returned with Bob a few days later. Bob was sleazy looking, young, but I felt God had shown me the complete way to accomplish what I intended.

Zee, who had been ambivalent with Charley, did not like Bob Ford at all and when she got me alone told me in no uncertain terms that he must go. I told her that I needed him for a bank robbery. This did not satisfy Zee and I broke down and told Zee everything. She cried and then stopped crying and asked to be a part of that last time. I told her that she must be strong; without me she and the children would be safe, not have to hide and be taken care of by the family. No matter what she said I had made up my mind. It was about then that the Fords came home and she merely stated that we would talk of it later.

Later never came.

The End

I had the feeling that I would know when the time for the end was at hand and act accordingly. How I knew this I don't know, I just plain felt it. Maybe there would be one more bank robbery before that time would come, but it couldn't be far off.

It was April 3, 1882 and there were six of us living in the house on the hill – the four Howards and our "cousins" Charley and Bob Ford. Bob had been there just three days, but we had explained the plan for the robbing of the Platte City Bank to him and all was understood. We were to leave that night and rob the bank the next day. The night before, I had given Bob one of my favorite guns, a 44, and I knew that it worked perfectly and was accurate. Bob seemed quite pleased with it.

Also, the night before, an interesting thing had happened. Bob Ford had come into our bedroom and just as he entered I heard the footsteps and I guess scared him half to death. He was walking lightly and I grabbed the 45 that was under my pillow at all times and before Bob took another step, the gun was levelled at him and cocked ready to discharge. It took only a split second and Bob saw all. He turned white and after I didn't shoot and all calmed down, he asked me if I was that skittish and I told him that I always slept with one ear and one eye open with my revolver within a few inches and he was darn lucky he hadn't been shot.

I was thinking about the incident that morning and wondering if maybe I had scared Bob so much that he and Charley would never attempt to kill me, even from the back. I had sort of thought that maybe somewhere on the ride to or from the robbery, the opportunity might arise for that bullet from the back, had I quashed that situation last night by merely reacting as I always did so quickly?

In any event it was late in the morning. The day was giving its first hint of spring and I decided to open the window and let the fresh warm air in. Zee and my son were in the next room and I could hear them talking. Mary was in the crib and asleep. Both Charley and Bob were in the room with me and, of course, both were wearing their guns. Bob had the 44 I had given him the night before in the holster and strapped to his side. If it had not been so serious I would have laughed.

I *KNEW* that this was it, this was the time. I looked up at the religious text on the wall. I remarked that it was dusty. I unbuckled my guns, laid them where they could not be seen from outside and proceeded to walk over, pick up the duster and get on the chair to dust the picture. As I did, I silently prayed, "Oh God, let this be the time. I'm ready to meet my maker."

It was the time. I heard the cocking of the hammer and thought "I wonder if it's the 44 I gave Bob last night?"

I heard the explosion and my body fell to the floor. As it hit I saw Zee and Jesse Edwards James rush into the room. As they did I heard Zee exclaim, "You've killed him, Bob Ford!"

Bob started for the door with his equally cowardly brother Charley following, both with guns drawn and in their hands.

I wondered why they were leaving so hurriedly and then I saw Jesse Jr., who somehow had gotten to the Winchester and was trying to point it at Bob Ford. Fortunately, Zee was able to grab him and take the rifle as she

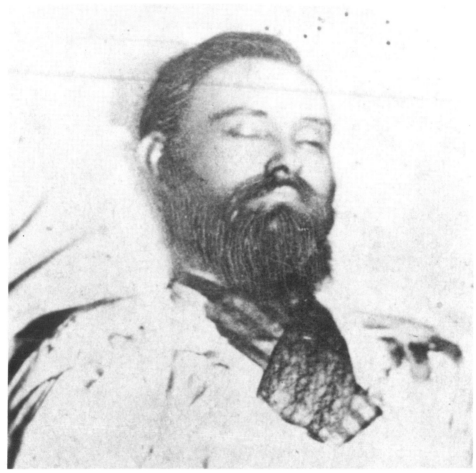

Jesse James in death.

screamed, "My God, I don't want to lose both Jesses in the same day!"
Those were the last words I heard on this earth.

Epilog

Did I get my wish? Did I wash clean my sins by fulfilling the dreams?
There were two diametrically opposed views of my death, and they were as follows:
The first view was that of the Governer of the State of Missouri, the man who had posted the $20,000 reward when he gave an interview to the Jefferson City Republican on April 6, 1882:

Robert Newton Ford the "dirty little coward that shot poor Mr. Howard", of the popular song. Born January 31st 1862, assassinated Jesse James on April 3rd 1882. Upon the conviction of himself and his brother Charles of Jesse's murder, he was pardoned by Gov. Crittenden. Died at the hand of Ed O'Kelley, an admirer of the James boys, who shot and killed him at his place of business on June 8th 1892. Jesse James Jnr. reported in his book written in 1898, that Charley Ford begged the forgiveness of Mrs. Samuel when they met accidentally in Kansas City three years after the murder. Eleven months later, Charley Ford died at his own hand.

Epilog

"In an interview with Governor Crittenden today his excellency stated that neither Craig Timberlake nor himself were aware that Jesse James was residing at St. Joseph but supposed he still lived in Kansas City, and that he was inclined to discredit the first telegram he received of the killing of Jesse James, because it came from St. Joseph, not believing he had gone there for any purpose. He now understands the reason James selected such a locality. It was to the bold outlaw a commanding position from which he could operate in Kansas and Missouri. 'The House,' said the governor, 'was situated admirably for protection and escape, presenting means of concealment for his stolen plunder and himself, and a convenient stable in which he lodged his stolen horses. A good general always looks when preparing for battle as well for accessible means of retreat as of attack'."

The Governor said, "The honest, good people of Missouri should stand by the Ford boys, and will, I verily believe, as soon as the excitement incident to the death of James has subsided. Why should anyone with a proper appreciation of honest citizenship aside from consideration regarding his own mother and loving little family regret his death? If not killed when he was, he would have attacked the bank at Platte City, and in perpetrating the robbery would have killed in all probability, some one or more officials in the ill-fated bank; then would have gone to Kansas, returned and attacked the bank at Forrest City and killed one or more of its officials.

Should not these things be considered? Must we overlook not only his past but anticipated robberies and murders in the future and grieve over his deprivations; I say no, a thousand times no. I have no excuses to make, no apologies to this bloody drama, nor has Crain nor Timberlake. The life of one honest law-abiding man however humble is worth more to society and a state than a legion of Jesse Jameses. One is a blessing. The other a living, breathing, putrid curse. I am no admirer of any of the acts of the outlaw. He may have occasionally done a good deed; if so, like the corsair it was 'one virtue linked with a thousand crimes.'

I am not regretful of his death, and have no words of censure for the boys who removed him. They deserve credit in my candid solemn opinion.

When John U. Waring, one of the bloodiest murderers who ever disgraced Kentucky, was shot down in the streets of Versailles, in that

Zerelda James with her children Jesse Edwards, and Mary Susan James. On the death of her husband, 'Zee' James was left with only $250 to keep herself and her family. Jesse Jnr. worked from a young age to support his mother and sister, and through his own efforts, graduated in law.

state, in 1835, by a well-known man concealed in the upper room of the courthouse (and Waring was no worse than Jesse James), no legal examination was ever made in the case and no volumes of denunciations were ever heaped upon the murderer. All said he did a righteous act, as the victim was an outlaw, a hostis humanis. Why should these Ford boys be so abused? If they are guilty of a hideous sin against society, others are equally guilty. Without fear or favor I say these boys did an act that will rebound to the prosperity and advancement of Missouri and remove the great shadow that was hung too long over this great state. All honor to the brave officer who accomplished the work. If you want to know the value of the deed ask the managers of the banks, ask the owners of land in that part of the state, ask the managers of the many railroads constructed in this state, ask the ticket agents at St. Louis, Kansas City, and Chicago, ask the hotel keepers at St. Louis and Kansas City, ask the property owners and real estate agents in Kansas City and in Jackson County, ask those who own land in Clay and Platte, hear all of their responses and then say it was not a good deed on behalf of law, order, and general prosperity."

The second view was that of Major John Newman Edwards who wrote and stated:

"Not one among all the hired cowards, hard on the hunt for blood money, dared face this wonderful outlaw, one even against twenty, until he had disarmed himself and turned his back on his assassins, the first and only time in a career which has passed from the realms of an almost fabulous romance into that of history.

We called him an outlaw, and he was, but fate made him so. When the war came he was just turned fifteen. The border was all aflame with steel and fire and ambuscade and slaughter. He flung himself into a band which had a black flag for a banner and devils for riders. What he did he did and it was fearful. But it was war. It was Missouri against Kansas. It was Jim Lane and Jennison against Quantrill, Anderson and Todd.

When the war closed, Jesse James had no home. Proscribed, hunted, shot, driven away from his people, a price put on his head, what else could he do, with such a nature, except what he did do; he had to live. It was his country. The graves of his kindred were there. He refused to be banished from his birthright, and when he was hunted he turned savagely about and hunted his hunters. Would to God he were alive today to make a righteous butchery of a few more of them.

There was never a more cowardly and unnecessary murder committed in all America than this murder of Jesse James. It was done for money. He had been living in St. Joseph for months. The Fords were with him. He was in their toils, for they meant to betray him. He was in the heart of a large city. One word would have summoned 500 armed men for his capture or extermination. Not a single one of the attacking party need to have been hurt. If, when his house had been surrendered, he had refused to surrender, he could have been killed on the inside of it and at long range. The chances for him to escape were as one to 10,000 and not even that; but it was never intended that he should be captured. It was his blood the bloody wretches were after, blood that would bring money in the official market of Missouri.

And this great commonwealth leagued with a lot of self-confessed robbers, highwaymen, and prostitutes, to have one of its citizens as-sassinated, before it was positively known that he had ever committed a single crime worthy of death.

Of course, everything that can be said about the dead man to justify the manner of his killing will be said; but who is saying it? Those with the blood of Jesse James on their guilty souls. Those who conspired to murder him. Those who wanted the reward and would invent any lie or concoct any diabolical story to get it. They have succeeded, but such a cry of horror and indignation at the infernal deed is even now thundering over the land that if a single one of the miserable assassins had either manhood, conscience, or courage, he would go as another Judas and hang himself. But so sure as God reigns, there never was a dollar of blood money yet obtained which did not bring with it per-dition. Sooner or later here comes a day of vengeance. Some among the murderers were mere beasts of prey. These, of course, can only suffer through cold blood, hunger, or thirst; but whatever they dread most, that will happen. Others, again, among the murderers are sanctimonious devils, who plead the honor of the State, the value of law and order, the splendid courage required to shoot an unarmed man in the back of the head; and these will be stripped to their skin of all their pretentions and made to shiver and freeze, splotched as they are with blood, in the pitiless storm of public contempt and condem-nation. This to the leader will be worse than death.

Nor is the end yet. If Jesse James had been hunted down as any other criminal, and killed when trying to escape or in resisting arrest, not a word would have been said to the contrary. He had sinned and he had suffered. In his death the majesty of the law would have been vindicated; but here the law itself becomes a murderer; it leagues with murderers. It borrows money to pay rewards to murderers. It is itself a murderer – the most abject, the most infamous, the most cowardly ever known to history. Therefore, these so called executors of the law are outlaws. Therefore, let Jesse James' comrades and he has a few remaining worth all the Fords and Liddels that can be packed together between St. Louis and St. Joseph do unto them as they did unto him. Yes, the end is not yet nor should it be. The man put a price upon his head and hire a band of cut-throats and highwaymen to murder him for money? Anything can be told of men. The whole land is filled with liars, robbers and assassins. Murder is easy for $100. Nothing is safe that is pure, or unsuspecting, or just; but it is not to be supposed that the law will become an ally and a co-worker in this sort of civilization.

Jesse James has been murdered, first, because an immense price had been set on his head and there isn't a low lived scroundrel today in Missouri who wouldn't kill his own father for money; and second because he was made the scapegoat of every train robbery, footpad, and highwayman between Iowa and Texas. Worse men a thousand times than the dead man have been hired to do this thing. The very character of the instruments chosen show the infamous nature of the work required. The hand that slew him had to be a traitor's! Missouri with 117 sheriffs, as brave and as efficient on the average as any men on earth. Missouri, with watchful and vigilant marshals in every one of her principal towns and cities. Missouri, with every screw, and cog, and crank, and lever, and wheel of the administrative machinery in perfect working order. Boasting of law, order, progress, and development, had yet to surrender all these in the face of a single man – a hunted, lied-upon, proscribed, and outlawed man, trapped and located in the midst of 35,000 people, and ally with some five or six cut throats and prostitutes that the majesty of the law might be vindicated, and the goodname of the State reeks today with a double orgy; that of lust and that of murder. What the men failed to do the women accomplished. Tear the two bears from the flag of Missouri. Put thereon in place of them, as more appropriate, a thief blowing out the brains of an unarmed victim; and a brazen harlot,

*The picture that Jesse was dusting seconds before the
fatal shot from Robert Ford's gun killed him.*

naked to the waist and splashed to the brows in blood."

Whatever of the two positions one can take, which is the true one?
Did my allowing the killing from the back by a supposed friend cleanse my
sins? Am I today in heaven or hell?

No person on this earth knows, but if you were the final Judge, what
sayeth you?

POSTSCRIPT

FRANK JAMES

Not long after the death of Jesse James, Frank, assisted as ever by the industrious Major Edwards, embarked upon a course of action that would eventually allow him to turn his back on the outlaw life, and return to his family a free man. No one will ever know the true story of his secret negotiations with the authorities, but by September 1882 John Edwards felt confident enough to make his first public move.

Written in Frank's hand, but bearing the unmistakable stamp of Major Edwards' literary style, a letter was mailed to Governor Crittenden from St. Louis on September 30th 1882. In this missive, the original of which has only recently been found, Frank asked for amnesty on the grounds that the deprivations that he had suffered during his years of outlawry, were a worse punishment than any a court could impose. He also complained that many of the crimes of which he was accused, had been committed by others who found it easy, because of his reputation, to lay the blame at his door.

Governor Crittenden replied that it was not in his power to grant an amnesty, only a pardon. And then, only if he felt it was appropriate in the event of Frank surrendering himself for trial, and subsequently being found guilty. On October 15th 1882 at about five o'clock in the afternoon, Frank James, accompanied by Major John Newman Edwards, walked into Governor Crittenden's office. In the presence of the witnesses assembled there, he removed his gun belt which he told the governor "no living man except myself has been permitted to touch since 1861", and handing it to him, surrendered himself.

To defend his now penniless friend, Major Edwards had assembled a team of lawyers that money could not have bought. For the Gallatin Missouri trial it included Congressman (later Judge) John Phillips, at the time a commissioner of the Supreme Court of Missouri. In two separate trials, at Gallatin and then Huntsville, Alabama, juries twice acquitted Frank James of the crimes with which he was charged, thereby returning him to society, and the bosom of the family that he loved so well.

Pro-Confederate leanings and the sympathy engendered by Frank's surrender, had made conviction almost impossible. The people of Missouri had not forgotten the service done them by Quantrill and his men during the Civil War, when Lane and Jennison razed and pillaged Missouri until it became known as the "Burnt District". As the Sedalia "Weekly Democrat" so aptly put it, **The East had no Jennison, or it would have appreciated a Quantrill.**

For the rest of his life Frank James was an industrious member of society who did no harm to his fellow man. Working variously as a salesman, horse race official and actor, he eventually purchased a small homestead near Fletcher Oklahoma, only to return to the James Farm in Missouri on the death of his mother in 1911. Frank James passed away at his childhood home on February 18th 1915. Judge John Phillips, who had so many years before saved him from the gallows, delivered the graveside oration.

Frank James aged about 55 years.

LETTER FROM FRANK JAMES TO HIS WIFE
WHILE AWAITING TRIAL IN CUSTODY

Gallatin Missouri
Oct. 19th 1988

My Dear Wife,

bond has been refused and my case set for the third week in Dec- Two long months, it is just awful but you must try and not take it too hard at heart, I will make the best of it, I will not trust all I think to paper when I see you I can tell you all. I am getting thoroughly disgusted with every thing and every body, except you. When would you like to come up and see me? I am so anxious to have you with but on Robs account I suppose I must make up my mind to spend my two months alone. Darling you need not expect me to write anything of interest for the reason my letters are liable to get into the papers. If you will be just as cautious as you can be, at the same time we can't tell what will happen I felt as I should write you today although I am afraid you will not go to office before Tuesday and then you will get two for I intend to write Monday. Kiss my little man for me,

Love to all

from loving husband Ben

I have no heart to write by Monday I might feel better I hope

Ben.

ZERELDA SAMUEL

The mother of Frank and Jesse, condemned long and loud all those associated with the death of her son; and did so publicly. She neither forgave nor forgot, and supported her grandson when he was accused of a robbery he did not commit, as strongly as she had defended his father. Consider the following if you will, from "Jesse James My Father", by Jesse Edwards James published in 1899.

Zerelda Samuel was called to give evidence for her grandson who is accused unjustly, of the crime of train robbery. The court is in session as she enters to be sworn.

The tension in the court was great as Mrs. Samuel took her seat. As she sank back in the witness chair she faced the entire assemblage, and five hundred pairs of eyes were fixed upon her.

They noted the tremor of the aged hand, the glossy whiteness of the hair upon which rested a simple and becoming bonnet of black; the plain silk dress – everything. Every ear was on the alert to hear the words which she would utter.

"Hold up your right hand and be sworn," boomed forth the clerk of the court.

Up went the right arm, but the hand was missing! Nothing but an empty sleeve – empty nearly to the elbow – greeted the vision. The minds of all unconsciously reverted to the tragedy in which she lost her arm so many years ago, when Pinkerton detectives are said to have thrown a dynamite bomb into her house, killing an infant in her arms and maiming her for life.

"You hereby swear that everything you say will be the truth, the whole truth and nothing but the truth?"

"I do" There was nothing weak about this response. While given in a low voice, it was clear and distinct, and after its utterance the jaws closed with the snap of determination.

Proof, if it were needed, of this remarkable woman's iron determination, and her absolute loyalty to those she called her own.

Zerelda Samuel suffered a stroke returning home from a visit to her son Frank, then living in Oklahoma. Taken from the train by her daughter in law, Annie James, she died in Oklahoma City.

ZERELDA JAMES

The wife of Jesse, never remarried and lived out the rest of her days quietly as a semi-recluse. With the help of her son she made ends meet, but never seems to have completely recovered from the loss of her husband. On November 14th 1900, the Kansas City Times reported under the heading:

MRS JAMES IS DEAD – Passed away Yesterday Morning after Lingering Illness – Widow of the Famous Bandit. – Story of Devoted Wife and Mother Who Clung to Her Husband Through Every Exciting Incident.

the following story.

Mrs. Zerelda James, widow of Jesse James, died of sciatic rheumatism and nervous prostration at the home of her son, Jesse James Jr. Thirty Fourth Street and Tracey Avenue at 5.25 o'clock yesterday morning, after an illness that confined her to bed for nearly eleven months. She lapsed into unconsciousness on the night of November 9th, from which condition she was unable to rally. Mrs. James became ill the day following Christmas, 1899, at that time a comparatively strong woman.

Mrs. James has been a widow since April 3, 1882 when Jesse James, whom the world at large had for twenty years called an outlaw, bandit and train robber, finally met his death at the hands of betrayers and assassins in the city of St. Joseph, Missouri. Since that time she has made her home in Kansas City.

Mrs. Zerelda Samuel and Frank James attended the funeral. The earthly remains of 'Zee' James were interred with those of her husband, and both now rest in the little cemetery at Kearney, Missouri.

Mrs. Jesse James in later life.

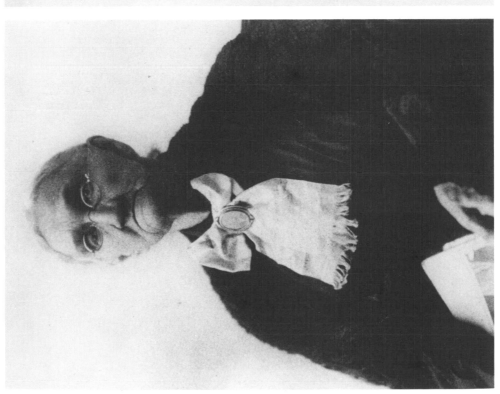

Zerelda Samuel. Despite her age, the iron will is still obvious from her bearing.